EDITED BOOK OF PHARMACEUTICAL ENGINEERING

[According to latest syllabus of B. Pharm – III semester of Pharmacy Council of India]

Dr. Surya Prakash Gupta

Professor & Director

Rajiv Gandhi Institute of Pharmacy,

Faculty of Pharmaceutical Science & Technology,

AKS University,

Satna (Madhya Pradesh)

Mrs. Neelam Singh

Assistant Professor

Rajiv Gandhi Institute of Pharmacy,

Faculty of Pharmaceutical Science & Technology,

AKS University,

Satna (Madhya Pradesh)

Mr. Ashutosh Jain

Assistant Professor

Rajiv Gandhi Institute of Pharmacy,

Faculty of Pharmaceutical Science & Technology,

AKS University,

Satna (Madhya Pradesh)

EDITED BOOK OF
PHARMACEUTICAL ENGINEERING

First Edition 2024

Published by:

NOTION PRESS
Publisher and distributor
Head office: Notion press Media Pvt. Ltd.
7, Red cross Road,
Egmore, Chennai,Tamil Nadu 60008
Website: www.notionpress.com

EDITED BOOK OF PHARMACEUTICAL ENGINEERING ABOUT THE EDITORS

Dr. Surya Prakash Gupta is a distinguished academician and currently serves as a Professor and Director at the Rajiv Gandhi Institute of Pharmacy, Constituent Unit of AKS University, Satna (M.P.). With an illustrious career spanning several years, Dr. Gupta has made significant contributions to the field of pharmacy education and research. He holds a Ph. D. in Pharmacy and is widely respected for his expertise in the field. Dr. Gupta's academic journey is marked by numerous achievements, and he has played a pivotal role in shaping the careers of aspiring pharmacists. As the Director of the Rajiv Gandhi Institute of Pharmacy, Dr. Gupta has been instrumental in implementing innovative teaching methodologies and fostering an environment conducive to research and learning. Under his guidance, the institute has achieved new heights of excellence. Dr. Surya Prakash Gupta is not only a proficient academician but also an inspiring mentor who is dedicated to the advancement of pharmacy education in India. His commitment to academic excellence and research makes him a highly regarded figure in the field.

Mrs. Neelam Singh is currently working as Assistant Professor in Rajiv Gandhi Institute of Pharmacy, AKS University Satna. She has actively participated in academic & research work. She did her M. Pharm in Pharmaceutical Chemistry from premier institute. She has presented paper in various National & International conferences. She is also engaged in various extracurricular activities to the pharmacy profession.

Mr. Ashutosh Jain is working as a Assistant Professor in Rajiv Gandhi institute of pharmacy, AKS University, Satna, MP. He has completed his M. Pharm from LNCT, University Bhopal, MP. He has attended various National and International conferences.

TEXT BOOK OF PHARMACEUTICAL ENGINEERING

NOTION PRESS

PREFACE

The authors feel great pleasure in presenting the first edition of the book **"Edited Book of Pharmaceutical Engineering"** for graduate and post graduate students. The present book on **Edited Book of Pharmaceutical Engineering** has been written according to the syllabus of B. Pharm – III semester of Pharmacy Council of India and covers full course of the subject.

THE SALIENT FEATURES OF THE BOOK ARE:-

- *Easy to understand style of writing* which makes the book a self-study material.
- *Each new concept has been introduced through day-today problem of interest* to the students which makes the subject matter interesting.
- *The language of the book, on the whole, is lucid and easy to understand.*
- Wherever needed *neatly labeled figures have been drawn*.

The authors hope that the students, teachers and other readers will find the book interesting and to the point covering the course. We hope that the students will receive the book warmly.

I express a sincere thank you to the Management of Rajiv Gandhi Institute of Pharmacy, Faculty of Pharmaceutical Science & Technology, AKS University, for their support during the writing of this book.

Every effort is made to keep the book error free. The author will gratefully acknowledge the suggestions to improve the book to make it more useful.

Wishing our readers success in examination and life ahead. The authors feel that their efforts will be fully rewarded if the book serves the purpose for which it is written.

EDITED BOOK OF PHARMACEUTICAL ENGINEERING

CONTENT

CHAPTER – 1

FLOW OF FLUIDS

Dr. Surya Prakash Gupta

Professor & Director, Rajiv Gandhi Institute of Pharmacy, Faculty of Pharmaceutical Science & Technology, AKS University, Satna, MP-India

---

Abstract:

"Flow of fluids" is a broad term that encompasses the movement of liquids and gases through various mediums, such as pipes, channels, or open spaces. Understanding fluid flow is crucial in numerous engineering disciplines, including mechanical, chemical, civil, and environmental engineering. Here's a detailed introduction to the topic:

Fundamentals of Fluid Flow:

1. **Fluid Properties:**
   a. Fluids can be classified into two main categories: liquids and gases. They both exhibit similar behaviors under flow conditions but differ in density and compressibility.
   b. Important properties include density, viscosity, pressure, temperature, and specific gravity, which affect how fluids flow.
2. **Types of Flow:**
   a. **Laminar Flow**: Smooth, orderly flow characterized by parallel layers of fluid moving in the same direction.
   b. **Turbulent Flow**: Chaotic, irregular flow characterized by swirling motion and mixing of fluid particles.
   c. **Transitional Flow**: A mix of laminar and turbulent flow, often occurring during a transition between laminar and turbulent regimes.
3. **Fluid Dynamics Equations:**

a. The fundamental equations governing fluid flow are the Navier-Stokes equations. These equations describe the conservation of momentum for a fluid.

b. In most practical applications, solving the full Navier-Stokes equations is complex, so simplified versions or empirical correlations are often used.

Factors Affecting Fluid Flow:

1. **Velocity Profile:**
    a. The velocity of a fluid across a pipe or channel isn't uniform. It typically follows a velocity profile, with maximum velocity at the center and decreasing towards the walls in laminar flow.
    b. In turbulent flow, the velocity profile is more complex due to mixing and swirling.
2. **Pressure Gradient:**
    a. Fluid flow occurs due to a pressure difference along the flow direction. This pressure gradient drives the flow from regions of high pressure to low pressure.
    b. Pressure drops occur due to frictional losses, fittings, bends, and other obstructions in the flow path.
3. **Viscosity:**
    a. Viscosity is a measure of a fluid's resistance to flow. Higher viscosity fluids flow more slowly than lower viscosity fluids under the same conditions.
    b. Viscosity affects both laminar and turbulent flow regimes.

Flow Characteristics:

1. **Reynolds Number:**
    a. The Reynolds number (Re) is a dimensionless parameter that characterizes the flow regime.

b. It's defined as the ratio of inertial forces to viscous forces and determines whether flow is laminar, transitional, or turbulent.

2. **Boundary Layers:**
    a. Boundary layers form at the interface between a solid surface and a flowing fluid.
    b. In laminar flow, the boundary layer is thin and smooth, while in turbulent flow, it's thicker and more chaotic.

3. **Flow Regimes and Patterns:**
    a. Different flow patterns can emerge depending on the geometry of the flow system, Reynolds number, and other factors.
    b. Examples include plug flow, fully developed flow, and separated flow.

Applications:

1. **Engineering Systems:**
    a. Fluid flow principles are applied in various engineering systems such as pipelines, HVAC systems, hydraulic systems, and chemical processing plants.
    b. Understanding fluid flow is essential for designing efficient and reliable systems.

2. **Environmental Impact:**
    a. Understanding fluid flow is crucial in environmental engineering for studying natural phenomena like river flow, ocean currents, and atmospheric circulation.
    b. It's also important for modeling pollutant dispersion and controlling environmental impacts.

3. **Biological Systems:**
    a. Fluid flow principles are relevant in understanding biological systems such as blood flow in arteries, airflow in the respiratory system, and fluid dynamics in organisms like fish and birds.

MANOMETERS

Manometers are devices used to measure fluid pressure by balancing the pressure of the fluid against a column of a known fluid (usually a liquid) in a vertical or inclined tube. They are widely used in various industries and applications to monitor pressure levels in pipelines, vessels, and other systems.

TYPES OF MANOMETERS

Here are the details of different types of manometers commonly used in the flow of fluids:

1. U-Tube Manometer:

a. **Principle:** It consists of a U-shaped tube filled with a liquid (usually a manometric fluid like mercury or water) and connected to the system where pressure needs to be measured.

b. **Working:** When the system pressure differs from atmospheric pressure, it causes a displacement of the manometric fluid in one leg of the U-tube, creating a height difference between the two fluid columns. The pressure difference can be determined by measuring the height difference between the two fluid levels.

c. **Types:**

I. **Simple U-Tube Manometer**: The simplest form where both ends of the U-tube are open to the atmosphere.

II. **Differential U-Tube Manometer**: Used to measure the pressure difference between two points in a system. One end of the U-tube is connected to the high-pressure point, while the other end is connected to the low-pressure point.

2. Inclined Tube Manometer:

a. **Principle**: Similar to the U-tube manometer but with one leg of the tube inclined at an angle.

b. **Working**: The inclined angle allows for more sensitive measurement of small pressure differences since a greater vertical displacement of the fluid column occurs for the same pressure difference.

c. **Types:**

   I. **Piezometer Tube**: A simple form of an inclined tube manometer used for measuring high pressures, typically found in hydraulic systems.

3. **Well-Type Manometer:**

   a. **Principle**: Consists of a reservoir or well connected to the system where pressure is to be measured and a vertical tube connected to the reservoir.

   b. **Working:** The pressure difference between the system and the atmosphere causes the manometric fluid in the well to rise or fall in the vertical tube. The pressure difference is determined by measuring the height difference between the fluid levels in the well and the tube.

   c. **Application**s: Commonly used in industries where pressure measurements at high temperatures or corrosive environments are required.

4. **Micromanometer:**

   a. **Principle:** Utilizes a small diameter tube to measure very small pressure differences accurately.

   b. **Working:** Similar to U-tube manometers but with narrower tubes, allowing for higher sensitivity.

   c. **Application**s: Used in precision instruments and laboratory setups where precise pressure measurements are essential, such as in airflow measurements and aerodynamic studies.

5. **Differential Pressure Gauge:**

   a. **Principle:** A more advanced device that measures the difference in pressure between two points in a system.

b. **Working**: It typically consists of two separate pressure chambers connected to the system at different points. The pressure difference causes a diaphragm or piston to move, which is then converted into a readable pressure value.
c. **Applications**: Widely used in industrial processes, HVAC systems, and fluid flow measurement systems.

REYNOLDS NUMBER AND ITS SIGNIFICANCE

The Reynolds number (Re) is a dimensionless parameter used to predict the flow regime of a fluid and is named after the British scientist Osborne Reynolds, who first described its significance in fluid dynamics. It plays a crucial role in understanding and analyzing the behavior of fluid flow in various engineering and scientific applications. Here's a detailed explanation of the Reynolds number and its significance:

1. Definition of Reynolds Number:

The Reynolds number is defined as the ratio of inertial forces to viscous forces within a fluid flow system. It is mathematically expressed as:

$$Re = \rho \cdot v \cdot l / \mu$$

Where:

ρ is the density of the fluid.

v is the velocity of the fluid relative to the object.

L is a characteristic length (e.g., diameter of a pipe or characteristic length of an object).

μ is the dynamic viscosity of the fluid.

2. Significance of Reynolds Number:

The Reynolds number provides valuable information about the flow regime and behavior of fluids in various situations:

a. Flow Regime Prediction:

1. **Laminar Flow (Re < 2000)**: In this regime, fluid particles move in parallel layers with minimal mixing. The flow is smooth and predictable, and viscous forces dominate over inertial forces.
2. **Transitional Flow (2000 < Re < 4000)**: Flow regime that occurs during the transition from laminar to turbulent flow. Characteristics of both laminar and turbulent flow may be present.
3. **Turbulent Flow (Re > 4000):** In this regime, fluid particles move chaotically with mixing and eddy formations. Inertial forces dominate over viscous forces, resulting in highly irregular and unpredictable flow patterns.

b. Flow Behavior Prediction:

1. **Laminar Flow**: Characterized by smooth flow patterns with low energy loss. Suitable for applications where precise control and low turbulence are desired, such as in microfluidics and some industrial processes.
2. **Turbulent Flow**: Exhibits high energy dissipation and mixing, making it suitable for applications requiring efficient heat or mass transfer, such as in chemical reactors, mixing tanks, and combustion chambers.

c. Drag and Heat Transfer Prediction:

1. **Laminar Flow**: Generally associated with lower drag and heat transfer coefficients compared to turbulent flow. This is because laminar flow creates less disturbance to the surrounding fluid.
2. **Turbulent Flow:** Results in higher drag and heat transfer coefficients due to increased mixing and agitation of the fluid. Turbulent flow enhances convective heat transfer and mixing processes.

3. Practical Applications:

1. **Pipe Flow**: Reynolds number helps in determining whether the flow in a pipe is laminar, transitional, or turbulent, which is essential for designing efficient piping systems.

2. **Aerodynamics**: It predicts the flow regime around objects like airfoils and vehicles, helping in designing streamlined shapes to minimize drag and optimize lift.
3. **Biomechanics**: Reynolds number is used to understand blood flow in arteries and veins, respiratory airflow in lungs, and fluid dynamics in aquatic organisms.
4. **Industrial Processes**: It assists in optimizing mixing, heat transfer, and fluid distribution in processes like chemical engineering, food processing, and wastewater treatment.

BERNOULLI'S THEOREM AND ITS APPLICATIONS

Bernoulli's theorem, named after the Swiss mathematician Daniel Bernoulli, is a fundamental principle in fluid dynamics that describes the relationship between the pressure, velocity, and elevation of a fluid within a streamline. It's based on the conservation of energy along a streamline and is widely used in various engineering and scientific applications involving fluid flow. Here's a detailed explanation of Bernoulli's theorem and its applications:

1. Bernoulli's Theorem:

Bernoulli's theorem states that for an ideal, incompressible, and steady flow of a fluid along a streamline, the total mechanical energy per unit mass (sum of pressure energy, kinetic energy, and potential energy) remains constant along that streamline. Mathematically, it can be expressed as:

$$P + 1/2\rho v^2 + \rho gh = \text{constant}$$

Where:

P is the pressure of the fluid.

ρ is the density of the fluid.

v is the velocity of the fluid.

g is the acceleration due to gravity.

h is the height above a reference plane (potential energy per unit mass).

2. Assumptions of Bernoulli's Theorem:

a. The fluid is ideal (non-viscous and incompressible).
b. The flow is steady (does not change with time).
c. The flow is along a streamline (no cross-flow).
d. There are no external forces acting on the fluid, except gravity.

3. Applications of Bernoulli's Theorem:

a. Venturi Effect:

Bernoulli's theorem explains the Venturi effect, which occurs when a fluid flows through a constricted section of a pipe. As the cross-sectional area decreases, the fluid velocity increases, resulting in a decrease in pressure according to Bernoulli's theorem. This principle is utilized in devices such as Venturi meters and carburetors.

b. Airplane Wings and Lift:

Bernoulli's theorem helps explain how airplane wings generate lift. The shape of an airplane wing is designed such that the air moves faster over the curved upper surface compared to the flat lower surface. According to Bernoulli's theorem, this difference in velocity results in lower pressure on the upper surface and higher pressure on the lower surface, creating lift.

c. Pitot-Static Tubes:

Pitot tubes use Bernoulli's theorem to measure the velocity of a fluid stream, such as airspeed in aircraft or water flow in pipes. They consist of two tubes—one facing the flow (Pitot tube) and one perpendicular to the flow (static tube). The difference in pressure between the two tubes is used to calculate the velocity of the fluid.

d. Water Towers and Hydraulic Jumps:

Bernoulli's theorem is used to analyze water towers and hydraulic jumps. In a water tower, the height of the tower determines the pressure at the base, allowing water to flow at high pressure to lower elevations. Hydraulic jumps occur when a high-velocity flow encounters a lower-velocity flow, and the resulting energy dissipation can be analyzed using Bernoulli's theorem.

e. Blood Flow in Arteries:

Bernoulli's theorem helps understand blood flow in arteries. When blood flows through narrow arteries, its velocity increases, causing a decrease in pressure according to Bernoulli's theorem. This principle is relevant in medical applications, such as diagnosing stenosis (narrowing) in blood vessels.

Conclusion:

Bernoulli's theorem is a powerful principle in fluid dynamics with numerous practical applications across various fields, including engineering, physics, and medicine. By understanding the relationship between pressure, velocity, and elevation in a fluid flow, engineers and scientists can design efficient systems, analyze complex flows, and solve practical problems related to fluid dynamics.

ENERGY LOSSES

In fluid dynamics, energy losses occur when the energy of a flowing fluid is dissipated due to various factors such as friction, turbulence, changes in flow direction, and fluid properties. Understanding and quantifying energy losses are essential in designing efficient fluid systems, optimizing processes, and minimizing wastage. Here's a detailed explanation of the different types of energy losses in the flow of fluids:

1. Frictional Losses:

Frictional losses occur due to the resistance encountered by a fluid as it flows through a conduit or along a surface. This resistance is caused by the interaction between the fluid and the walls of the conduit or surface and results in a loss of energy in the form of heat. Frictional losses can be further classified into:

a. **Pipe Friction**: Losses due to the roughness of the pipe walls, which cause a shear stress on the fluid and result in a pressure drop along the length of the pipe.

b. **Boundary Layer Friction**: Losses due to the boundary layer formed at the interface between the fluid and a solid surface, resulting in shear stresses that retard the flow.

2. Expansion and Contraction Losses:

When a fluid flows from a larger cross-sectional area to a smaller one (contraction) or vice versa (expansion), energy losses occur due to changes in flow velocity and pressure. These losses are caused by flow separation, turbulence, and vortices that develop during the expansion or contraction process.

3. Fitting and Bend Losses:

Losses occur at fittings, valves, elbows, bends, and other obstructions in the flow path due to changes in flow direction, turbulence generation, and additional frictional effects. These losses can be significant, especially in complex piping systems with numerous fittings and bends.

4. Viscous Dissipation:

Viscous dissipation refers to the conversion of mechanical energy into heat within the fluid due to internal friction and molecular interactions. This loss of energy is proportional to the viscosity of the fluid and the rate of deformation, particularly significant in highly viscous fluids or at high flow velocities.

5. Hydraulic Jump:

In open-channel flow, a hydraulic jump occurs when a high-velocity flow encounters a lower-velocity flow, leading to a sudden increase in water depth and energy dissipation. Energy losses in hydraulic jumps result from turbulence and mixing as the kinetic energy of the flowing water is converted into potential and thermal energy.

6. Sudden Enlargement and Contraction Losses:

Sudden changes in pipe diameter, such as expansions or contractions, cause energy losses due to flow separation, turbulence, and pressure changes. These losses are particularly pronounced in cases where the change in diameter is abrupt and not properly designed.

7. Heat Transfer Losses:

In certain fluid systems, energy losses occur due to heat transfer between the fluid and the surroundings or between different fluid streams. Heat transfer losses can result in temperature changes within the fluid, affecting its properties and overall performance.

ORIFICE METER

An orifice meter is a device used to measure the rate of flow of a fluid within a pipeline by utilizing the principle of differential pressure across an orifice plate inserted into the flow stream. It's one of the most common flow meters used in industries for measuring the flow of liquids, gases, and steam. Here's a detailed explanation of the orifice meter, its components, working principle, advantages, and limitations:

Components of an Orifice Meter:

1. **Orifice Plate**: A thin, flat plate with a precisely machined hole (or orifice) in the center. The orifice plate is installed perpendicular to the flow direction within the pipeline.
2. **Pressure Taps**: Small holes drilled into the pipeline upstream and downstream of the orifice plate to measure the pressure difference across the orifice.
3. **Pressure Transmitters or Gauges**: Devices used to measure the pressure at the upstream and downstream taps and transmit the readings to a control system or display unit.

Working Principle:

1. **Flow Restriction**: When the fluid flows through the orifice plate, it experiences a restriction due to the presence of the small orifice. This restriction causes an increase in fluid velocity and a corresponding decrease in pressure according to Bernoulli's principle.
2. **Differential Pressure Measurement**: The pressure difference (ΔP) between the upstream and downstream taps is measured using pressure transmitters or gauges. This differential pressure is proportional to the

square of the flow rate (Q) through the orifice, as per the Bernoulli equation.

3. **Calculation of Flow Rate**: The flow rate is calculated using a flow equation that relates the differential pressure, fluid properties, orifice diameter, and other factors. Common equations used include the ISO 5167 standard equations or empirical correlations derived from experimental data.

Advantages of Orifice Meters:

1. **Simple Design**: Orifice meters have a simple and robust design, making them cost-effective and easy to install and maintain.
2. **Wide Range of Applications**: They can be used for measuring the flow of various fluids, including liquids, gases, and steam, in a wide range of industrial processes.
3. **Reliable Performance**: Orifice meters provide accurate and repeatable measurements under a wide range of flow conditions when properly installed and calibrated.

Limitations of Orifice Meters:

1. **Permanent Pressure Loss**: Orifice meters cause a permanent pressure drop across the orifice plate, leading to energy losses in the system.
2. **Limited Turndown Ratio**: Orifice meters have a limited turndown ratio (the ratio of maximum flow rate to minimum flow rate), which may not be suitable for applications with widely varying flow rates.
3. **Sensitive to Installation Conditions**: Proper installation and alignment of the orifice plate and pressure taps are crucial for accurate measurements. Any disturbances or irregularities in the flow profile upstream of the orifice can affect the measurement accuracy.

Applications of Orifice Meters:

1. **Oil and Gas Industry**: Used for measuring the flow of natural gas, crude oil, and refined petroleum products in pipelines and refineries.

2. **Chemical Processing**: Used in chemical plants for monitoring the flow of liquids and gases in various processes, such as chemical reactions and distillation.
3. **Water and Wastewater Treatment**: Applied in water treatment plants and sewage systems for measuring the flow of water, sludge, and other fluids.

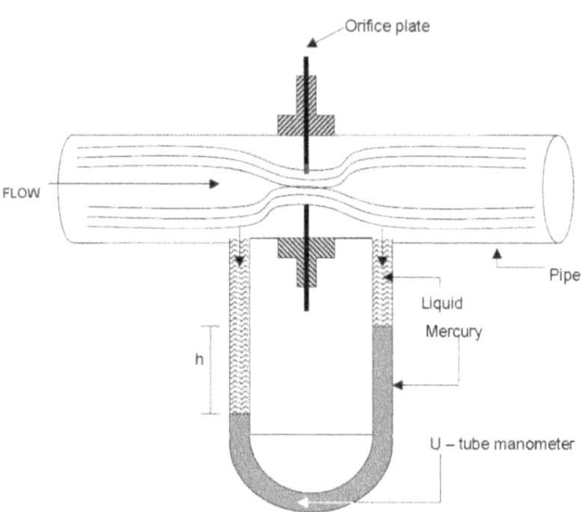

VENTURIMETER

A venturi meter is a flow measurement device used to determine the flow rate of a fluid in a pipeline. It operates on the principle of Bernoulli's equation, which relates the pressure and velocity of a fluid in a flowing stream. A venturi meter consists of a converging section, a throat, and a diverging section. Here's a detailed explanation of the venturi meter, its components, working principle, advantages, and limitations:

Components of a Venturi Meter:

1. **Inlet (Converging Section):** The upstream section of the venturi meter where the diameter of the pipeline gradually decreases. This section increases the velocity of the fluid and decreases its pressure.

2. **Throat**: The narrowest part of the venturi meter where the fluid reaches its maximum velocity. This is the point of lowest pressure in the venturi meter.
3. **Outlet (Diverging Section):** The downstream section where the diameter of the pipeline gradually increases again. This section reduces the velocity of the fluid and increases its pressure back to near the upstream level.
4. **Pressure Taps**: Small holes drilled into the pipeline at the entrance and throat of the venturi meter. These taps are used to measure the pressure difference (ΔP) between the entrance and throat.

Working Principle:

1. **Pressure Difference**: As the fluid flows through the converging section of the venturi meter, its velocity increases, leading to a decrease in pressure according to Bernoulli's principle.
2. **Maximum Velocity at Throat**: The fluid reaches its maximum velocity at the throat of the venturi meter due to the constriction of the flow area.
3. **Pressure Recovery**: In the diverging section, the velocity of the fluid decreases, causing a corresponding increase in pressure. This pressure recovery occurs as the kinetic energy of the fluid is converted back into pressure energy.
4. **Measurement of Pressure Difference**: The pressure taps at the entrance and throat of the venturi meter measure the pressure difference (ΔP) caused by the change in velocity and pressure. This pressure difference is proportional to the square of the flow rate (Q) through the venturi meter.
5. **Calculation of Flow Rate:** Using the measured pressure difference and the known properties of the fluid and venturi meter, the flow rate can be calculated using empirical equations or standard tables.

Advantages of Venturi Meters:

1. **High Accuracy**: Venturi meters offer high accuracy and repeatability in flow measurements compared to other flow measurement devices.
2. **Low Permanent Pressure Loss**: Venturi meters have lower permanent pressure loss compared to orifice meters, making them suitable for applications where energy conservation is important.
3. **Wide Range of Applications**: They can be used to measure the flow of various fluids, including liquids, gases, and steam, in a wide range of industrial processes.

Limitations of Venturi Meters:

1. **Complex Design:** Venturi meters have a more complex design compared to orifice meters, which can make them more expensive to manufacture and install.
2. **Sensitive to Installation Conditions**: Proper installation and alignment of the venturi meter are crucial for accurate measurements. Any disturbances or irregularities in the flow profile upstream of the venturi meter can affect measurement accuracy.
3. **Limited Turndown Ratio**: Venturi meters have a limited turndown ratio, which may not be suitable for applications with widely varying flow rates.

Applications of Venturi Meters:

1. **Water Supply Systems:** Used for measuring the flow of water in municipal water supply systems, irrigation systems, and wastewater treatment plants.
2. **Oil and Gas Industry**: Applied in oil and gas production, refining, and transportation for measuring the flow of crude oil, natural gas, and refined petroleum products.
3. **Chemical Processing**: Utilized in chemical plants for monitoring the flow of various liquids and gases in chemical reactions, mixing processes, and distillation.

Conclusion:

Venturi meters are widely used flow measurement devices that offer high accuracy, low permanent pressure loss, and versatility for a variety of industrial applications. While they have certain limitations, proper installation, calibration, and maintenance can ensure accurate and reliable flow measurements in fluid systems. Advanced techniques, such as computational fluid dynamics (CFD), are often employed to optimize the design and performance of venturi meters in specific applications.

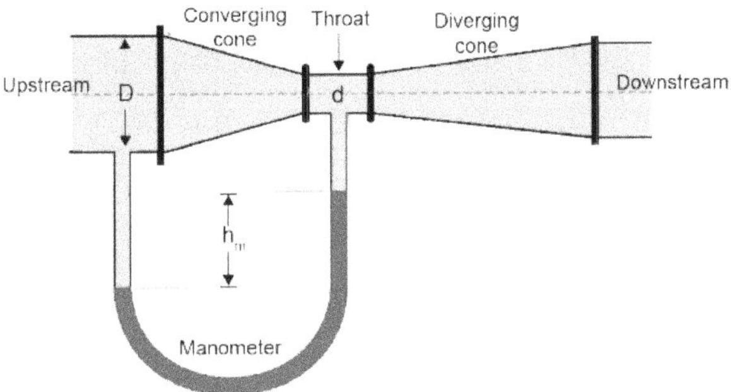

PITOT TUBE AND ROTOMETER

Pitot Tube:

A Pitot tube is a simple and commonly used instrument for measuring fluid flow velocity, particularly in applications involving gases or air. It operates based on the principle of stagnation pressure, which is the pressure exerted by a fluid when it comes to a complete stop (stagnates). Here's a detailed overview:

Components of a Pitot Tube:

1. **Tube Assembly**: The main body of the Pitot tube, typically made of stainless steel or another durable material, with a hollow tube extending into the fluid flow.
2. **Stagnation (Impact) Port**: Located at the front of the tube, this port is positioned directly facing the flow. It captures the stagnation pressure of the fluid.

3. **Static Pressure Port**: Located on the side of the tube, perpendicular to the flow direction. It measures the static pressure of the fluid, unaffected by its velocity.

Working Principle:

1. **Stagnation Pressure**: As fluid flows into the Pitot tube, its velocity increases, and the fluid comes to a stop at the stagnation port, resulting in the highest pressure, known as the stagnation pressure.
2. **Static Pressure**: The static pressure port, positioned away from the flow direction, measures the pressure of the fluid unaffected by its velocity.
3. **Differential Pressure**: The difference between the stagnation pressure and static pressure is directly proportional to the velocity of the fluid flow, according to Bernoulli's principle.
4. **Calculation of Velocity**: Using the measured differential pressure and the fluid properties, the velocity of the fluid flow can be calculated using appropriate equations or conversion factors.

Applications:

1. **Aircraft:** Pitot tubes are widely used in aircraft to measure airspeed (velocity of the aircraft relative to the surrounding air).
2. **HVAC Systems**: Used to measure air velocity in heating, ventilation, and air conditioning (HVAC) systems for indoor air quality control.
3. **Weather Monitoring**: Pitot tubes are utilized in weather instruments such as anemometers for measuring wind speed.

ROTAMETER:

A Rotameter, also known as a variable-area flowmeter, is a device used to measure the flow rate of a fluid by measuring the position of a freely moving float inside a tapered tube. The principle of operation is based on balancing the gravitational force acting on the float with the drag force exerted by the flowing fluid. Here's a detailed explanation:

Components of a Rotameter:

1. **Tapered Tube**: The main body of the Rotameter, usually made of glass or transparent plastic, with a uniform taper from top to bottom.
2. **Float:** A buoyant object, often shaped like a sphere or cylinder, which moves freely inside the tapered tube in response to the fluid flow.
3. **Scale**: A calibrated scale marked on the outside of the tube, indicating the flow rate corresponding to the position of the float.

Working Principle:

1. **Balancing Forces:** As fluid flows upward through the tapered tube, it exerts a drag force on the float, causing it to rise. The gravitational force acting on the float opposes this upward motion.
2. **Equilibrium Position**: The float reaches an equilibrium position where the gravitational force and the drag force are balanced. The position of the float within the tube corresponds to a specific flow rate.
3. **Flow Rate Measurement**: By observing the position of the float relative to the scale on the tube, the flow rate of the fluid can be determined.

Applications:

1. **Laboratory Experiments**: Rotameters are commonly used in laboratory settings for measuring the flow rates of gases and liquids in experiments and research.
2. **Industrial Processes**: Widely used in industrial applications such as chemical processing, pharmaceutical manufacturing, and water treatment for monitoring and controlling fluid flow rates.
3. **Pilot Plants**: Used in pilot plants and small-scale production facilities for process development and optimization.

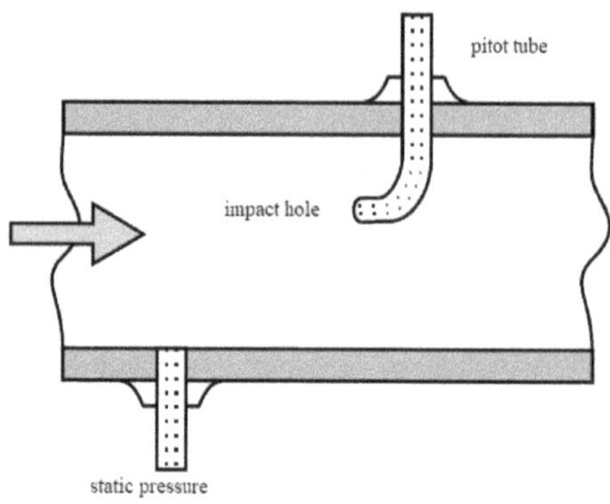

PITOT TUBE

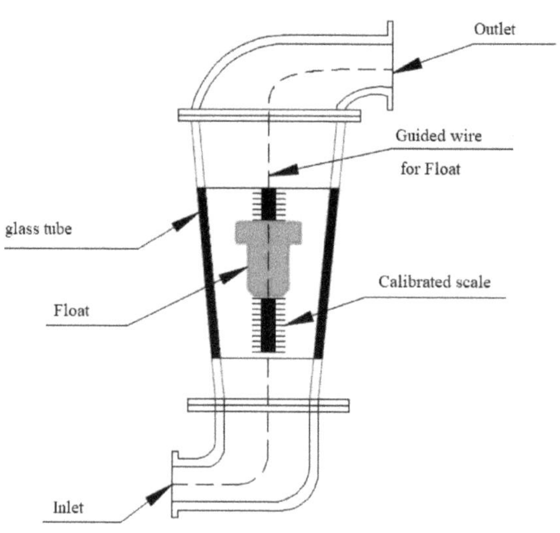

ROTAMERE

CHAPTER – 2

SIZE REDUCTION – I

Dr. Gopal Garg

Professor, Rajiv Gandhi Institute of Pharmacy, Faculty of Pharmaceutical Science & Technology, AKS University Satna, MP-India

---

Abstract:

Size reduction, a crucial process in various industries, aims to decrease the size of solid particles to enhance processing efficiency and product quality. This objective is achieved through mechanisms such as compression, impact, attrition, and cutting. The choice of mechanism depends on the material properties and the desired particle size. Governing laws, such as Rittinger's, Kick's, and Bond's laws, describe the energy requirements for size reduction, emphasizing the relationship between energy input and particle size decrease. Several factors affect size reduction, including material hardness, moisture content, feed size, and machine type. Understanding these factors and applying the appropriate laws and mechanisms ensures optimal size reduction, enhancing efficiency and product consistency across various applications.

Introduction

Size reduction is a fundamental process in various industries, including pharmaceuticals, food processing, mining, and recycling. It involves reducing the size of solid materials into smaller particles or pieces.

This process is crucial for several reasons:

1. **Ease of Handling**: Smaller particles are often easier to handle, transport, and store. They occupy less space and are more convenient for further processing or packaging.
2. **Increased Surface Area**: Size reduction increases the surface area of the material, which can be advantageous for processes like dissolution,

extraction, and chemical reactions. This is particularly important in industries such as pharmaceuticals and food, where the efficacy of the product depends on its surface area.

3. **Improved Uniformity**: Size reduction helps in achieving uniformity in particle size, which is vital for consistent product quality and performance.
4. **Enhanced Reactivity**: In chemical and biochemical processes, reducing particle size can enhance reactivity by exposing more reactive sites on the material's surface.
5. **Ease of Mixing**: Smaller particles mix more easily and uniformly with other materials, facilitating processes like blending and homogenization.

There are various methods employed for size reduction, each suitable for different materials and desired particle sizes. Some of the commonly used methods include:

1. **Crushing**: This involves applying compressive force to break large particles into smaller ones. Crushers, such as jaw crushers, gyratory crushers, and cone crushers, are commonly used for this purpose.
2. **Grinding**: Grinding is a process of reducing the size of particles by applying shear, impact, or attrition forces. It's commonly used for reducing the particle size of materials such as grains, spices, and minerals. Equipment like ball mills, hammer mills, and attrition mills are used for grinding.
3. **Milling**: Milling is similar to grinding but typically involves more controlled processes to achieve specific particle sizes and shapes. It's commonly used in industries such as pharmaceuticals and chemicals.
4. **Cutting and Chopping**: Cutting and chopping involve physically shearing or slicing materials into smaller pieces. Equipment like knives, blades, and cutters are used for this purpose, and it's commonly employed in the food processing industry.

5. **Shredding**: Shredding is a specialized form of size reduction that involves tearing materials into smaller pieces using sharp blades or teeth. It's commonly used for recycling applications, such as shredding plastic or paper waste.
6. **Pulverization**: Pulverization involves reducing materials to very fine particles or powders. It's often used in industries such as pharmaceuticals and cosmetics to achieve precise particle sizes.

The choice of method depends on factors such as the properties of the material, desired particle size distribution, and the specific requirements of the end product. Additionally, considerations such as energy efficiency, equipment cost, and maintenance requirements play a crucial role in selecting the appropriate size reduction method for a given application.

OBJECTIVES, MECHANISMS & LAWS GOVERNING SIZE REDUCTION

Objectives of Size Reduction:

1. **Particle Size Reduction**: The primary objective is to reduce the size of solid materials into smaller particles or pieces, often to achieve specific particle size distributions required for various applications.
2. **Enhanced Surface Area**: Increasing the surface area of the material facilitates processes like dissolution, extraction, and chemical reactions. Thus, one objective is to maximize the material's surface area by reducing particle size.
3. **Improving Process Efficiency**: Size reduction aims to enhance the efficiency of subsequent processes, such as mixing, blending, compaction, and granulation, by reducing particle size and achieving uniformity.
4. **Improved Product Performance**: In industries like pharmaceuticals and food processing, size reduction is crucial for improving product

performance, such as bioavailability of drugs or texture and taste of food products.

Mechanisms of Size Reduction:

1. **Compression**: This mechanism involves applying compressive forces to break large particles into smaller ones. It's commonly observed in processes like crushing, where materials are subjected to high pressure between two surfaces.
2. **Impact:** Impact occurs when particles are struck by a moving object or subjected to sudden shock or collision forces. This mechanism is prevalent in processes like grinding and milling, where particles are reduced in size by the impact of rapidly moving grinding media or hammers.
3. **Shear:** Shear forces cause materials to deform or break by sliding or tearing along planes of weakness within the material. Cutting, chopping, and shredding processes primarily rely on shear mechanisms to reduce particle size.
4. **Attrition**: Attrition involves the wearing down or gradual reduction of particle size due to frictional forces between particles or between particles and the surfaces of equipment. It's commonly observed in processes like milling and grinding, where particles are continuously subjected to abrasive forces.

Laws Governing Size Reduction:

1. **Kick's Law**: Proposed by German scientist, Kick's Law states that the energy required for size reduction is directly proportional to the size reduction ratio. In other words, the energy required to reduce the particle size by a certain amount is proportional to the initial size of the particles.
2. **Rittinger's Law**: Proposed by German engineer, Rittinger's Law states that the energy required for size reduction is directly proportional to the increase in surface area. This law applies to fine grinding processes where

the size reduction is primarily due to surface area increase rather than volume reduction.

3. **Bond's Law**: Proposed by British chemist, Bond's Law states that the energy required for size reduction is inversely proportional to the square root of the particle size. It's commonly used in the analysis of grinding processes and helps in estimating the energy consumption for size reduction operations.

Factors affecting size reduction

The size reduction process is influenced by various factors that can affect the efficiency and effectiveness of the operation. Here's a detailed exploration of the factors affecting size reduction:

1. Properties of Feed Material:

a. **Hardness**: Harder materials require more energy for size reduction compared to softer ones. Materials with high hardness may necessitate the use of tougher equipment or abrasion-resistant materials for efficient size reduction.

b. **Brittleness**: Brittle materials tend to fracture easily under stress, making them suitable for processes like crushing and impact grinding. Ductile materials, on the other hand, may deform rather than fracture, requiring different size reduction techniques.

c. **Moisture Content**: Moisture content affects the behavior of materials during size reduction. High moisture content can lead to material sticking and agglomeration, reducing the efficiency of size reduction processes like grinding and milling.

d. **Fat Content**: In food processing, the fat content of materials can affect their behavior during size reduction. Higher fat content may lead to material sticking and clogging in equipment, necessitating adjustments in processing parameters.

2. Equipment Design and Operating Parameters:

a. **Type of Equipment**: Different types of equipment, such as crushers, grinders, and shredders, have unique mechanisms of action and are suitable for specific size reduction applications. Selecting the appropriate equipment is crucial for achieving desired particle sizes efficiently.

b. **Speed and Feed Rate**: The speed at which the equipment operates and the rate at which feed material is supplied can significantly impact the effectiveness of size reduction. Optimal speed and feed rates ensure efficient particle size reduction while minimizing energy consumption and equipment wear.

c. **Screen Size and Configuration**: In processes like milling and grinding, the size and configuration of screens or perforated plates can influence the particle size distribution of the final product. Fine-tuning screen size and configuration allows for control over the desired particle size range.

d. **Rotor Design and Hammer Configuration**: For impact mills and crushers, the design of the rotor and the configuration of hammers or impactors play a crucial role in determining particle size distribution and throughput. Optimizing rotor design and hammer configuration can enhance size reduction efficiency.

3. Operating Conditions:

a. **Temperature:** Temperature can affect the properties of materials and the performance of size reduction equipment. Elevated temperatures may soften materials, reducing their resistance to size reduction, while excessively low temperatures can increase material brittleness.

b. **Pressure**: In processes like compression and extrusion, pressure plays a significant role in size reduction. Controlling pressure levels is essential for achieving desired particle sizes and preventing equipment damage.

c. **Environment**: Factors such as humidity and air flow can influence the behavior of materials during size reduction. Proper environmental control is necessary to prevent material sticking, agglomeration, or degradation.

4. Material Feed Size and Shape:

a. **Initial Particle Size:** The initial size of the feed material affects the energy consumption and efficiency of size reduction processes. Larger particles may require more energy to break down into smaller sizes.

b. **Particle Shape**: Irregularly shaped particles may resist size reduction more than spherical or cuboidal particles. Understanding the particle shape is essential for selecting appropriate size reduction techniques and equipment.

5. Material Handling and Feeding:

a. **Uniformity of Feed**: Uniform feeding of materials into size reduction equipment ensures consistent particle size distribution in the final product. Irregular or uneven feeding can lead to variations in particle size and reduced process efficiency.

b. **Material Flow Properties**: The flow properties of materials, such as cohesion, adhesion, and friction, influence their behavior during size reduction and feeding. Understanding these properties helps in optimizing material handling and feeding systems.

HAMMER MILL

Principles of Hammer Mill:

A hammer mill operates on the principle of impact where particles are struck by rapidly moving hammers attached to a rotating shaft. The hammers impact the feed material, causing it to break into smaller pieces. The size of the final product is determined by the size and configuration of the hammer mill's screen or perforated grate through which the particles must pass.

Construction of Hammer Mill:

a. **Rotor:** The rotor is the main component of the hammer mill and consists of a series of hammers mounted on a central shaft. These hammers can be fixed or swinging depending on the design of the mill.
b. **Hammers**: The hammers are typically made of hardened steel and come in various shapes and sizes. They are arranged around the rotor and are free to swing or rotate freely.
c. **Screen or Perforated Grate**: Beneath the rotor, there is a screen or perforated grate that determines the size of the final product. The perforations or holes in the screen allow particles smaller than the desired size to pass through while larger particles are retained and further reduced by the hammers.
d. **Housing:** The housing of the hammer mill encloses the rotor and other internal components and provides support and protection. It may include access doors for maintenance and inspection.

Working of Hammer Mill:

a. **Feeding**: Feed material is introduced into the hammer mill through an inlet chute or hopper.
b. **Impact**: As the rotor rotates at high speed, the hammers swing or rotate, striking the feed material with significant force.
c. **Size Reduction**: The impact of the hammers breaks the feed material into smaller particles. The size of the particles is determined by the size of the openings in the screen or perforated grate.
d. **Discharge**: The smaller particles pass through the screen or grate and are discharged from the bottom of the hammer mill, while larger particles are continuously reduced until they reach the desired size.

Uses of Hammer Mill:

a. **Size Reduction**: Hammer mills are widely used for size reduction in industries such as agriculture, food processing, pharmaceuticals, and mining. They can reduce a variety of materials including grains, herbs, spices, wood, biomass, and minerals.

b. **Grinding**: Hammer mills are also used for grinding operations where finer particle sizes are desired, such as in the production of animal feeds and fine powders.

c. **Shredding:** Some hammer mills are designed for shredding applications, such as shredding waste materials like cardboard, paper, and plastic.

Merits of Hammer Mill:

a. **Versatility**: Hammer mills can handle a wide range of materials and particle sizes, making them versatile for various applications.

b. **High Production Rate:** Hammer mills can achieve high production rates with relatively low energy consumption, making them efficient for size reduction operations.

c. **Simple Design**: Hammer mills have a simple design, which makes them easy to operate, maintain, and clean.

Demerits of Hammer Mill:

a. **High Wear and Maintenance**: The high-speed impact and abrasion involved in hammer mill operation can lead to significant wear and tear on the hammers, screens, and other components, requiring frequent maintenance and replacement.

b. **Particle Size Variation**: Achieving precise particle size control can be challenging with hammer mills, as the size of the final product depends on factors such as hammer speed, screen size, and feed rate.

c. **Dust Generation**: Hammer milling operations can generate a significant amount of dust, which may pose safety and environmental hazards if not properly controlled.

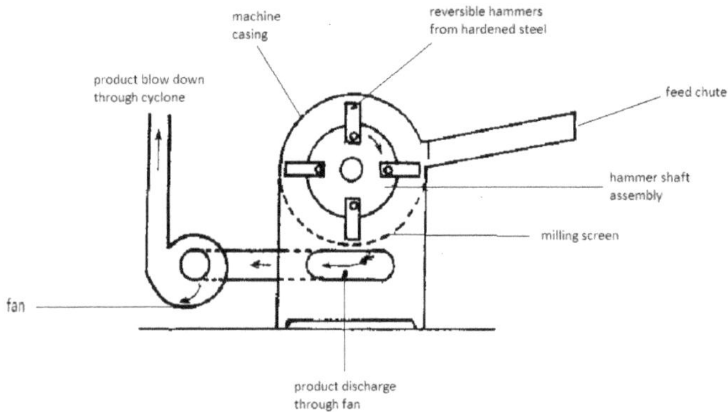

BALL MILL

Principles of Ball Mill:

A ball mill operates on the principle of impact and attrition, where the grinding media (usually metallic balls) impact the feed material, causing it to break or disintegrate. The grinding media and the material to be ground are placed in a rotating cylindrical shell. As the shell rotates, the grinding media cascade and tumble onto the material, effectively crushing and grinding it.

Construction of Ball Mill:

a. **Cylindrical Shell**: The ball mill consists of a hollow cylindrical shell that rotates about its axis. The shell is made of steel or other materials and is lined with wear-resistant liners to protect it from abrasion.

b. **Grinding Media**: Inside the shell, grinding media such as steel balls are placed. The size and composition of the grinding media vary depending on the desired fineness of the final product and the characteristics of the material being ground.

c. **Drive System**: A motor and gearbox are used to rotate the cylindrical shell of the ball mill. The speed of rotation can be adjusted to control the grinding process.

d. **Discharge System**: At the discharge end of the ball mill, a grate or screen is typically used to control the size of the final product. The ground material is discharged through the grate while the grinding media are retained inside the mill.

Working of Ball Mill:

a. **Loading:** The feed material, along with the grinding media, is loaded into the ball mill.
b. **Rotation:** The cylindrical shell of the ball mill rotates about its axis, causing the grinding media to cascade and tumble onto the feed material.
c. **Impact and Attrition**: As the grinding media impact the feed material, it is crushed and ground into smaller particles through a combination of impact and attrition forces.
d. **Size Reduction**: The grinding process continues until the desired fineness of the final product is achieved. The size of the final product is determined by factors such as the size and composition of the grinding media, the speed of rotation, and the duration of milling.
e. **Discharge**: The ground material passes through the grate or screen at the discharge end of the ball mill, while the grinding media are retained inside the mill for further grinding.

Uses of Ball Mill:

a. **Grinding:** Ball mills are widely used for grinding various materials into fine powders. They are commonly used in industries such as cement, ceramics, metallurgy, and mineral processing to grind materials ranging from ores and minerals to chemicals and pigments.
b. **Mixing and Blending**: Ball mills can also be used for mixing and blending purposes, where different materials are combined to form homogeneous mixtures.
c. **Size Reduction**: Ball mills are effective for size reduction of both coarse and fine materials, making them suitable for a wide range of applications requiring particle size reduction.

Merits of Ball Mill:

a. **High Efficiency**: Ball mills offer high grinding efficiency due to their relatively large grinding surface area and efficient collision of grinding media with the feed material.

b. **Versatility**: Ball mills can be used for both wet and dry grinding operations, making them versatile for various processing applications.

c. **Uniform Product Size Distribution**: Ball mills produce a uniform product size distribution, ensuring consistent product quality and performance.

Demerits of Ball Mill:

a. **High Energy Consumption**: Ball milling can consume a significant amount of energy, especially for fine grinding operations, leading to high operating costs.

b. **Wear and Maintenance**: The grinding media and liners inside the ball mill are subject to wear and require regular maintenance and replacement, increasing downtime and maintenance costs.

c. **Size Limitations:** Ball mills have limitations on the maximum feed size and the fineness of the final product, which may restrict their applicability in certain size reduction applications.

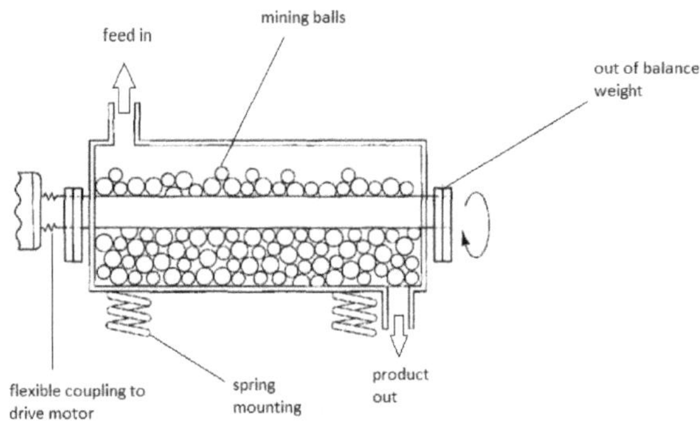

CHAPTER – 3

SIZE REDUCTION – II

Mrs. Kiran Shukla

Associate Professor, Rajiv Gandhi Institute of Pharmacy, Faculty of Pharmaceutical Science & Technology, AKS University Satna, MP-India

---

Abstract:

Size reduction is essential in numerous industries, enabling the transformation of bulk materials into finer particles for improved processing and product quality. One advanced method for achieving fine particle sizes is the fluid energy mill, which utilizes high-velocity air or steam jets to induce particle collisions and fractures. This method is particularly effective for producing extremely fine powders with narrow particle size distributions. The edge runner mill and end runner mill are traditional size reduction machines that operate on different principles. The edge runner mill consists of a horizontal grinding table and heavy wheels that roll over the material, applying shear and compressive forces to achieve size reduction. In contrast, the end runner mill features a vertical, cylindrical vessel with a rotating pestle that grinds the material against the vessel walls, utilizing impact and attrition forces. Each of these mills is suited to specific applications, depending on the material properties and desired final particle size. By selecting the appropriate milling equipment and understanding the mechanisms involved, industries can achieve efficient and consistent size reduction, optimizing the performance and quality of their products.

FLUID ENERGY MILL

Principles of Fluid Energy Mill:

A fluid energy mill operates on the principle of fluid energy milling, where a high-velocity stream of gas (usually air) is used to impart energy to particles, causing them to fracture and reduce in size. The feed material is introduced into the mill along with the high-velocity gas stream, and the particles are subjected to intense collisions and attrition within the milling chamber.

Construction of Fluid Energy Mill:

a. **Milling Chamber**: The fluid energy mill consists of a cylindrical milling chamber where the size reduction process takes place. The chamber is typically constructed of stainless steel or other materials resistant to corrosion and abrasion.

b. **Injector Nozzle**: At the entrance of the milling chamber, there is an injector nozzle through which the high-velocity gas stream is introduced. The gas stream carries the feed material into the milling chamber and provides the energy necessary for size reduction.

c. **Classifier**: Inside the milling chamber, a classifier is used to separate fine particles from coarser ones. The classifier may be integrated into the mill or positioned externally, depending on the design.

Working of Fluid Energy Mill:

a. **Feed Introduction**: The feed material is introduced into the fluid energy mill along with the high-velocity gas stream through the injector nozzle.

b. **Particle Size Reduction**: As the feed material enters the milling chamber, it is subjected to intense collisions and attrition with the gas stream and other particles. This energy imparted by the gas stream causes the particles to fracture and reduce in size.

c. **Classification**: Fine particles generated during the milling process are carried by the gas stream and separated from the coarser particles by the classifier. The fine particles are collected as the product, while the coarser particles may undergo further milling or be recycled for further processing.

d. **Gas Exhaust:** After passing through the milling chamber, the gas stream, along with the fine particles, exits the mill and may be directed to a cyclone separator or filter for separation of the particles from the gas stream.

Uses of Fluid Energy Mill:

a. **Fine Grinding**: Fluid energy mills are commonly used for fine grinding and micronization of dry powders and crystalline materials. They are particularly suitable for grinding heat-sensitive and friable materials.
b. **Particle Size Reduction**: Fluid energy mills are effective for reducing particle size distribution and achieving narrow particle size distributions, making them suitable for applications requiring precise control over particle size.
c. **Milling of Abrasive Materials**: Fluid energy mills are often used for milling abrasive materials that may damage other types of milling equipment due to their gentle grinding action.

Merits of Fluid Energy Mill:

a. **High Efficiency**: Fluid energy mills offer high grinding efficiency due to the intense collisions and attrition experienced by particles within the milling chamber.
b. **Low Heat Generation**: The low-temperature milling environment in fluid energy mills minimizes the risk of thermal degradation or agglomeration of heat-sensitive materials.
c. **Versatility:** Fluid energy mills can handle a wide range of materials, including heat-sensitive, friable, and abrasive materials, making them versatile for various applications.

Demerits of Fluid Energy Mill:

a. **High Energy Consumption**: Fluid energy milling can consume a significant amount of energy, especially when processing fine particles, leading to high operating costs.

b. **Equipment Complexity**: Fluid energy mills may be more complex and expensive to operate and maintain compared to some other size reduction equipment, requiring skilled operators and regular maintenance.
c. **Particle Size Limitations**: Fluid energy mills may have limitations on the maximum feed size and the fineness of the final product, which may restrict their applicability in certain size reduction applications.

Despite these limitations, fluid energy mills are widely used in industries such as pharmaceuticals, chemicals, and food processing for their ability to achieve fine particle sizes and narrow particle size distributions efficiently. Proper selection, operation, and maintenance are essential for maximizing the performance and efficiency of fluid energy mills in size reduction applications.

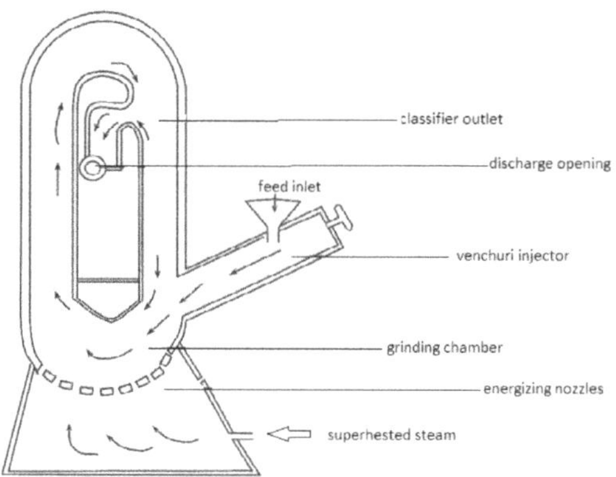

EDGE RUNNER MILL

Principles of Edge Runner Mill:

An edge runner mill, also known as a runner stone mill, operates on the principle of grinding materials between two heavy wheels or stones mounted on a horizontal axle. The material to be ground is fed into the gap between the rotating wheels, where it is subjected to crushing, shearing, and grinding actions. The weight of the rotating wheels and the friction between the material and the wheels facilitate the size reduction process.

Construction of Edge Runner Mill:

a. **Runner Stones**: The key components of an edge runner mill are the two heavy wheels or stones, known as runner stones, which are typically made of granite or other hard materials. The runner stones are mounted on a horizontal axle and rotate in a circular motion.
b. **Base Plate:** The runner stones are mounted on a base plate or bed, which provides support and stability for the mill. The base plate may be made of wood, metal, or concrete, depending on the size and design of the mill.
c. **Feed Hopper**: A feed hopper is used to introduce the material to be ground into the gap between the runner stones. The material is fed manually or by gravity into the center of the rotating wheels.
d. **Drive Mechanism**: The rotation of the runner stones is typically driven by a motor or a manual crank connected to the axle. The speed of rotation can be adjusted to control the grinding process.

Working of Edge Runner Mill:

a. **Feed Introduction:** The material to be ground is fed into the gap between the rotating runner stones either manually or by gravity through the feed hopper.
b. **Crushing and Grinding**: As the runner stones rotate, they crush, shear, and grind the material between them. The weight of the rotating stones and the friction between the material and the stones facilitate the size reduction process.
c. **Particle Size Reduction**: The material undergoes size reduction as it passes through the gap between the runner stones. The size of the final product is determined by the gap between the stones and the duration of milling.
d. **Discharge**: The ground material is discharged from the edge of the runner stones, either continuously or intermittently, depending on the design of the mill.

Uses of Edge Runner Mill:

a. **Grinding and Crushing**: Edge runner mills are commonly used for grinding and crushing various materials, including ores, minerals, pigments, and chemicals.
b. **Mixing and Homogenization**: Edge runner mills can also be used for mixing and homogenizing materials to achieve uniformity in particle size and composition.
c. **Wet Grinding**: Edge runner mills are particularly suitable for wet grinding operations, where the material to be ground is in the form of a slurry or paste.

Merits of Edge Runner Mill:

a. **Simple Design**: Edge runner mills have a simple and robust design, making them easy to operate and maintain.
b. **High Efficiency**: Edge runner mills offer high grinding efficiency, especially for wet grinding operations, due to the large grinding surface area provided by the rotating stones.
c. **Versatility**: Edgc runner mills can handle a wide range of materials and particle sizes, making them versatile for various grinding and crushing applications.

Demerits of Edge Runner Mill:

a. **High Wear and Maintenance**: The runner stones and other components of edge runner mills are subject to wear and may require frequent maintenance and replacement.
b. **Limited Fineness**: Edge runner mills may have limitations on the fineness of the final product, especially for fine grinding applications, due to the gap between the rotating stones.
c. **Manual Operation:** Some edge runner mills may require manual operation, which can be labor-intensive and time-consuming.

Despite these limitations, edge runner mills are widely used in industries such as mining, ceramics, and pharmaceuticals for their effectiveness in grinding and crushing various materials efficiently. Proper selection, operation, and maintenance are essential for maximizing the performance and longevity of edge runner mills in size reduction applications.

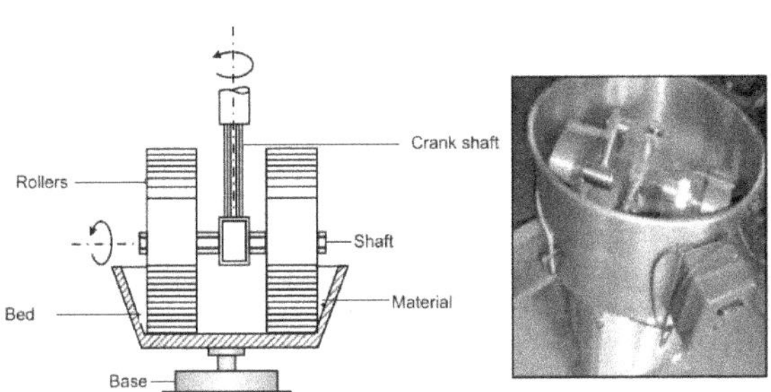

END RUNNER MILL

Principles of End Runner Mill:

An end runner mill, also known as a pestle and mortar mill, operates on the principle of grinding materials between a stationary cylindrical mortar containing rotating pestles. The material to be ground is fed into the mortar, and the rotating pestles crush, grind, and mix the material against the inner surface of the mortar. The size of the final product is determined by the gap between the pestles and the mortar and the duration of milling.

Construction of End Runner Mill:

a. **Mortar**: The mortar is a stationary cylindrical container made of hard materials such as stone, granite, or metal. It has a flat or slightly concave bottom surface where the material to be ground is placed.
b. **Pestles:** The pestles are cylindrical rods or shafts made of hard materials, such as metal or wood, with a heavy and flat bottom surface. They are

mounted horizontally on a central shaft or axle and rotate around their axis within the mortar.

c. **Drive Mechanism**: The rotation of the pestles is typically driven by a motor or manual crank connected to the central shaft. The speed of rotation can be adjusted to control the grinding process.

Working of End Runner Mill:

a. **Feed Introduction**: The material to be ground is placed into the mortar of the end runner mill.
b. **Grinding and Crushing**: As the pestles rotate within the mortar, they crush, grind, and mix the material against the inner surface of the mortar. The weight of the rotating pestles and the friction between the material and the mortar facilitate the size reduction process.
c. **Particle Size Reduction**: The material undergoes size reduction as it is crushed and ground between the rotating pestles and the mortar. The size of the final product is determined by the gap between the pestles and the mortar and the duration of milling.
d. **Discharge:** The ground material is discharged from the bottom of the mortar, either continuously or intermittently, depending on the design of the mill.

Uses of End Runner Mill:

a. **Grinding and Crushing**: End runner mills are commonly used for grinding and crushing various materials, including pharmaceuticals, food products, herbs, and spices.
b. **Mixing and Homogenization:** End runner mills can also be used for mixing and homogenizing materials to achieve uniformity in particle size and composition.
c. **Wet Grinding**: End runner mills are particularly suitable for wet grinding operations, where the material to be ground is in the form of a slurry or paste.

Merits of End Runner Mill:

a. **Simple Design**: End runner mills have a simple and robust design, making them easy to operate and maintain.
b. **High Efficiency**: End runner mills offer high grinding efficiency due to the large grinding surface area provided by the rotating pestles.
c. **Versatility**: End runner mills can handle a wide range of materials and particle sizes, making them versatile for various grinding and crushing applications.

Demerits of End Runner Mill:

a. **High Wear and Maintenance**: The pestles and other components of end runner mills are subject to wear and may require frequent maintenance and replacement.
b. **Limited Fineness**: End runner mills may have limitations on the fineness of the final product, especially for fine grinding applications, due to the gap between the rotating pestles and the mortar.
c. **Manual Operation**: Some end runner mills may require manual operation, which can be labor-intensive and time-consuming.

Despite these limitations, end runner mills are widely used in industries such as pharmaceuticals, food processing, and cosmetics for their effectiveness in grinding and crushing various materials efficiently. Proper selection, operation, and maintenance are essential for maximizing the performance and longevity of end runner mills in size reduction applications.

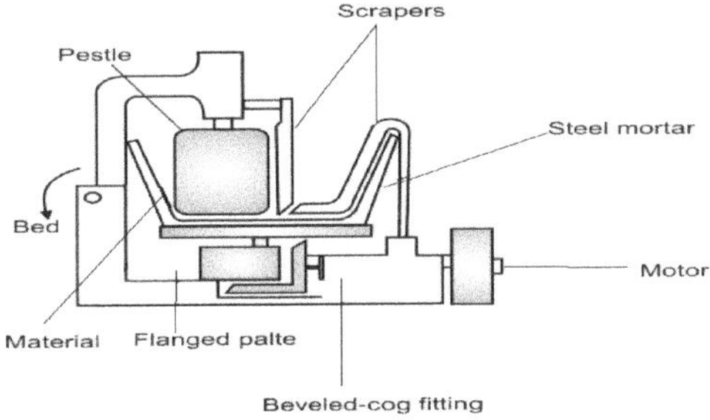

CHAPTER – 4

SIZE SEPARATION – I

Mrs. Shaily Goyal

Associate Professor, Rajiv Gandhi Institute of Pharmacy, Faculty of Pharmaceutical Science & Technology, AKS University Satna, MP-India

---

ABSTRACT:

Size separation, also known as sieving or classification, is a critical process in various industries to sort particles based on size. This process ensures uniformity and quality in final products by removing oversized or undersized particles. Techniques for size separation include sieving, air classification, and sedimentation. Sieving involves passing materials through screens with specific mesh sizes, separating particles accordingly. Air classification uses air flow to segregate particles based on their size and density, while sedimentation relies on the settling rates of particles in a fluid. Factors such as particle shape, density, and moisture content influence the efficiency of size separation. Implementing effective size separation techniques improves product quality, enhances process efficiency, and ensures compliance with industry standards, making it an indispensable part of material processing.

INTRODUCTION

Size separation is a fundamental process used in various fields, including chemical engineering, environmental science, pharmaceuticals, and mining, among others. It involves separating particles or components of a mixture based on their size or particle size distribution. This process is crucial for various industrial processes and research applications.

Principles of Size Separation:

1. **Size Exclusion**: Also known as sieving, it's the simplest method of size separation. It involves passing a mixture through a sieve or mesh with

specific openings. Particles smaller than the openings pass through, while larger particles are retained.

2. **Gravity Separation**: This method relies on the differences in the settling velocities of particles in a fluid medium. Heavier particles settle faster than lighter ones. Techniques like sedimentation and centrifugation utilize gravity separation.
3. **Centrifugation:** In this method, centrifugal force is used to separate particles based on their size and density. High-speed rotation causes denser and larger particles to sediment more rapidly than smaller or less dense particles.
4. **Filtration**: Filtration involves passing a mixture through a porous medium, where particles larger than the pores are retained, and the smaller ones pass through. It's commonly used in various industries, such as water treatment and pharmaceuticals.
5. **Hydrocyclones**: Hydrocyclones use centrifugal force to separate particles of different sizes in a liquid suspension. They are widely used in mineral processing, oil and gas industry, and environmental engineering.
6. **Electrophoresis:** This technique separates particles based on their electrophoretic mobility, which is influenced by their size and charge. It's extensively used in molecular biology and biochemistry for separating DNA fragments, proteins, and other biomolecules.

Factors Affecting Size Separation:

1. **Particle Size Distribution**: The range of particle sizes present in the mixture influences the choice of separation method and equipment.
2. **Particle Density**: Differences in particle density affect their settling rates in gravity-based separation methods.
3. **Fluid Properties**: Properties like viscosity and density of the fluid medium influence particle settling and separation efficiency.

4. **Equipment Design:** The design and operating parameters of separation equipment play a crucial role in determining separation efficiency.
5. **Operating Conditions**: Factors such as flow rate, temperature, and pressure can affect the performance of size separation processes.

Applications:

1. **Mining and Mineral Processing**: Size separation is used to concentrate valuable minerals from ore and to remove waste materials.
2. **Particle Size Analysis:** In research and quality control, size separation is used to determine the particle size distribution of a sample.
3. **Environmental Engineering**: It's used in water and wastewater treatment for separating suspended solids from liquids.
4. **Pharmaceuticals**: Size separation is crucial in pharmaceutical manufacturing for particle size control and purification of drugs.
5. **Food Industry**: It's used for separating food particles, such as flour milling, cereal processing, and in the production of beverages.

OBJECTIVES, APPLICATIONS & MECHANISM OF SIZE SEPARA TION

Objectives of Size Separation:

1. **Purification:** One of the primary objectives of size separation is to purify mixtures by removing unwanted particles or components based on their size.
2. **Particle Size Analysis:** Size separation is often used to analyze the particle size distribution of a sample, which is crucial for understanding the properties and behavior of materials.
3. **Concentration:** Size separation is employed to concentrate valuable components by separating them from the bulk of the mixture.
4. **Particle Size Control**: In various industries, maintaining precise control over particle size is essential for ensuring product quality and performance.

Applications of Size Separation:

1. **Mining and Mineral Processing**: Size separation is extensively used in mining and mineral processing to concentrate valuable minerals and to remove gangue materials.
2. **Environmental Engineering**: In water and wastewater treatment, size separation is employed to remove suspended solids, colloids, and other contaminants.
3. **Food Industry**: Size separation is crucial in food processing for separating different components such as flour, sugar, and grains, and for controlling the texture and quality of food products.
4. **Pharmaceuticals:** Size separation plays a critical role in pharmaceutical manufacturing for particle size control, purification of drugs, and formulation of dosage forms.
5. **Biotechnology and Life Sciences**: Techniques like centrifugation and electrophoresis are widely used for separating biomolecules such as DNA, proteins, and cells.
6. **Chemical Engineering**: Size separation is applied in various chemical processes such as crystallization, filtration, and distillation for separating solids from liquids or gases.

Mechanisms of Size Separation:

1. **Sieving**: This mechanism relies on the size exclusion principle, where particles smaller than the openings of a sieve pass through, while larger particles are retained.
2. **Gravity Separation**: It utilizes the differences in settling velocities of particles in a fluid medium. Heavier and larger particles settle faster than lighter and smaller ones.
3. **Centrifugation**: Centrifugal force is used to separate particles based on their size and density. Denser and larger particles sediment more rapidly under high-speed rotation.

4. **Filtration**: Filtration involves passing a mixture through a porous medium, where particles larger than the pores are retained, and the smaller ones pass through.
5. **Hydrocyclones**: Hydrocyclones use centrifugal force to separate particles of different sizes in a liquid suspension based on their mass and size.
6. **Electrophoresis**: This technique separates particles based on their electrophoretic mobility, which is influenced by their size and charge.

OFFICIAL STANDARDS OF POWDERS, SIEVES

Official standards for powders and sieves play a crucial role in ensuring consistency, accuracy, and quality in size separation processes. These standards provide guidelines and specifications for the manufacturing, testing, and use of powders and sieves, ensuring their suitability for various applications. Here's a detailed overview:

Standards for Powders:

1. **ISO 4490**: This standard specifies terms and definitions relating to test sieving using test sieves of woven wire cloth and perforated metal plate.
2. **ISO 10069**: It provides guidelines for the preparation of steel substrates before application of paints and related products.
3. **ISO 9276**: This standard specifies a method for the measurement of the particle size distribution of solid materials using test sieving techniques.
4. **ASTM B214**: It specifies the sieve sizes and designations for the American National Standard for Testing Materials (ASTM) E11 Test Sieve Standard.
5. **ISO 3310-1**: This standard specifies test sieves of metal wire cloth and perforated metal plate.
6. **ASTM B214**: It provides standard test methods for testing powder metals.

Standards for Sieves:

1. **ISO 3310-1:** This standard specifies the technical requirements and testing methods for test sieves of metal wire cloth and perforated metal plate.
2. **ASTM E11**: It covers the designations for test sieves of various materials, including woven wire cloth and perforated plate.
3. **ASTM B214**: This standard provides guidelines for the designation of test sieves and for determining the particle size distribution of metal powders.
4. **ISO 565**: It specifies the standard sieves and aperture sizes for test sieves used in test sieving.
5. **ASTM E161:** This standard specifies the designations for test sieves used in testing aggregates for concrete.
6. **ISO 10601**: It specifies test sieves of perforated metal plate.

Importance of Standards:

1. **Quality Assurance**: Standards ensure that powders and sieves meet specific quality criteria, leading to consistent and reliable results in size separation processes.
2. **Interoperability**: Standardized sieves allow for compatibility and interchangeability across different equipment and manufacturers, enhancing efficiency and reducing costs.
3. **Accuracy and Precision**: By specifying requirements for sieve construction and calibration, standards help maintain accuracy and precision in particle size analysis.
4. **Regulatory Compliance**: Compliance with international standards is often required for regulatory approval and certification in industries such as pharmaceuticals, food processing, and environmental testing.
5. **Uniformity**: Standards promote uniformity in the manufacturing and testing of powders and sieves, facilitating fair competition and market access.

6. **Safety**: Adherence to standards ensures the safety of operators and users by providing guidelines for the design and construction of sieves and related equipment.

SIZE SEPARATION PRINCIPLES

Size separation principles form the foundation of various techniques used to separate particles or components of a mixture based on their size or particle size distribution. These principles are fundamental to numerous industries and research fields. Here's a detailed overview of the key principles:

1. Sieving:

a. **Principle:** Sieving relies on the size exclusion principle, where particles smaller than the openings of a sieve pass through, while larger particles are retained.

b. **Mechanism:** A mixture is passed through a sieve or mesh with specific openings. Particles smaller than the openings fall through, while larger particles are retained on the sieve.

c. **Applications:** Sieving is widely used in industries such as pharmaceuticals, food processing, mining, and environmental engineering for particle size analysis, quality control, and separation of solid particles from a bulk material.

2. Gravity Separation:

a. **Principle**: Gravity separation exploits the differences in the settling velocities of particles in a fluid medium under the influence of gravity.

b. **Mechanism**: Heavier and larger particles settle faster than lighter and smaller ones in a fluid medium. This principle is used in sedimentation, where particles settle under gravity, and in centrifugation, where centrifugal force enhances particle separation.

c. **Applications:** Gravity separation is employed in mineral processing, wastewater treatment, oil and gas industry, and environmental engineering for separating particles based on their density and size.

3. Centrifugation:

a. **Principle:** Centrifugation utilizes centrifugal force generated by high-speed rotation to separate particles based on their size, shape, and density.

b. **Mechanism:** In a centrifuge, particles suspended in a liquid medium are subjected to centrifugal force, causing denser and larger particles to sediment more rapidly than smaller or less dense particles.

c. **Applications**: Centrifugation is used in molecular biology, biotechnology, pharmaceuticals, and industrial processes such as separation of cells, purification of biomolecules, and clarification of liquids.

4. Filtration:

a. **Principle**: Filtration involves passing a mixture through a porous medium, where particles larger than the pores are retained, and the smaller ones pass through.

b. **Mechanism**: The size of the particles retained depends on the pore size of the filter medium. Filtration can be achieved through various methods, including gravity filtration, vacuum filtration, and pressure filtration.

c. **Applications:** Filtration is widely used in water and wastewater treatment, air pollution control, food and beverage processing, and pharmaceutical manufacturing for separating solids from liquids or gases.

5. Hydrocyclones:

a. **Principle:** Hydrocyclones use centrifugal force to separate particles of different sizes in a liquid suspension based on their mass and size.

b. **Mechanism**: The mixture enters a cylindrical inlet section tangentially, creating a vortex. Under centrifugal force, larger and denser particles move outward and downward, while smaller and lighter particles move inward and upward.

c. **Applications:** Hydrocyclones are used in mineral processing, oil and gas industry, and environmental engineering for particle classification, dewatering, and desliming.

SIEVE SHAKER

Construction of Sieve Shaker:

1. **Base and Frame**: The base provides stability to the sieve shaker, while the frame supports the sieve stack during operation.
2. **Motor and Drive Mechanism**: An electric motor provides the necessary rotational motion to the sieve stack. The drive mechanism transmits the motor's rotational energy to the sieves via a shaft or belt.
3. **Sieve Stack**: The sieve stack consists of multiple sieves of different mesh sizes stacked vertically. Each sieve is held securely in place within the sieve shaker to prevent shifting during operation.
4. **Clamping System**: A clamping system holds the sieves in position and ensures uniform distribution of vibration across the entire stack.
5. **Vibration Mechanism**: The vibration mechanism imparts mechanical agitation to the sieve stack, facilitating the separation of particles based on size.

Working Principle of Sieve Shaker:

1. **Loading Sieves**: The sample to be sieved is evenly distributed across the top sieve of the stack.
2. **Adjustment of Settings**: The desired settings, including vibration intensity and duration, are selected based on the characteristics of the sample and the sieving requirements.
3. **Operation**: When the sieve shaker is turned on, the motor generates vibrations that are transmitted to the sieve stack. These vibrations cause the particles to move rapidly and bounce off the sieve surfaces, effectively separating them based on size.
4. **Sieving Process**: As the particles pass through the openings in the sieves, they are sorted into different fractions according to their size. The finer particles pass through the lower mesh sieves, while the coarser particles are retained on the upper sieves.
5. **Analysis**: After sieving is complete, the retained particles on each sieve are carefully collected and weighed, allowing for the determination of the particle size distribution of the sample.

Uses of Sieve Shaker:

1. **Particle Size Analysis**: Sieve shakers are commonly used in laboratories and quality control facilities for determining the particle size distribution of granular materials.
2. **Quality Control**: They are employed in various industries, including pharmaceuticals, food processing, mining, and construction, to ensure the consistency and quality of raw materials and finished products.
3. **Research and Development**: Sieve shakers play a crucial role in research and development activities, where precise control over particle size is necessary for experimentation and product development.
4. **Soil Analysis**: In geotechnical engineering, sieve shakers are used to analyze soil samples for determining their particle size distribution and classification.

Merits of Sieve Shaker:

1. **Efficiency:** Sieve shakers provide rapid and consistent sieving results, making them highly efficient for particle size analysis and quality control.
2. **Accuracy**: They offer precise control over sieving parameters, ensuring accurate determination of particle size distribution.
3. **Versatility**: Sieve shakers can accommodate a wide range of sieve sizes and types, allowing for versatility in particle size analysis.
4. **Ease of Use**: They are user-friendly devices that require minimal training for operation, making them suitable for use in various settings.

Demerits of Sieve Shaker:

1. **Size Limitations**: Sieve shakers are typically limited to relatively small sample sizes, which may not be suitable for large-scale industrial applications.
2. **Noise and Vibration**: The operation of sieve shakers can produce noise and vibration, which may require appropriate measures to minimize workplace disruption and ensure operator safety.
3. **Maintenance**: Regular maintenance is required to ensure the proper functioning of sieve shakers, including cleaning, lubrication, and inspection of components.
4. **Cost:** High-quality sieve shakers can be expensive to purchase and maintain, particularly for smaller laboratories or facilities with limited budgets.

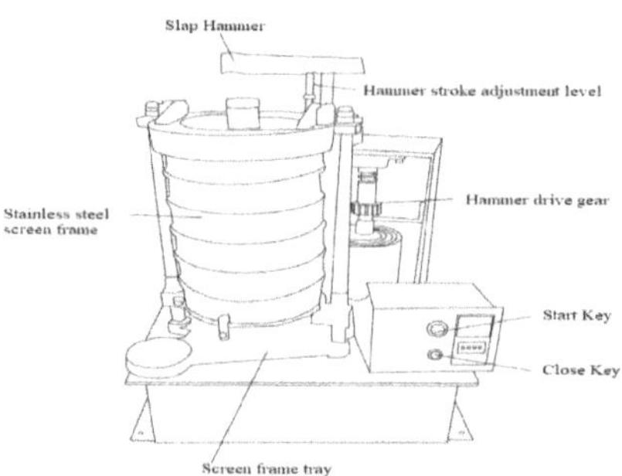

CHAPTER – 5

SIZE SEPARATION – II

Mr. Prabhakar Tiwari

Associate Professor, Rajiv Gandhi Institute of Pharmacy, Faculty of Pharmaceutical Science & Technology, AKS University Satna, MP-India

---

ABSTRACT:

Size separation is a vital process in industries for sorting particles by size to ensure product uniformity and quality. Various equipment is employed for this purpose, including cyclone separators, air separators, bag filters, and elutriation tanks. Cyclone separators use centrifugal forces to separate particles from air or gas streams based on their size and density. Air separators rely on airflow to classify particles, often used in conjunction with grinding operations. Bag filters capture fine particles from air streams, utilizing filter bags that trap particulate matter while allowing clean air to pass through. Elutriation tanks separate particles by allowing them to settle at different rates in a fluid, typically water. These size separation techniques are chosen based on the specific material characteristics and desired separation outcomes, ensuring optimal efficiency and product quality in industrial processes.

CYCLONE SEPARATOR

Construction of Cyclone Separator:

1. **Cylindrical Body**: The main body of the cyclone separator is typically cylindrical in shape, with a conical bottom section. This design allows for the efficient separation of particles from the gas or liquid stream.
2. **Inlet and Outlet Ports**: The inlet port is located at the top of the cyclone separator, where the mixture of particles and fluid enters. The outlet port

is situated at the bottom of the conical section, through which the separated particles and fluid exit.

3. **Tangential Entry:** The inlet port is tangentially oriented to the cylindrical body, creating a swirling motion within the separator. This swirling motion generates centrifugal forces that drive particle separation.
4. **Vortex Finder**: A vortex finder, typically located near the top of the cyclone separator, helps to direct the separated fluid stream towards the outlet port while allowing the particles to be collected in the bottom section.
5. **Collection Chamber**: The conical bottom section serves as a collection chamber where the separated particles accumulate. These particles can be discharged periodically or continuously, depending on the specific application.

Working Principle of Cyclone Separator:

1. **Tangential Entry**: The mixture of particles and fluid enters the cyclone separator through the tangentially oriented inlet port.
2. **Centrifugal Force**: As the mixture enters the cyclone separator, it is forced to rotate rapidly around the cylindrical body due to the tangential entry. This rotation generates centrifugal forces, causing the heavier particles to move towards the outer wall of the cyclone separator.
3. **Particle Separation**: The centrifugal forces act on the particles, causing them to move outward and downward towards the conical bottom section of the separator. Meanwhile, the lighter fluid moves upward towards the center of the cyclone.
4. **Collection**: The separated particles collect at the bottom of the cyclone separator, forming a dense slurry or solid mass. The separated fluid exits the cyclone through the vortex finder and outlet port.

5. **Adjustment:** The efficiency of particle separation in a cyclone separator can be adjusted by varying parameters such as the inlet velocity, cyclone geometry, and particle size distribution.

Uses of Cyclone Separator:

1. **Dust Collection**: Cyclone separators are widely used in industries such as woodworking, metalworking, and agriculture to remove dust and particulate matter from air or gas streams.
2. **Gas-Liquid Separation**: They are employed in oil and gas production facilities to separate oil, water, and gas phases from multiphase fluid streams.
3. **Particle Classification**: Cyclone separators can be used to classify particles based on size or density, making them useful in mineral processing, powder handling, and pharmaceutical manufacturing.
4. **Environmental Control**: They are used in pollution control systems to remove particulate pollutants from industrial exhaust gases before discharge into the atmosphere.

Merits of Cyclone Separator:

1. **Simple Design**: Cyclone separators have a simple design and are relatively easy to install and operate.
2. **High Efficiency:** They offer high separation efficiency for a wide range of particle sizes and densities.
3. **Low Maintenance**: Cyclone separators have few moving parts and require minimal maintenance compared to other separation devices.
4. **Versatility**: They can be adapted for various applications and operating conditions by adjusting parameters such as inlet velocity and cyclone geometry.

Demerits of Cyclone Separator:

1. **Limited Particle Size Range**: Cyclone separators are most effective for separating particles within a certain size range, and their efficiency may decrease for extremely fine or coarse particles.
2. **Pressure Drop**: Cyclone separators typically incur a pressure drop across the device, which can affect system performance and energy consumption.
3. **Particle Re-entrainment**: In some cases, separated particles may be re-entrained into the fluid stream, reducing separation efficiency.
4. **Space Requirement**: Cyclone separators may require significant space for installation, especially for large-scale industrial applications.

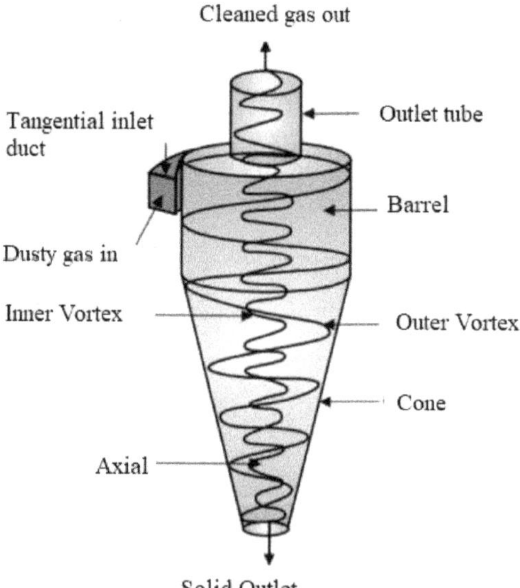

AIR SEPARATOR

Construction of Air Separator:

1. **Inlet:** The mixture to be separated enters the air separator through an inlet, usually located at the top of the device.

2. **Distribution Plate**: The inlet leads to a distribution plate or distributor, which evenly distributes the incoming mixture across the cross-section of the separator.
3. **Air Distribution System**: The separator contains an air distribution system, typically consisting of fans or blowers, which supply air to the device. This air flow is crucial for the separation process.
4. **Classifier Wheel**: The heart of the air separator is the classifier wheel or rotor, which is typically mounted on a shaft and rotates at high speed. The classifier wheel has blades or vanes that impart centrifugal forces to the particles.
5. **Fine Particle Outlet**: At the center of the classifier wheel, there is an outlet for fine particles. These particles are entrained by the air flow and are typically collected in a cyclone or bag filter.
6. **Coarse Particle Outlet**: Around the periphery of the classifier wheel, there is an outlet for coarse particles. These particles are separated due to their inability to follow the airflow around the classifier wheel and are collected separately.

Working Principle of Air Separator:

1. **Inlet and Distribution**: The mixture to be separated enters the air separator through the inlet and is evenly distributed across the cross-section of the device by the distribution plate.
2. **Centrifugal Separation**: As the mixture flows through the air separator, it encounters the rapidly rotating classifier wheel. The centrifugal forces generated by the rotation of the wheel cause the particles to move outward.
3. **Particle Separation**: Fine particles, which are smaller and lighter, are carried by the air flow towards the center of the classifier wheel and exit through the fine particle outlet. Coarse particles, which are larger and

heavier, cannot follow the airflow and are directed towards the periphery of the classifier wheel, where they exit through the coarse particle outlet.

4. **Airflow Control**: The air flow rate and velocity within the separator can be adjusted to optimize the separation process and achieve the desired particle size distribution.

Uses of Air Separator:

1. **Powder Processing**: Air separators are commonly used in industries such as pharmaceuticals, food processing, and chemical manufacturing for separating powders into different size fractions.
2. **Mineral Processing**: They are employed in mineral processing plants for separating minerals based on their size and density, as well as for removing impurities from ores and concentrates.
3. **Recycling**: Air separators are used in recycling facilities to separate different types of materials, such as plastics, metals, and paper, based on their size and density.
4. **Environmental Control**: They are used in pollution control systems to remove particulate matter and other contaminants from air and gas streams before they are discharged into the atmosphere.

Merits of Air Separator:

1. **High Efficiency:** Air separators offer high separation efficiency and can effectively separate particles over a wide range of sizes and densities.
2. **Versatility**: They can be used for a variety of applications and can handle different types of materials, including powders, granules, and solids.
3. **Continuous Operation**: Air separators can operate continuously, allowing for consistent and reliable performance in industrial processes.
4. **Adjustability**: The air flow rate and other operating parameters of air separators can be adjusted to optimize performance and meet specific process requirements.

Demerits of Air Separator:

1. **Energy Consumption**: Air separators typically require energy-intensive fans or blowers to generate the air flow needed for particle separation, leading to higher energy consumption.
2. **Maintenance:** The rotating parts of air separators, such as the classifier wheel, may require regular maintenance and inspection to ensure proper functioning and prevent wear and tear.
3. **Particle Attrition**: In some cases, the high-speed rotation of the classifier wheel may cause attrition or breakage of particles, leading to product degradation or loss of fines.
4. **Capital Cost**: Air separators can be relatively expensive to purchase and install, especially for larger industrial-scale applications.

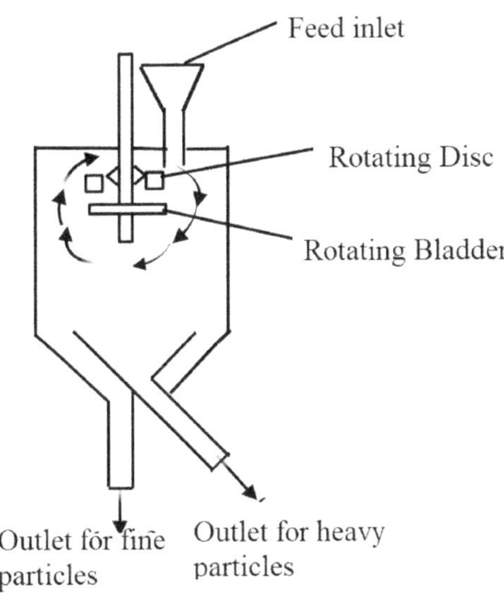

BAG FILTER

Construction of Bag Filter:

1. **Housing**: The bag filter typically consists of a housing, which is a large cylindrical or rectangular vessel made of metal or reinforced plastic. This housing contains the filter bags and provides structural support.
2. **Filter Bags:** The filter bags are the primary filtration medium in a bag filter. They are cylindrical bags made of porous material, such as woven or non-woven fabric, with a high surface area for particle capture. The bags are suspended vertically within the housing.
3. **Inlet:** The contaminated gas or air stream enters the bag filter through an inlet port located at the bottom or side of the housing.
4. **Outlet:** The clean gas or air exits the bag filter through an outlet port located at the top or side of the housing, after passing through the filter bags.
5. **Support Cage**: Each filter bag is typically supported by a cage or frame, which helps to maintain its shape and prevent collapse under the pressure of the gas flow.
6. **Cleaning Mechanism**: Some bag filters include a cleaning mechanism, such as reverse air flow or mechanical shaking, to dislodge and remove accumulated particles from the filter bags.

Working Principle of Bag Filter:

1. **Contaminated Gas Entry**: The gas or air stream containing particulate matter enters the bag filter through the inlet port.
2. **Filtration:** As the gas flows through the filter bags, the particulate matter is captured on the surface of the bags, while the clean gas passes through the porous material.
3. **Particle Accumulation:** Over time, the particulate matter accumulates on the surface of the filter bags, forming a layer of dust or cake.

4. **Cleaning Process**: To maintain optimal filtration efficiency, the accumulated particles must be periodically removed from the filter bags. This is typically achieved using a cleaning mechanism, such as reverse air flow or mechanical shaking.
5. **Clean Gas Exit**: After the cleaning process, the clean gas exits the bag filter through the outlet port, while the separated particles are collected in a hopper or bin at the bottom of the housing.

Uses of Bag Filter:

1. **Air Pollution Control**: Bag filters are widely used in industries such as cement manufacturing, power generation, and steel production to control air pollution by removing particulate matter from exhaust gases.
2. **Dust Collection**: They are employed in woodworking shops, metalworking facilities, and other industrial environments for dust collection and containment.
3. **Ventilation Systems**: Bag filters are used in ventilation systems for commercial buildings, hospitals, and laboratories to maintain indoor air quality by removing airborne contaminants.
4. **Product Recovery**: They are used in food processing, pharmaceutical manufacturing, and chemical production for recovering product powder or granules from exhaust streams.

Merits of Bag Filter:

1. **High Efficiency:** Bag filters offer high filtration efficiency for a wide range of particle sizes and concentrations.
2. **Versatility:** They can handle a variety of applications and can be customized to suit specific process requirements.
3. **Low Maintenance**: Bag filters require minimal maintenance compared to other filtration systems, especially if equipped with automatic cleaning mechanisms.

4. **Compact Design**: Bag filters have a relatively compact footprint compared to other filtration systems, making them suitable for installation in tight spaces.

Demerits of Bag Filter:

1. **Limited Temperature and Chemical Resistance**: Bag filters may not be suitable for high-temperature or corrosive gas streams, as they can degrade the filter material and reduce performance.
2. **Pressure Drop:** The accumulation of dust on the filter bags can increase the pressure drop across the filter, leading to higher energy consumption and reduced airflow.
3. **Bag Replacement**: Over time, the filter bags may become clogged or damaged and require replacement, which can incur additional maintenance costs.
4. **Particle Re-entrainment:** In some cases, particles dislodged during the cleaning process may re-enter the gas stream, reducing filtration efficiency.

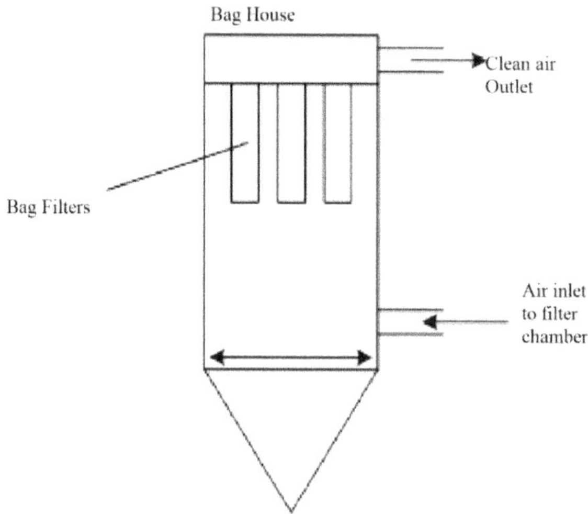

ELUTRIATION TANK

Construction of Elutriation Tank:

1. **Tank Structure**: An elutriation tank typically consists of a vertical cylindrical vessel made of metal or reinforced plastic. The tank is designed to withstand the pressure and flow of the liquid medium.
2. **Inlet**: The mixture to be separated is introduced into the elutriation tank through an inlet pipe or nozzle, typically located near the top of the tank.
3. **Overflow Weir**: Near the top of the tank, there is an overflow weir or baffle that directs the liquid flow and prevents the mixture from overflowing out of the tank.
4. **Settling Zone**: The lower portion of the tank serves as the settling zone, where particles settle under the influence of gravity.
5. **Underflow Outlet**: At the bottom of the tank, there is an underflow outlet through which the settled particles are discharged from the tank.
6. **Overflow Outlet**: Near the top of the tank, there is an overflow outlet through which the clarified liquid exits the tank.

Working Principle of Elutriation Tank:

1. **Introduction of Mixture**: The mixture to be separated, consisting of particles of different sizes and densities suspended in a liquid medium, is introduced into the elutriation tank through the inlet.
2. **Liquid Flow**: The liquid medium, typically water or a solvent, is continuously fed into the tank, creating an upward flow that suspends the particles within the tank.
3. **Settling**: As the particles move upward with the liquid flow, they experience gravitational forces that cause them to settle downward towards the bottom of the tank.
4. **Particle Separation**: Due to differences in size and density, larger and denser particles settle more quickly and reach the bottom of the tank first, while smaller and lighter particles remain suspended for a longer period.

5. **Underflow Discharge**: The settled particles are collected and discharged from the tank through the underflow outlet, typically at the bottom of the tank.
6. **Overflow Discharge**: The clarified liquid, free from suspended particles, overflows out of the tank through the overflow outlet, usually located near the top.

Uses of Elutriation Tank:

1. **Mineral Processing**: Elutriation tanks are commonly used in mineral processing plants for separating minerals based on their size and density, such as in the concentration of heavy minerals like gold, tin, and coal.
2. **Particle Classification**: They are employed in laboratories and research facilities for particle classification and size separation experiments, allowing for the determination of particle size distribution.
3. **Water Treatment**: Elutriation tanks are used in water treatment facilities for removing suspended solids and particulate matter from water streams, contributing to the purification of drinking water and wastewater treatment.

Merits of Elutriation Tank:

1. **High Efficiency**: Elutriation tanks offer high separation efficiency for a wide range of particle sizes and densities.
2. **Continuous Operation**: They can operate continuously, allowing for continuous separation and collection of particles from the liquid medium.
3. **Simple Design**: Elutriation tanks have a relatively simple design and are easy to install and operate.
4. **Low Maintenance**: They require minimal maintenance compared to other separation devices, reducing downtime and operational costs.

Demerits of Elutriation Tank:

1. **Limited Scalability**: Elutriation tanks may not be suitable for large-scale industrial applications due to limitations in throughput and scalability.

2. **Space Requirement**: They may require significant space for installation, especially for large tanks needed to achieve higher throughput.
3. **Energy Consumption**: Elutriation tanks require energy to maintain the liquid flow and suspension of particles, leading to energy consumption and operational costs.

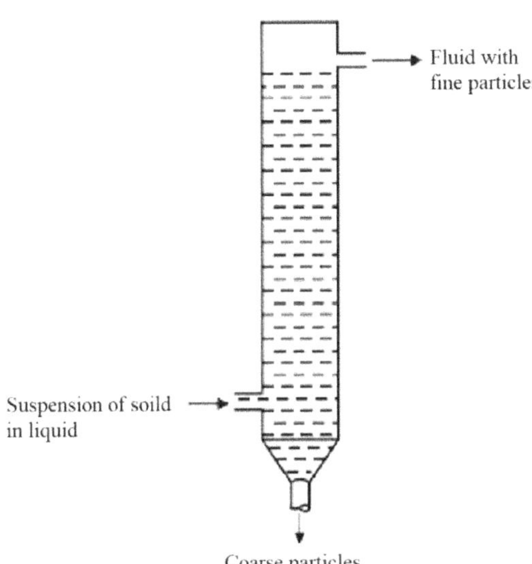

CHAPTER – 6

HEAT TRANSFER

Mrs. Priyanka Gupta

Associate Professor, Rajiv Gandhi Institute of Pharmacy, Faculty of Pharmaceutical Science & Technology, AKS University Satna, MP-India

---

ABSTRACT:

Heat transfer is a fundamental process in which thermal energy is exchanged between physical systems, playing a crucial role in various industrial and engineering applications. It occurs through three primary mechanisms: conduction, convection, and radiation. Conduction involves the transfer of heat through direct contact between molecules in a solid or between solids in contact. Convection is the movement of heat through fluids (liquids or gases) driven by the fluid's movement, often enhanced by fans or pumps. Radiation is the transfer of energy through electromagnetic waves, requiring no medium and occurring even in a vacuum. Factors such as material properties, temperature gradients, and surface areas influence the efficiency of heat transfer. Understanding these mechanisms and their influencing factors allows engineers to design effective thermal management systems, ensuring optimal performance and energy efficiency in applications ranging from industrial processes to everyday appliances.

INTRODUCTION

Heat transfer is the process of exchanging thermal energy between physical systems, typically from a higher temperature region to a lower temperature region. It plays a fundamental role in various natural phenomena and engineering applications, influencing the temperature distribution within objects and systems. Let's explore the concept of heat transfer in detail:

Modes of Heat Transfer:

1. **Conduction**: Conduction occurs when heat flows through a material due to a temperature gradient. In this mode, heat is transferred by molecular collisions within the material, with energy transferred from higher-energy particles to lower-energy particles. Materials with high thermal conductivity, such as metals, are efficient conductors of heat.
2. **Convection**: Convection involves the transfer of heat through the movement of fluids (liquids or gases). It occurs through a combination of fluid motion and thermal conduction. Convection can be natural (free convection) or forced (forced convection) depending on whether external forces such as gravity or mechanical devices are involved.
3. **Radiation:** Radiation is the transfer of heat in the form of electromagnetic waves, such as infrared radiation, without the need for a medium. All objects emit and absorb electromagnetic radiation based on their temperature and emissivity. Radiation can occur through vacuum and is the primary mode of heat transfer in space.

Governing Equations:

1. **Fourier's Law of Heat Conduction**: This law describes the rate of heat transfer through a material by conduction and is given by

$$q=-kAdTdx$$

where

a. q is the heat flux,

b. k is the thermal conductivity of the material,

c. A is the cross-sectional area, and $dTdx$ is the temperature gradient.

2. **Newton's Law of Cooling**: This law describes the rate of heat transfer between a solid surface and a fluid (liquid or gas) by convection and is given by

$$q=hA(Ts-T\infty)$$

where

a. q is the heat transfer rate,

b. h is the convective heat transfer coefficient,

c. A is the surface area, Ts is the surface temperature, and $T\infty$ is the fluid temperature.

3. **Stefan-Boltzmann Law**: This law relates the radiant heat flux emitted by an object to its temperature and emissivity and is given by

$$q=\varepsilon\sigma AT4$$

where

a. q is the radiant heat flux,

b. ε is the emissivity,

c. σ is the Stefan-Boltzmann constant,

d. A is the surface area, and

e. T is the absolute temperature.

Applications of Heat Transfer:

1. **Thermal Management**: Heat transfer is crucial in thermal management systems for electronic devices, engines, and industrial processes to maintain safe operating temperatures and prevent overheating.
2. **Energy Conversion**: Heat transfer plays a vital role in energy conversion processes such as combustion, refrigeration, and power generation, where heat is converted into mechanical or electrical energy.
3. **Building Design**: Understanding heat transfer is essential in building design to optimize insulation, HVAC systems, and energy efficiency, ensuring comfortable indoor environments.
4. **Climate Science**: Heat transfer influences weather patterns, ocean currents, and climate dynamics on Earth and other planets, contributing to our understanding of climate change and global warming.

Merits and Demerits of Heat Transfer:

1. **Merits:**
   a. Facilitates energy transfer and conversion in various processes.
   b. Enables the regulation of temperature in systems and environments.
   c. Essential for natural phenomena such as weather patterns and planetary climate.
2. **Demerits:**
   a. Inefficient heat transfer can lead to energy loss and reduced system efficiency.
   b. Poor thermal management can result in equipment failure and safety hazards.
   c. Anthropogenic activities contributing to excessive heat transfer can exacerbate climate change and environmental degradation.

OBJECTIVES, APPLICATIONS & HEAT TRANSFER MECHANISMS

Objectives of Heat Transfer:

1. **Efficient Energy Utilization**: One of the primary objectives of heat transfer is to facilitate the efficient utilization and conversion of thermal energy in various engineering systems and processes, minimizing energy waste and maximizing performance.
2. **Temperature Regulation**: Heat transfer plays a crucial role in maintaining temperature control within systems, ensuring that components operate within safe temperature limits and preventing overheating or freezing.
3. **Thermal Comfort**: In buildings and vehicles, heat transfer is essential for providing thermal comfort to occupants by regulating indoor temperatures and humidity levels.

4. **Industrial Processes**: Heat transfer is integral to numerous industrial processes, including heating, cooling, drying, distillation, and chemical reactions, contributing to the production of goods and materials.
5. **Environmental Control**: Understanding heat transfer is vital for addressing environmental challenges such as climate change, air pollution, and energy sustainability, informing policies and technologies aimed at mitigating environmental impacts.

Applications of Heat Transfer:

1. **Thermal Management in Electronics**: Heat transfer is crucial for dissipating heat generated by electronic devices such as computers, smartphones, and servers, preventing overheating and maintaining optimal performance.
2. **Heat Exchangers**: Heat transfer is utilized in heat exchangers for exchanging thermal energy between fluids or between a fluid and a solid surface, commonly used in HVAC systems, refrigeration, and industrial processes.
3. **Power Generation**: Heat transfer is central to power generation processes such as combustion, steam turbines, and nuclear reactors, where heat energy is converted into mechanical or electrical energy.
4. **Transportation Systems**: Heat transfer influences the performance of vehicles, aircraft, and spacecraft by affecting engine efficiency, aerodynamics, and thermal protection systems.
5. **Biomedical Applications**: Heat transfer is applied in medical devices such as MRI machines, laser systems, and thermal therapy devices for diagnostics, treatment, and research in healthcare.

Heat Transfer Mechanisms:

1. **Conduction**: Conduction is the transfer of heat through a material by molecular collisions. It occurs when adjacent particles with different temperatures exchange kinetic energy, leading to the flow of heat from

regions of higher temperature to regions of lower temperature. Materials with high thermal conductivity, such as metals, are efficient conductors of heat.

2. **Convection**: Convection involves the transfer of heat through the movement of fluids (liquids or gases). It occurs through a combination of fluid motion and thermal conduction, where hotter fluid rises and cooler fluid sinks, creating circulation patterns. Convection can be natural (free convection) or forced (forced convection) depending on external forces such as gravity or mechanical devices.
3. **Radiation**: Radiation is the transfer of heat in the form of electromagnetic waves, such as infrared radiation, without the need for a medium. All objects emit and absorb electromagnetic radiation based on their temperature and emissivity. Radiation can occur through vacuum and is the primary mode of heat transfer in space.

FOURIER'S LAW

Fourier's law of heat conduction is a fundamental principle governing the transfer of heat through a solid material by conduction. It quantifies the rate of heat transfer per unit area through a material in response to a temperature gradient. Fourier's law is named after the French mathematician and physicist Joseph Fourier, who formulated the law in the early 19th century. Let's delve into Fourier's law in detail:

Fourier's Law Equation:

Mathematically, Fourier's law can be expressed as:

$$q{=}{-}kAdTdx$$

Where:

q is the heat flux, which represents the rate of heat transfer per unit area (W/m^2).

k is the thermal conductivity of the material, which quantifies the material's ability to conduct heat (W/(m·K)).

A is the cross-sectional area perpendicular to the direction of heat flow (m^2).

$dTdx$ is the temperature gradient, which represents the rate of change of temperature with respect to distance along the direction of heat flow (K/m).

Interpretation of Fourier's Law:

1. **Heat Flux (q):** The heat flux represents the amount of heat transferred per unit area per unit time. It indicates the rate at which thermal energy flows through the material. A higher heat flux corresponds to a greater rate of heat transfer.
2. **Thermal Conductivity (k)**: The thermal conductivity is a material property that characterizes the ability of a material to conduct heat. Materials with higher thermal conductivity values conduct heat more efficiently. For example, metals such as copper and aluminum have high thermal conductivity, while insulating materials like wood and plastic have lower thermal conductivity.
3. **Temperature Gradient ($dTdx$)**: The temperature gradient indicates how quickly the temperature changes with distance along the direction of heat flow. A steeper temperature gradient corresponds to a more rapid change in temperature over a given distance, leading to a higher rate of heat transfer.

Assumptions and Limitations:

a. Fourier's law assumes that heat conduction occurs in a stationary medium with constant properties and uniform temperature gradients.

b. It is valid for isotropic materials (materials with uniform properties in all directions) under steady-state conditions.

c. Fourier's law is applicable to conduction through solids, but it may also be used to approximate heat transfer in fluids under certain conditions.

Applications of Fourier's Law:

1. **Heat Transfer Analysis**: Fourier's law is widely used in engineering and physics to analyze and predict heat transfer phenomena in various systems and materials, including heat exchangers, electronic devices, building materials, and thermal insulation.
2. **Material Characterization**: Thermal conductivity measurements based on Fourier's law are used to characterize the thermal properties of materials and assess their suitability for specific applications, such as in construction, manufacturing, and thermal management.
3. **Design and Optimization**: Engineers use Fourier's law to design and optimize heat transfer systems, such as thermal insulation, heat sinks, and cooling systems, to achieve desired performance and efficiency.

HEAT TRANSFER BY CONDUCTION, CONVECTION & RADIATION

Heat transfer plays a critical role in various processes and phenomena, and it occurs through three primary mechanisms: conduction, convection, and radiation. Each mechanism operates differently and has distinct characteristics. Let's explore these mechanisms in detail:

1. Conduction:

Definition: Conduction is the transfer of heat through a material by molecular collisions without any bulk motion of the material itself. In other words, heat is transferred from the hotter end of an object to the cooler end by the vibration and collisions of neighboring molecules.

Key Points:

a. Conduction occurs primarily in solids, where molecules are closely packed and have strong interactions.
b. Materials with high thermal conductivity conduct heat more effectively. Metals, for example, typically have higher thermal conductivity than insulators like wood or plastic.
c. Conduction rate depends on the temperature difference (ΔT), the cross-sectional area (A) perpendicular to the direction of heat flow, and the

distance (Δx) over which the heat is transferred, as described by Fourier's law.

Applications:

Heat conduction is commonly observed in cooking utensils (e.g., metal pans), building materials (e.g., brick walls), and electronic devices (e.g., computer processors).

2. Convection:

Definition: Convection is the transfer of heat through the movement of fluids (liquids or gases). It involves a combination of fluid motion and thermal conduction.

Key Points:

a. Convection occurs in fluids, where heat is transferred by the movement of hot fluid (which becomes less dense and rises) and the cooler fluid (which becomes denser and sinks).
b. Convection can be either natural (free convection), driven by buoyancy forces due to density differences, or forced (forced convection), induced by external forces such as fans or pumps.
c. Heat transfer rate in convection depends on factors like fluid velocity, fluid properties, surface geometry, and temperature difference between the fluid and the surface.

Applications:

Convection is prevalent in processes such as boiling, where heat is transferred from a solid surface to a liquid, and in forced-air heating and cooling systems commonly used in buildings and vehicles.

3. Radiation:

Definition: Radiation is the transfer of heat through electromagnetic waves without requiring a medium. It can occur through a vacuum and does not depend on the presence of matter.

Key Points:

a. All objects emit and absorb electromagnetic radiation based on their temperature and emissivity. Emissivity is a measure of an object's ability to emit and absorb radiation.
b. Radiation heat transfer is governed by Stefan-Boltzmann's law, which states that the rate of radiant heat transfer is proportional to the fourth power of the absolute temperature of the radiating surface.
c. Unlike conduction and convection, radiation can occur across empty space and is the primary mechanism of heat transfer in vacuum environments.

Applications:

a. Radiation is essential in various processes, including heating (e.g., solar heating), cooling (e.g., radiative cooling), and thermal imaging (e.g., infrared cameras).
b. It is a crucial factor in designing energy-efficient buildings, spacecraft thermal control systems, and solar energy harvesting technologies.

Comparison:

1. **Dominant Medium:**
    a. **Conduction:** Solids
    b. **Convection**: Fluids (liquids and gases)
    c. **Radiation:** Occurs through vacuum or any medium
2. **Mechanism:**
    a. **Conduction:** Molecular collisions
    b. **Convection:** Fluid motion and conduction
    c. **Radiation**: Electromagnetic waves
3. **Dependence on Medium:**
    a. **Conduction**: Medium-dependent
    b. **Convection:** Medium-dependent
    c. **Radiation**: Medium-independen.

HEAT INTERCHANGERS

Heat exchangers play a crucial role in various industrial, commercial, and residential applications where heating, cooling, or heat recovery is required. Let's explore heat exchangers in detail:

Types of Heat Exchangers:

1. **Shell and Tube Heat Exchangers:**
    a. Consist of a bundle of tubes enclosed within a shell.
    b. One fluid flows through the tubes (tube-side fluid), while the other fluid flows through the space surrounding the tubes (shell-side fluid).
    c. Commonly used in power plants, chemical processing, HVAC systems, and refrigeration.
2. **Plate Heat Exchangers:**
    a. Consist of multiple plates arranged in parallel and held together in a frame.
    b. Fluids flow alternatively between the plates, allowing for efficient heat transfer.
    c. Compact design and high heat transfer efficiency make them suitable for applications with space constraints, such as food and beverage processing, HVAC, and automotive cooling systems.
3. **Double-Pipe Heat Exchangers:**
    a. Simplest type of heat exchanger, consisting of two concentric pipes.
    b. One fluid flows through the inner pipe, while the other fluid flows in the annular space between the inner and outer pipes.
    c. Widely used in small-scale applications, such as domestic water heaters, air conditioning systems, and heat recovery units.
4. **Cross-Flow Heat Exchangers:**

a. Fluids flow perpendicular to each other, with one fluid passing through a series of tubes or channels while the other fluid flows across the tubes or channels.
b. Used in applications where one fluid needs to be heated or cooled while the other fluid remains relatively unchanged in temperature, such as in air-cooled condensers and HVAC systems.

5. **Regenerative Heat Exchangers:**
    a. Utilize a heat storage medium, such as a matrix of porous material or a rotating wheel, to absorb heat from one fluid stream and transfer it to another.
    b. Commonly used in energy recovery systems, such as in industrial processes, power plants, and ventilation systems, to improve energy efficiency and reduce operating costs.

Working Principle:

a. Heat exchangers operate based on the principle of heat transfer between fluids or between a fluid and a solid surface. The fluids involved may be gases, liquids, or multiphase mixtures.
b. Heat transfer occurs due to the temperature difference between the two fluids, causing thermal energy to transfer from the hot fluid to the cold fluid.
c. The design and configuration of the heat exchanger determine the efficiency of heat transfer, the pressure drop across the exchanger, and other performance characteristics.

Applications:

1. Heat exchangers are used in a wide range of industries and applications, including:
    a. HVAC systems for heating, cooling, and ventilation.
    b. Power generation plants for steam generation and turbine cooling.

c. Chemical processing plants for heat recovery and process heating/cooling.
d. Refrigeration and air conditioning systems for cooling and dehumidification.
e. Food and beverage processing for pasteurization, sterilization, and cooling.
f. Automotive and aerospace industries for engine cooling and cabin heating.

Merits and Demerits:

1. **Merits:**
   a. Efficient heat transfer between fluids.
   b. Energy savings and reduced operating costs.
   c. Versatility in design and application.
   d. Compact and space-saving designs available.
2. **Demerits:**
   a. Initial capital cost can be high, depending on the type and size of the heat exchanger.
   b. Maintenance and cleaning requirements to prevent fouling and corrosion.
   c. Possibility of leakage and pressure drop issues if not properly installed or maintained.

HEAT EXCHANGERS

Heat exchangers are crucial devices designed to transfer heat from one fluid (liquid or gas) to another fluid or to a solid surface. They play a vital role in various industries and applications where heating, cooling, or temperature control is required. Let's delve into heat exchangers in detail:

Working Principle:

a. **Heat Transfer Mechanisms**: Heat exchangers facilitate heat transfer through one or more of the following mechanisms: conduction, convection, and radiation, depending on the design and operating conditions.

b. **Temperature Difference**: Heat transfer occurs due to the temperature difference between the hot and cold fluids or between the fluid and the solid surface. Thermal energy flows from the hotter medium to the cooler medium until thermal equilibrium is reached.

c. **Fluid Flow**: The hot and cold fluids flow through separate channels or passages within the heat exchanger, ensuring thermal contact while preventing mixing. The fluid flow may be arranged in parallel, counterflow, or crossflow configurations, optimizing heat transfer efficiency.

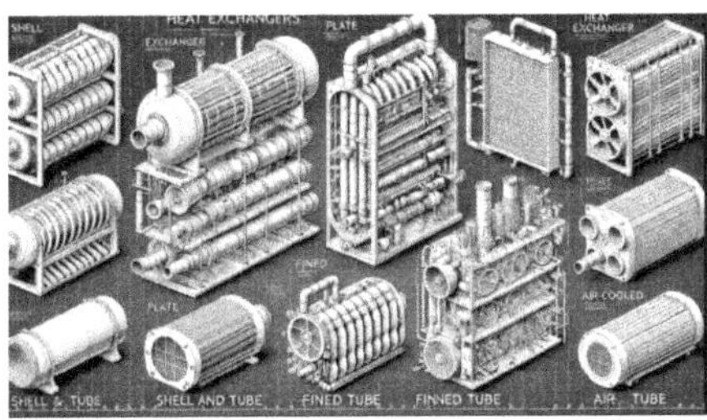

Types of Heat Exchangers:

1. **Shell and Tube Heat Exchangers:**
    a. Consist of a shell (outer vessel) containing a bundle of tubes.
    b. One fluid flows through the tubes (tube-side fluid), while the other fluid flows around the tubes within the shell (shell-side fluid).
    c. Commonly used in industrial applications due to their versatility, high heat transfer efficiency, and robust construction.
2. **Plate Heat Exchangers:**
    a. Comprise multiple thin plates with alternating corrugated patterns, stacked together and clamped within a frame.

b. Fluids flow alternately between adjacent plates, promoting turbulent flow and enhancing heat transfer.
c. Compact design, high heat transfer rates, and ease of maintenance make them suitable for applications with space constraints.

3. **Double-Pipe Heat Exchangers:**
    a. Simplest type of heat exchanger, consisting of two concentric pipes.
    b. One fluid flows through the inner pipe, while the other fluid flows in the annular space between the inner and outer pipes.
    c. Widely used in small-scale applications, such as domestic water heaters and process heating systems.
4. **Shell and Coil Heat Exchangers:**
    a. Similar to shell and tube heat exchangers but with a coil-shaped tube bundle instead of straight tubes.
    b. Coil arrangement enhances heat transfer efficiency and allows for compact designs, suitable for high-pressure or high-temperature applications.
5. **Regenerative Heat Exchangers:**
    a. Utilize a heat storage medium, such as a matrix of porous material or a rotating wheel, to absorb heat from one fluid stream and transfer it to another.
    b. Ideal for energy recovery applications, such as waste heat recovery and air-to-air heat exchange in HVAC systems.

Applications:

a. **Industrial Processes**: Heat exchangers are widely used in chemical processing, petroleum refining, power generation, and manufacturing industries for heating, cooling, condensation, and evaporation processes.

b. **HVAC Systems**: Heat exchangers play a critical role in heating, ventilation, and air conditioning (HVAC) systems for temperature control, humidity regulation, and energy recovery in buildings, commercial spaces, and residential dwellings.
c. **Refrigeration and Air Conditioning**: Heat exchangers are integral components in refrigeration cycles, air conditioning systems, and heat pumps for cooling and dehumidification purposes.
d. **Power Generation**: Heat exchangers are employed in power plants for steam generation, turbine cooling, and condensation of exhaust gases, enhancing overall efficiency and performance.

Merits and Demerits:

1. **Merits:**
   a. Efficient heat transfer between fluids or between a fluid and a solid surface.
   b. Energy savings and reduced operating costs.
   c. Versatility in design and application for various industries and processes.
   d. Compact and space-saving designs available for diverse applications.
2. **Demerits:**
   a. Initial capital investment can be high, particularly for specialized or custom-designed heat exchangers.
   b. Maintenance requirements, including cleaning, inspection, and repair, to prevent fouling, corrosion, and performance degradation.
   c. Possibility of leakage, pressure drop, and flow maldistribution if not properly installed, operated, or maintained.

CHAPTER – 7

EVAPORATION – I

Ms. Neha Goel

Associate Professor, Rajiv Gandhi Institute of Pharmacy, Faculty of Pharmaceutical Science & Technology, AKS University Satna, MP-India

---

ABSTRACT:

Evaporation is the process where liquid molecules gain sufficient energy to transition into the vapor phase, playing a vital role in various natural and industrial processes. It occurs when the surface molecules of a liquid absorb enough heat to overcome intermolecular forces and escape into the air. Factors such as temperature, surface area, air movement, and humidity significantly influence the rate of evaporation. In industrial applications, evaporation is utilized in processes like concentrating solutions, drying materials, and producing pure substances through distillation. Efficient evaporation techniques are essential in sectors like food processing, pharmaceuticals, and chemical manufacturing, where precise control over moisture content is crucial. By optimizing conditions such as heat supply and airflow, industries can enhance evaporation rates, improving process efficiency and product quality.

Introduction

Evaporation is the process by which a liquid transforms into a gas or vapor state. It occurs at the surface of the liquid, where molecules with sufficient kinetic energy break free from the liquid phase and enter the gas phase. This process is essential in various natural phenomena and industrial applications. Let's delve into the details:

Mechanism of Evaporation:

1. Molecular Kinetics: Evaporation is driven by the kinetic energy of molecules. In a liquid, molecules are in constant motion due to thermal energy. Some molecules at the surface gain enough kinetic energy to overcome the intermolecular forces holding them in the liquid phase, allowing them to escape into the gas phase.
2. Energy Exchange: As molecules transition from liquid to gas, they absorb energy from the surroundings, leading to a decrease in the average kinetic energy (and therefore temperature) of the remaining liquid molecules. This cooling effect is evident in processes like sweating, where evaporation of sweat from the skin's surface cools the body.

Factors Affecting Evaporation:

1. Temperature: Higher temperatures provide more energy to liquid molecules, increasing the rate of evaporation.
2. Surface Area: Evaporation occurs primarily at the liquid's surface. A larger surface area allows more molecules to escape simultaneously, speeding up the process.
3. Humidity: The presence of water vapor in the air affects evaporation. In a dry environment, the concentration gradient between the liquid and the air is higher, promoting faster evaporation. Conversely, in a humid environment, the air already contains a significant amount of water vapor, slowing down evaporation.
4. Airflow: Moving air can carry away newly evaporated molecules from the liquid's surface, maintaining a lower concentration of vapor near the liquid and enhancing the rate of evaporation.

Applications of Evaporation:

1. Cooling Systems: Evaporative cooling is utilized in various systems, including refrigeration and air conditioning, where a liquid evaporates, absorbing heat from its surroundings and cooling the environment.

2. Drying Processes: Industries use evaporation for drying various materials such as food products, textiles, and chemicals. By exposing the material to warm, dry air or vacuum conditions, moisture evaporates, leaving behind the dry substance.
3. Water Purification: Evaporation is a crucial step in desalination processes, where seawater is evaporated to separate the salt from the water, producing fresh water.
4. Natural Phenomena: Evaporation plays a vital role in the water cycle, where water evaporates from oceans, lakes, and rivers, forming clouds and eventually returning to the Earth's surface as precipitation.

Objectives, applications and factors influencing evaporation

Objectives of Evaporation:

1. Phase Transition: Evaporation facilitates the transition of a liquid substance into its gaseous state. This change of phase is essential in various natural processes and industrial applications.
2. Cooling: One of the primary objectives of evaporation is to dissipate heat from a system. When a liquid evaporates, it absorbs heat from its surroundings, leading to a cooling effect. This principle is utilized in cooling systems like evaporative coolers and air conditioning units.
3. Separation: Evaporation can be employed to separate substances from a mixture based on differences in volatility. By evaporating the more volatile components, it's possible to isolate desired substances from a solution or mixture.
4. Concentration: Evaporation can concentrate solutions by removing the solvent (typically water) from a solution, leaving behind a more concentrated solute. This process is widely used in industries such as food processing and chemical manufacturing.

Applications of Evaporation:

1. Industrial Drying: Evaporation is extensively used in industries for drying various materials such as food products, pharmaceuticals, chemicals, and textiles. By exposing wet materials to controlled conditions, moisture evaporates, leaving behind dry products.
2. Water Treatment: Evaporation plays a crucial role in water treatment processes, including desalination. By evaporating seawater and subsequently condensing the vapor, it's possible to produce freshwater from saline sources.
3. Cooling Systems: Evaporative cooling is employed in refrigeration and air conditioning systems. By evaporating a refrigerant at low pressure, heat is absorbed from the surroundings, leading to a cooling effect.
4. Salt Production: Evaporation ponds are commonly used to produce salt from seawater or brine. As water evaporates from the ponds, salt crystals precipitate out, which can be harvested for various purposes.

Factors Influencing Evaporation:

1. Temperature: Higher temperatures generally lead to faster evaporation rates since they provide more energy to liquid molecules, allowing them to escape into the gas phase.
2. Surface Area: Evaporation primarily occurs at the surface of a liquid. Increasing the surface area of the liquid enhances the rate of evaporation by providing more space for molecules to escape.
3. Humidity: The presence of water vapor in the air affects evaporation. In a dry environment, with low humidity, the concentration gradient between the liquid and the air is higher, promoting faster evaporation. Conversely, high humidity slows down evaporation since the air is already saturated with moisture.

4. Airflow: Moving air can carry away newly evaporated molecules from the liquid's surface, maintaining a lower concentration of vapor near the liquid and enhancing the rate of evaporation.
5. Pressure: Changes in pressure can influence evaporation rates. Lowering the pressure above a liquid can decrease its boiling point, facilitating evaporation at lower temperatures.

Differences between evaporation and other heat process

Evaporation is a specific heat process that involves the transformation of a liquid into its vapor or gaseous state, driven primarily by the transfer of thermal energy from the surroundings to the liquid molecules. While evaporation shares some similarities with other heat processes, such as boiling and condensation, there are distinct differences between them:

Evaporation vs. Boiling:

1. Temperature Requirement: Evaporation can occur at any temperature below the boiling point of the liquid. In contrast, boiling occurs when the entire liquid reaches its boiling point, resulting in rapid vaporization throughout the bulk of the liquid.
2. Location of Occurrence: Evaporation occurs at the surface of the liquid, while boiling occurs throughout the bulk of the liquid, with bubbles forming and rising to the surface.
3. Rate of Vaporization: Boiling leads to a much faster rate of vaporization compared to evaporation since it involves vaporization throughout the entire liquid volume.
4. Energy Requirement: Boiling requires a significant amount of energy input to reach the boiling point and sustain the process, while evaporation occurs spontaneously as long as there is a temperature difference between the liquid and its surroundings.

Evaporation vs. Condensation:

1. Direction of Heat Transfer: Evaporation involves the transfer of thermal energy from the surroundings to the liquid, leading to the vaporization of the liquid molecules. In contrast, condensation involves the transfer of thermal energy from the vapor or gas to the surroundings, resulting in the conversion of the vapor into its liquid state.
2. Location of Occurrence: Evaporation typically occurs at the surface of the liquid, whereas condensation can occur on surfaces (as in the case of dew formation) or within a volume of gas (as in the formation of clouds).
3. Phase Transition: Evaporation represents the transition from the liquid phase to the vapor phase, while condensation represents the reverse process, transitioning from the vapor phase to the liquid phase.
4. Energy Release: During condensation, energy is released into the surroundings in the form of latent heat, contributing to the warming of the surrounding environment. In contrast, evaporation absorbs energy from the surroundings, resulting in cooling.

Evaporation vs. Sublimation:

1. Phase Transition: Evaporation involves the transition from the liquid phase to the vapor phase, while sublimation involves the direct transition from the solid phase to the vapor phase, skipping the liquid phase altogether.
2. Temperature Range: Evaporation typically occurs at temperatures below the boiling point of the liquid, while sublimation occurs at temperatures where the solid phase can transition directly to the vapor phase without melting.
3. Examples: Evaporation commonly occurs with liquids such as water, whereas sublimation is observed in substances like dry ice (solid carbon dioxide) and mothballs (naphthalene).

Steam jacketed kettle

The steam jacketed kettle is a versatile piece of equipment used in various industries for cooking, heating, and evaporation processes. Let's delve into its principles, construction, working, uses, as well as its merits and demerits:

Principles:

The steam jacketed kettle operates based on the principle of indirect heating. Steam is circulated through the jacket surrounding the kettle's inner chamber. This jacketed design allows for uniform heating of the kettle's contents, whether it's liquid, semi-liquid, or solid, without direct contact with the heating medium. Heat transfer occurs through the metal walls of the kettle, ensuring efficient and controlled heating or evaporation processes.

Construction:

1. Inner Kettle: The inner chamber of the kettle is typically made of stainless steel or other corrosion-resistant materials. It holds the substance being heated or processed.
2. Steam Jacket: Surrounding the inner kettle is a jacket filled with steam. This jacket is also made of stainless steel and is designed to distribute heat evenly around the inner chamber.
3. Agitator: Many steam jacketed kettles are equipped with agitators or stirrers to ensure uniform mixing and heating of the contents.
4. Controls: The kettle may have temperature and pressure controls to regulate the steam flow and maintain precise operating conditions.

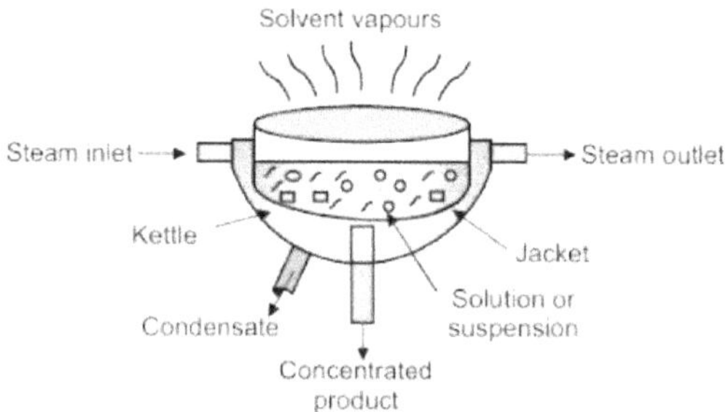

Working:

1. Steam Supply: Steam is supplied to the jacket through inlet ports. The pressure and flow of steam are controlled to maintain the desired temperature inside the kettle.
2. Heat Transfer: Steam circulating in the jacket transfers heat to the inner chamber through the metal walls. The substance inside the kettle absorbs this heat, leading to heating, cooking, or evaporation as required.
3. Agitation: If equipped with an agitator, it rotates to ensure uniform mixing and heating of the contents.
4. Evaporation: In evaporation processes, the steam jacketed kettle facilitates the removal of liquid from a solution or mixture by applying heat indirectly, causing the liquid to vaporize and leave behind a concentrated product.

Uses:

1. Food Processing: Steam jacketed kettles are widely used in food processing for cooking, simmering, and blending various food products such as soups, sauces, stews, and confectionery.
2. Pharmaceuticals: They are utilized in pharmaceutical manufacturing for the preparation of ointments, creams, gels, and other medicinal products.
3. Chemical Industry: Steam jacketed kettles are employed in the chemical industry for mixing, heating, and evaporation processes in the production of adhesives, coatings, and other chemical compounds.
4. Cosmetics: They are used in cosmetic manufacturing for blending and heating ingredients in the production of creams, lotions, and other beauty products.

Merits:

1. Uniform Heating: The steam jacketed design ensures even distribution of heat, preventing hot spots and ensuring consistent product quality.

2. Controlled Heating: Temperature and pressure controls allow for precise regulation of the heating process, reducing the risk of overheating or burning the contents.
3. Efficiency: Indirect heating through steam circulation is energy-efficient and reduces the risk of product contamination compared to direct heating methods.
4. Versatility: Steam jacketed kettles are versatile and can be used for a wide range of cooking, heating, and evaporation applications in various industries.

Demerits:

1. Initial Cost: Steam jacketed kettles can have a higher initial cost compared to other types of cooking or heating equipment.
2. Maintenance: Regular maintenance is required to ensure proper functioning of the kettle, including cleaning, inspection, and repair of steam valves, seals, and agitators.
3. Space Requirements: They may require more space due to their larger size and the need for steam supply infrastructure.
4. Complexity: The controls and operating mechanisms of steam jacketed kettles can be complex, requiring trained personnel for operation and maintenance.

Despite these potential drawbacks, the benefits of uniform heating, controlled operation, and versatility make steam jacketed kettles an indispensable tool in many industrial processes involving cooking, heating, and evaporation.

CHAPTER – 8

EVAPORATION – II

Mrs. Priya Diwedi

Assistant Professor, Rajiv Gandhi Institute of Pharmacy, Faculty of Pharmaceutical Science & Technology, AKS University Satna, MP-India

---

ABSTRACT:

Evaporation is a critical process in many industries, transforming liquids into vapor for purposes such as concentration, purification, and drying. Different types of evaporators are designed to optimize this process under various conditions. The horizontal tube evaporator features tubes where the liquid flows inside while steam heats the outside, facilitating efficient heat transfer and evaporation. The climbing film evaporator, on the other hand, uses vertical tubes where the liquid forms a thin film that ascends due to vapor formation, ideal for heat-sensitive materials due to its short residence time. Forced circulation evaporators employ pumps to circulate the liquid through a heat exchanger, ensuring uniform heating and preventing fouling, making them suitable for viscous or crystallizing solutions. Each type of evaporator offers distinct advantages tailored to specific industrial needs, ensuring effective and efficient evaporation for diverse applications.

HORIZONTAL TUBE EVAPORATOR

Horizontal tube evaporators are widely used in industries for concentrating liquid solutions by removing solvent through the process of evaporation. Let's explore the principles, construction, working, uses, as well as the merits and demerits of horizontal tube evaporators in detail:

Principles:

Horizontal tube evaporators operate on the principle of evaporation under vacuum conditions. The liquid solution to be concentrated is heated in a chamber while maintaining a vacuum to lower the boiling point of the liquid. Heat is supplied to the solution, causing the solvent to vaporize and leave behind a concentrated product. The vapor is then condensed and collected for further processing or disposal.

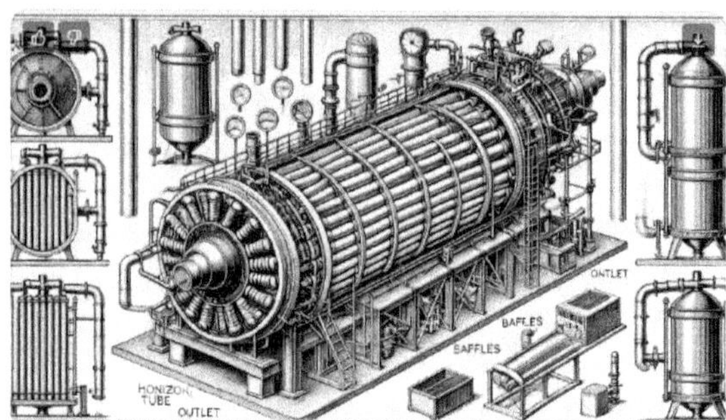

Construction:

1. Horizontal Tubes: The evaporator consists of a series of horizontal tubes arranged in a bundle within a chamber. These tubes provide a large surface area for heat transfer and evaporation.
2. Steam or Hot Water Jacket: Surrounding the tubes is a jacket through which steam or hot water is circulated to provide heat to the tubes.
3. Vacuum System: A vacuum system is connected to the evaporator chamber to maintain the desired vacuum pressure, lowering the boiling point of the liquid solution.
4. Condenser: The vapor generated during evaporation is condensed back into liquid form in a separate condenser unit.
5. Agitator: Some horizontal tube evaporators may include an agitator to ensure uniform heating and mixing of the solution.

Working:

1. Heat Transfer: Steam or hot water is circulated through the jacket surrounding the horizontal tubes. Heat is transferred from the jacket to the tubes, heating the liquid solution inside.
2. Evaporation: The heat applied to the solution causes the solvent to vaporize, leaving behind a concentrated product. The vacuum maintained in the chamber lowers the boiling point of the liquid, facilitating evaporation at lower temperatures.
3. Vapor Collection: The vapor generated during evaporation is drawn out of the chamber and condensed into liquid form in a separate condenser unit.
4. Concentrated Product Removal: The concentrated product remaining in the evaporator chamber is periodically removed for further processing or storage.

Uses:

1. Food and Beverage Industry: Horizontal tube evaporators are used for concentrating fruit juices, dairy products, and other liquid food items.
2. Chemical Industry: They are employed in chemical manufacturing for concentrating solutions of various chemicals and solvents.
3. Pharmaceuticals: Horizontal tube evaporators are used in pharmaceutical production for concentrating medicinal solutions and extracts.
4. Wastewater Treatment: They are utilized in wastewater treatment plants for concentrating and recovering valuable chemicals from wastewater streams.

Merits:

1. High Efficiency: Horizontal tube evaporators offer high heat transfer rates due to their large surface area, resulting in efficient evaporation processes.

2. Versatility: They can handle a wide range of liquid solutions with varying viscosities and concentrations.
3. Continuous Operation: Horizontal tube evaporators can be operated continuously, allowing for consistent and uninterrupted production.
4. Energy Efficiency: The use of vacuum reduces the boiling point of the liquid, requiring less energy for evaporation compared to atmospheric evaporators.

Demerits:

1. Complex Maintenance: Maintenance of horizontal tube evaporators can be complex due to the intricate arrangement of tubes and the need to maintain vacuum conditions.
2. Scaling and Fouling: The tubes may be susceptible to scaling and fouling, which can reduce heat transfer efficiency and require frequent cleaning.
3. Initial Cost: Horizontal tube evaporators may have a higher initial cost compared to other types of evaporators due to their design and construction.
4. Limited Scalability: Scaling up the capacity of horizontal tube evaporators may pose challenges due to space constraints and increased complexity.

CLIMBING FILM EVAPORATOR

Climbing film evaporators are a type of falling film evaporator widely used in industries for the concentration of liquid solutions through the process of evaporation. Let's delve into the principles, construction, working, uses, as well as the merits and demerits of climbing film evaporators in detail:

Principles:

Climbing film evaporators operate on the principle of thin film evaporation. The liquid solution to be concentrated is fed onto the inner surface of vertical tubes or plates. Gravity causes the liquid to flow downwards as a thin film along the surface of the tubes or plates. Heat is supplied to the tubes or plates, causing the solvent to vaporize from the liquid film. The vapor is then separated from the remaining liquid and condensed to produce the concentrated product.

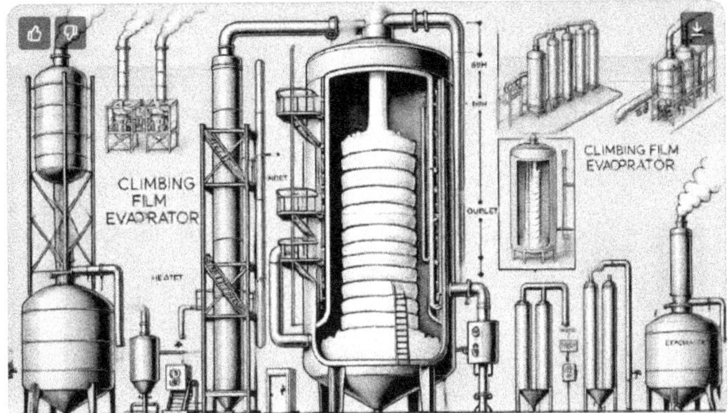

Construction:

1. Vertical Tubes or Plates: Climbing film evaporators consist of a series of vertical tubes or plates arranged in a vertical orientation. These tubes or plates provide a surface for the liquid film to flow downwards.
2. Steam or Hot Water Heating: Heat is supplied to the tubes or plates through a steam or hot water jacket surrounding the evaporator chamber.
3. Vapor Separator: A vapor separator at the top of the evaporator chamber separates the vapor generated during evaporation from the remaining liquid.
4. Condenser: The vapor collected from the vapor separator is condensed into liquid form in a separate condenser unit.

Working:

1. Liquid Feed: The liquid solution to be concentrated is fed onto the inner surface of the vertical tubes or plates.
2. Thin Film Formation: Gravity causes the liquid to flow downwards as a thin film along the surface of the tubes or plates. This thin film

maximizes the surface area for evaporation and minimizes the distance traveled by the liquid, ensuring efficient heat transfer.

3. Evaporation: Heat supplied to the tubes or plates causes the solvent to vaporize from the liquid film. The vapor rises upwards and is separated from the remaining liquid in the vapor separator.
4. Condensation: The vapor collected in the vapor separator is condensed into liquid form in a separate condenser unit. The condensed vapor is then collected as the concentrated product.

Uses:

1. Food and Beverage Industry: Climbing film evaporators are used for concentrating fruit juices, dairy products, and other liquid food items.
2. Chemical Industry: They are employed in chemical manufacturing for concentrating solutions of various chemicals and solvents.
3. Pharmaceuticals: Climbing film evaporators are used in pharmaceutical production for concentrating medicinal solutions and extracts.
4. Wastewater Treatment: They are utilized in wastewater treatment plants for concentrating and recovering valuable chemicals from wastewater streams.

Merits:

1. High Efficiency: Climbing film evaporators offer high heat transfer rates due to the thin film formation, resulting in efficient evaporation processes.
2. Compact Design: Their vertical orientation and compact design make climbing film evaporators suitable for applications where space is limited.
3. Uniform Concentration: The thin film formation ensures uniform concentration of the liquid solution, resulting in consistent product quality.

4. Low Residence Time: The short residence time of the liquid in the evaporator minimizes the risk of thermal degradation of sensitive products.

Demerits:

1. Potential for Fouling: Climbing film evaporators may be susceptible to fouling, particularly if the liquid solution contains suspended solids or precipitates.
2. Complex Maintenance: Maintenance of climbing film evaporators can be complex due to the arrangement of tubes or plates and the need to ensure uniform flow of the liquid film.
3. Limited Scalability: Scaling up the capacity of climbing film evaporators may pose challenges due to space constraints and increased complexity.
4. Initial Cost: Climbing film evaporators may have a higher initial cost compared to other types of evaporators due to their design and construction.

FORCED CIRCULATION EVAPORATOR

Forced circulation evaporators are widely used in industries for concentrating liquid solutions by evaporating the solvent under controlled conditions. Let's explore the principles, construction, working, uses, as well as the merits and demerits of forced circulation evaporators in detail:

Principles:

Forced circulation evaporators operate by continuously circulating the liquid solution through a heat exchanger to facilitate evaporation. The liquid solution is pumped under pressure through the heat exchanger, where it is heated by steam or another heating medium. As the liquid is heated, the solvent vaporizes, leaving behind a concentrated product. The vapor is then separated from the remaining liquid and condensed to produce the concentrated product.

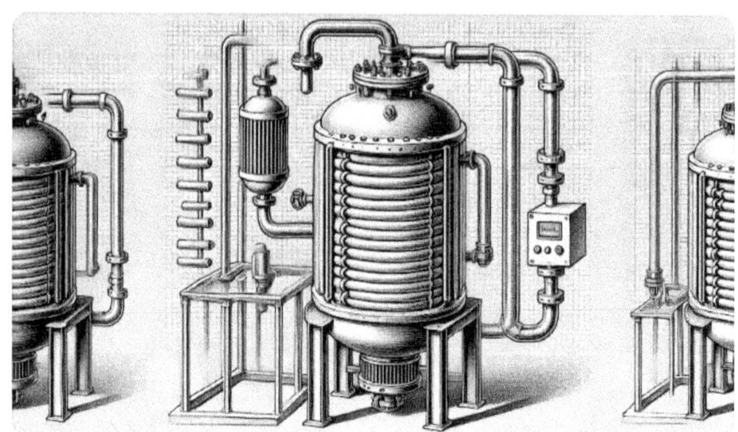

Construction:

1. Heat Exchanger: The core component of a forced circulation evaporator is the heat exchanger, which consists of a series of tubes or plates through which the liquid solution flows. The heat exchanger is typically made of stainless steel or another corrosion-resistant material.
2. Pump: A pump is used to circulate the liquid solution through the heat exchanger under pressure. The pump ensures a consistent flow rate and circulation of the solution.
3. Steam or Hot Water Heating: Heat is supplied to the heat exchanger through a steam or hot water jacket surrounding the evaporator chamber. The heating medium is circulated through the jacket to transfer heat to the liquid solution.
4. Vapor Separator: A vapor separator at the top of the evaporator chamber separates the vapor generated during evaporation from the remaining liquid.
5. Condenser: The vapor collected from the vapor separator is condensed into liquid form in a separate condenser unit. The condensed vapor is then collected as the concentrated product.

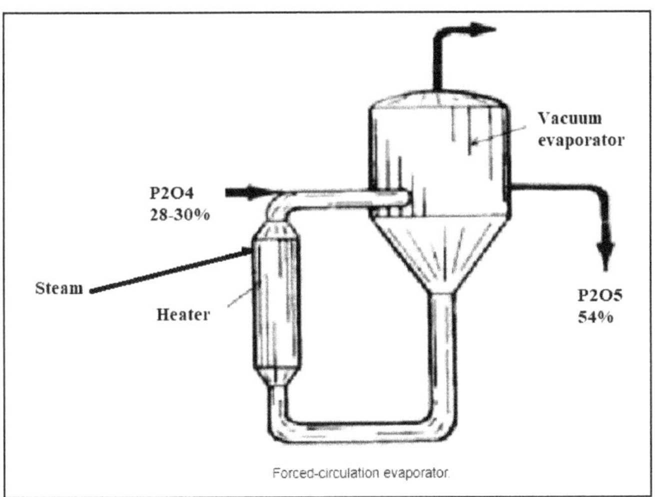

Forced-circulation evaporator

Working:

1. Liquid Feed: The liquid solution to be concentrated is pumped under pressure into the heat exchanger.
2. Heat Transfer: Steam or hot water is circulated through the jacket surrounding the heat exchanger, heating the liquid solution as it flows through the tubes or plates.
3. Evaporation: As the liquid solution is heated, the solvent vaporizes, leaving behind a concentrated product. The vapor generated during evaporation is separated from the remaining liquid in the vapor separator.
4. Condensation: The vapor collected in the vapor separator is condensed into liquid form in a separate condenser unit. The condensed vapor is then collected as the concentrated product.

Uses:

1. Food and Beverage Industry: Forced circulation evaporators are used for concentrating fruit juices, dairy products, and other liquid food items.
2. Chemical Industry: They are employed in chemical manufacturing for concentrating solutions of various chemicals and solvents.

3. Pharmaceuticals: Forced circulation evaporators are used in pharmaceutical production for concentrating medicinal solutions and extracts.
4. Wastewater Treatment: They are utilized in wastewater treatment plants for concentrating and recovering valuable chemicals from wastewater streams.

Merits:

1. High Efficiency: Forced circulation evaporators offer high heat transfer rates due to the forced circulation of the liquid solution through the heat exchanger.
2. Uniform Concentration: The controlled flow rate of the liquid solution ensures uniform concentration of the product, resulting in consistent product quality.
3. Compact Design: Forced circulation evaporators can be designed to be compact, making them suitable for applications where space is limited.
4. Continuous Operation: They can be operated continuously, allowing for consistent and uninterrupted production.

Demerits:

1. Potential for Fouling: Forced circulation evaporators may be susceptible to fouling, particularly if the liquid solution contains suspended solids or precipitates.
2. Complex Maintenance: Maintenance of forced circulation evaporators can be complex due to the arrangement of tubes or plates and the need to ensure uniform flow of the liquid solution.
3. Energy Consumption: The operation of the pump to circulate the liquid solution requires energy, which can contribute to operating costs.
4. Initial Cost: Forced circulation evaporators may have a higher initial cost compared to other types of evaporators due to their design and construction.

MULTIPLE EFFECT EVAPORATOR & ECONOMY OF MULTIPLE EFFECT EVAPORATOR

Multiple-effect evaporators are widely used in industries for the concentration of liquid solutions by sequentially utilizing the vapor generated in one effect to heat and evaporate the solution in subsequent effects. Let's explore the principles, construction, working, uses, merits, and demerits of multiple-effect evaporators, as well as the economy of their operation, in detail:

Principles:

Multiple-effect evaporators operate on the principle of heat recycling, where the vapor generated during evaporation in one effect is used to heat and evaporate the liquid solution in subsequent effects. Each effect consists of a separate evaporator vessel, and the vapor generated in one effect serves as the heating medium for the next effect. This process allows for significant energy savings compared to single-effect evaporators since the heat input is reused across multiple stages.

Construction:

1. Evaporator Vessels: Multiple-effect evaporators consist of multiple evaporator vessels arranged in series. Each vessel contains heating surfaces, such as tubes or plates, for heat transfer.
2. Vapor Separators: Vapor separators are installed between each effect to separate the vapor generated during evaporation from the remaining liquid solution.
3. Condensers: Condensers are used to condense the vapor generated in each effect back into liquid form for further processing or disposal.
4. Heat Exchangers: Heat exchangers are employed to transfer heat from the vapor generated in one effect to the liquid solution in the subsequent effect.

Working:

1. Feed Solution: The liquid solution to be concentrated is fed into the first effect of the multiple-effect evaporator.
2. Evaporation: Heat is supplied to the liquid solution in the first effect, causing the solvent to vaporize and leave behind a concentrated product. The vapor generated in the first effect is then used to heat and evaporate the liquid solution in the second effect.
3. Sequential Heating: The vapor generated in each effect serves as the heating medium for the subsequent effect, resulting in a series of evaporation stages.
4. Condensation: The vapor generated in each effect is condensed back into liquid form in separate condenser units. The condensed vapor is collected as the concentrated product.

Uses:

1. Food and Beverage Industry: Multiple-effect evaporators are used for concentrating fruit juices, dairy products, and other liquid food items.
2. Chemical Industry: They are employed in chemical manufacturing for concentrating solutions of various chemicals and solvents.
3. Pharmaceuticals: Multiple-effect evaporators are used in pharmaceutical production for concentrating medicinal solutions and extracts.
4. Wastewater Treatment: They are utilized in wastewater treatment plants for concentrating and recovering valuable chemicals from wastewater streams.

Merits:

1. Energy Efficiency: Multiple-effect evaporators offer significant energy savings compared to single-effect evaporators due to the reuse of heat across multiple stages.

2. High Concentration Ratio: Multiple-effect evaporators can achieve high concentration ratios by utilizing the vapor generated in one effect to heat and evaporate the solution in subsequent effects.
3. Compact Design: They can be designed to be compact, making efficient use of space in industrial facilities.
4. Continuous Operation: Multiple-effect evaporators can be operated continuously, allowing for consistent and uninterrupted production.

Demerits:

1. Complex Maintenance: Maintenance of multiple-effect evaporators can be complex due to the arrangement of vessels, heat exchangers, and condensers, as well as the need to ensure proper functioning of each effect.
2. Initial Cost: Multiple-effect evaporators may have a higher initial cost compared to single-effect evaporators due to their design and construction.
3. Scaling and Fouling: They may be susceptible to scaling and fouling, particularly if the liquid solution contains suspended solids or precipitates.
4. System Complexity: The operation of multiple-effect evaporators requires careful control and monitoring of each effect to ensure efficient heat transfer and evaporation.

ECONOMY OF MULTIPLE-EFFECT EVAPORATOR:

The economy of multiple-effect evaporators refers to their cost-effectiveness and efficiency in terms of energy consumption and production output. Multiple-effect evaporators offer several economic advantages:

1. Energy Savings: By reusing the heat across multiple stages, multiple-effect evaporators significantly reduce energy consumption compared to single-effect evaporators, resulting in lower operating costs.

2. High Production Output: Multiple-effect evaporators can achieve high concentration ratios, allowing for the production of a large volume of concentrated product with relatively low energy input.
3. Reduced Operating Costs: The efficient operation and continuous production capability of multiple-effect evaporators contribute to lower overall operating costs and increased profitability for industrial processes.
4. Long-Term Investment: Despite the higher initial cost, multiple-effect evaporators offer a favorable return on investment over the long term due to their energy efficiency and production output.

CHAPTER – 9

DISTILLATION – I

Mrs. Pooja Chauhan

Assistant Professor, Rajiv Gandhi Institute of Pharmacy, Faculty of Pharmaceutical Science & Technology, AKS University Satna, MP-India

---

ABSTRACT:

Distillation is a widely used separation process that exploits differences in boiling points to separate components of a liquid mixture. It involves heating the mixture to vaporize the more volatile components, then cooling the vapor to condense it back into a liquid, effectively separating it from less volatile substances. This process is fundamental in industries such as petrochemicals, pharmaceuticals, and beverage production. Simple distillation is suitable for separating components with significant boiling point differences, while fractional distillation is used for mixtures with closer boiling points, employing a fractionating column to achieve repeated vaporization-condensation cycles for higher purity. Vacuum distillation lowers the pressure to distill heat-sensitive compounds at reduced temperatures, preserving their integrity. Azeotropic distillation, on the other hand, is used to break azeotropes by adding another component to alter relative volatilities. Each distillation method is selected based on the specific properties of the mixture and the desired purity level of the separated components. Mastery of distillation techniques is crucial for ensuring the efficiency and quality of products across various applications, highlighting its importance in both laboratory and industrial settings.

INTRODUCTION

Distillation is a widely used separation technique in chemistry and industry for purifying liquids based on differences in their boiling points. It's a process that involves heating a mixture to vaporize its more volatile components, then condensing those vapors back into liquid form, thereby separating them from the less volatile components.

Here's a detailed introduction to distillation:

Principle of Distillation:

The principle behind distillation relies on the fact that different substances have different boiling points. When a mixture of liquids is heated, the component with the lower boiling point vaporizes first, leaving behind the components with higher boiling points. By controlling the temperature and pressure, it's possible to separate the components effectively.

Components of a Distillation Setup:

1. **Boiler or Distillation Flask**: This is where the mixture to be separated is heated.
2. **Condenser:** It cools down the vaporized components, causing them to condense back into liquid form.
3. **Collection Vessel**: The condensed liquid is collected here.
4. **Thermometer:** It measures the temperature of the vapor, helping to monitor the process.
5. **Fractionating Column (Optional):** In fractional distillation, a column with internal surfaces is used to increase the surface area for condensation and re-evaporation, allowing for more precise separation of components.

Types of Distillation:

1. **Simple Distillation**: It's used when the components have significantly different boiling points. The vapor from the boiling mixture is condensed and collected as a single fraction.
2. **Fractional Distillation**: This is employed when the boiling points of the components are close to each other. The fractional distillation column provides multiple condensation and vaporization cycles, allowing for better separation.

3. **Vacuum Distillation**: Used for compounds with high boiling points or those that decompose at high temperatures. Lowering the pressure lowers the boiling points of the components, preventing thermal degradation.
4. **Steam Distillation**: Suitable for separating temperature-sensitive compounds from non-volatile impurities. Steam is passed through the mixture, and the volatile compounds are carried over with the steam, then condensed back into liquid form.

Steps in Distillation Process:

1. **Heating:** The mixture is heated to the boiling point of the most volatile component.
2. **Vaporization:** The more volatile components vaporize, leaving behind the less volatile ones.
3. **Condensation**: The vapor is cooled and condensed back into liquid form.
4. **Collection**: The condensed liquid is collected in a separate vessel.
5. **Repeat (for fractional distillation)**: In fractional distillation, the process of vaporization and condensation is repeated multiple times within the fractionating column for better separation.

Applications of Distillation:

1. **Purification of Water:** Distillation is used to produce pure water from seawater or contaminated water.
2. **Separation of Alcohol**: Distillation is employed in the production of alcoholic beverages and in the refining of ethanol.
3. **Petroleum Refining**: Fractional distillation is used to separate crude oil into its various components such as gasoline, diesel, and kerosene.
4. **Pharmaceutical Industry**: It's used to purify and separate different chemical compounds.

SIMPLE DISTILLATION

Simple distillation is one of the fundamental techniques in the field of chemistry for separating and purifying liquid mixtures based on differences in their boiling points. Here's a detailed explanation of the basic principles and methodology of simple distillation:

Basic Principles:

Simple distillation is a fundamental separation technique used to separate two or more liquids from a mixture based on differences in their boiling points. It's one of the most common methods of distillation and is widely used in laboratories and industrial settings. Here's a detailed explanation of the basic principles involved in simple distillation:

1. Boiling Point Difference:

Simple distillation relies on the principle that different components of a mixture have different boiling points. The component with the lower boiling point will vaporize first, while the component with the higher boiling point will remain in the liquid phase. By heating the mixture, the more volatile component can be selectively vaporized and separated from the less volatile components.

2. Vapor-Liquid Equilibrium:

At the boiling point of a liquid, the vapor pressure of the liquid equals the pressure exerted on it by the surrounding atmosphere. This equilibrium state allows the liquid to vaporize and form a vapor phase. In simple distillation, the vapor phase contains a higher concentration of the more volatile component, while the liquid phase contains a higher concentration of the less volatile components.

3. Fractional Separation:

Simple distillation is effective for separating components with a significant difference in boiling points. However, if the boiling points of the components are too close, fractional distillation, which incorporates a fractionating column, may be necessary for better separation. The fractionating column provides multiple vaporization and condensation stages, allowing for more precise separation of closely boiling components.

4. Temperature Control:

Temperature control is crucial in simple distillation to ensure that the boiling point of the desired component is reached without overheating or decomposing the mixture. By monitoring the temperature of the distillation apparatus, the distillation process can be controlled to achieve optimal separation.

5. Vaporization and Condensation:

During simple distillation, the mixture is heated to its boiling point, causing the more volatile component to vaporize. The vapor rises through the distillation apparatus and enters a condenser, where it is cooled and condensed back into liquid form. The condensed liquid, enriched with the more volatile component, is collected as the distillate.

6. Separation and Collection:

The distillate collected during simple distillation contains the more volatile component of the mixture. The less volatile components, which remain in the original liquid phase, are left behind in the distillation apparatus. The distillate can be further processed or analyzed depending on the desired application.

Methodology:

The methodology of simple distillation involves a series of steps aimed at separating two or more liquids from a mixture based on differences in their boiling points. Here's a detailed explanation of the methodology involved in simple distillation:

1. Setup:

1. **Apparatus Assembly**: Assemble the distillation apparatus, which typically includes a distillation flask, a distillation head, a condenser, a receiver flask, and a heating source such as a heating mantle or a Bunsen burner.
2. **Boiling Flask Preparation**: Place the mixture to be distilled in the boiling flask. Ensure that the boiling flask is clean and properly attached to the rest of the apparatus.

2. Heating:

1. **Heat Application**: Apply heat to the boiling flask using the heating source. The heat causes the mixture to gradually reach its boiling point.
2. **Temperature Monitoring**: Monitor the temperature of the mixture using a thermometer or a temperature probe. The temperature should be increased gradually to avoid overheating or decomposition of the mixture.

3. Vaporization:

1. **Boiling**: As the temperature of the mixture rises, the component with the lower boiling point vaporizes first. This vaporization process occurs within the boiling flask.
2. **Rise of Vapor**: The vaporized component rises through the distillation head and enters the condenser.

4. Condensation:

1. **Cooling:** The vapor travels through the condenser, which is cooled either by circulating cold water or another cooling medium. The cooling causes the vapor to condense back into liquid form.
2. **Liquid Collection**: The condensed liquid, enriched with the more volatile component, is collected in the receiver flask. This liquid is referred to as the distillate.

5. Separation and Collection:

1. **Fractional Separation**: The distillate collected in the receiver flask contains the more volatile component of the mixture. The less volatile components remain in the boiling flask.
2. **Multiple Distillate Collection**: If the mixture contains multiple components with significantly different boiling points, multiple fractions of distillate may be collected at different temperature ranges.

6. Cleanup:

1. **Cooling Down**: Once the distillation process is complete, allow the apparatus to cool down before disassembly.

2. **Cleanup**: Disassemble the distillation apparatus and clean all glassware thoroughly to remove any residue from the distillation process.

Safety Considerations:

Safety considerations are paramount in any laboratory procedure, including simple distillation. Here's a detailed explanation of the safety considerations involved in simple distillation:

1. Heat and Fire Hazards:

1. **Flammable Liquids**: Some components being distilled may be flammable. Use caution and ensure proper ventilation to prevent the accumulation of flammable vapors. Avoid open flames near the distillation setup.
2. **Heating Equipment**: Use heating sources such as heating mantles or hot plates designed for laboratory use. Avoid using open flames such as Bunsen burners unless absolutely necessary, and ensure they are properly controlled.

2. **Pressure Build-Up**:

1. **Pressure R**elief: If the distillation setup is closed, ensure that there are pressure relief mechanisms in place to prevent pressure build-up. This could include pressure relief valves or venting systems.
2. **Vigilance**: Monitor the distillation setup closely for any signs of pressure build-up, such as leaks or bulging glassware. If pressure starts to rise unexpectedly, stop heating immediately and address the issue before continuing.

3. **Chemical Exposure**:

1. **Volatile Compounds**: Some components being distilled may be hazardous if inhaled or come into contact with skin or eyes. Always work in a well-ventilated area or in a fume hood, and wear appropriate personal protective equipment (PPE) such as safety glasses, gloves, and lab coats.

2. **Chemical Compatibility**: Be aware of the chemicals being used and their potential hazards. Ensure that the materials used in the distillation apparatus are compatible with the chemicals being distilled to prevent reactions or corrosion.

4. **Glassware Safety**:
   1. **Handling Glassware**: Handle glassware with care to prevent breakage or cuts. Inspect glassware for any defects or damage before use, and replace any damaged glassware immediately.
   2. **Hot Surfaces**: Glassware and heating equipment can become very hot during the distillation process. Use appropriate protective equipment such as insulated gloves or tongs when handling hot glassware or equipment.

5. **Electrical Safety:**
   1. **Electrical Equipment**: Ensure that all electrical equipment used in the distillation setup is in good working condition and properly grounded. Avoid using damaged or frayed electrical cords, and keep electrical equipment away from water or other liquids.
   2. **Water Baths:** If using a water bath for heating, ensure that it is properly insulated and that the electrical connections are protected from water.

6. **Emergency Procedures:**
   1. **Emergency Response**: Know the location of emergency equipment such as fire extinguishers, eye wash stations, and safety showers. Familiarize yourself with emergency procedures and know how to respond in case of accidents or spills.
   2. **Safety Training**: Ensure that all personnel involved in the distillation process are properly trained in safety procedures and emergency response protocols.

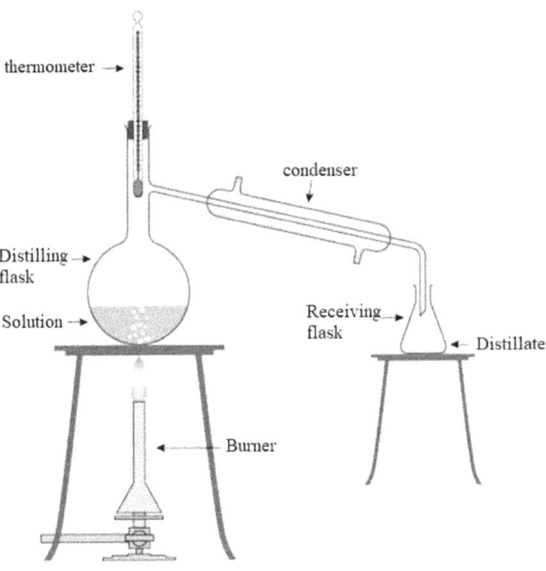

FLASH DISTILLATION

Flash distillation is a separation process commonly used in chemical engineering to separate a mixture of liquids into its individual components based on differences in their vapor pressures. This method is particularly useful when dealing with mixtures of volatile components that have different boiling points. Here's a detailed explanation of the basic principles and methodology of flash distillation:

Flash distillation is a separation process used to separate a liquid mixture into its individual components by exploiting differences in their volatility. It's commonly employed in various industries, including petrochemical, chemical, and food processing, for separating mixtures with components that have significantly different boiling points. Here's a detailed explanation of the basic principles, methodology, and applications of flash distillation:

Basic Principles:

Flash distillation is a separation process used to separate a liquid mixture into its individual components by exploiting differences in their volatility. It involves the rapid vaporization of a liquid mixture followed by immediate condensation to separate the more volatile components from the less volatile ones. Here's a detailed explanation of the basic principles involved in flash distillation:

1. Vapor-Liquid Equilibrium:

Flash distillation operates based on the principle of vapor-liquid equilibrium. At a given temperature and pressure, a mixture of liquids reaches equilibrium, where the vapor phase and the liquid phase contain the same composition of components. This equilibrium allows for the volatilization of components with lower boiling points.

2. Pressure Drop:

The key principle behind flash distillation is the sudden drop in pressure. By reducing the pressure in the distillation apparatus, the boiling points of the components are lowered, allowing for rapid vaporization of the more volatile components. This pressure drop can be achieved by passing the liquid mixture through a control valve or by applying heat to the mixture.

3. Partial Vaporization:

In flash distillation, the liquid mixture is partially vaporized as it enters the flash drum or flash separator. The sudden reduction in pressure or increase in temperature causes the more volatile components to vaporize rapidly, while the less volatile components remain in the liquid phase.

4. Vapor-Liquid Separation:

Inside the flash drum or flash separator, the vapor and liquid phases separate. The vapor, enriched with the more volatile components, rises to the top, while the liquid, containing the less volatile components, settles at the bottom. This separation occurs due to differences in the vapor pressures of the components.

5. Vapor Recovery:

The vapor phase, containing the more volatile components, is typically recovered from the top of the flash drum or flash separator. It may be condensed back into liquid form using a condenser and collected for further processing or disposal. This condensed vapor, known as the distillate, contains the separated components with lower boiling points.

Methodology of Flash Distillation:

1. **Setup:**
    a. Flash distillation typically involves a flash drum or flash separator, a feed inlet, a vapor outlet, a liquid outlet, and sometimes a heat source.
    b. The liquid mixture to be separated is fed into the flash drum through the feed inlet.
2. **Pressure Reduction:**
    a. The pressure inside the flash drum is reduced suddenly, either by passing the liquid mixture through a control valve or by applying heat to the mixture.
    b. This rapid pressure drop lowers the boiling points of the components, allowing for rapid vaporization of the more volatile components.
3. **Partial Vaporization:**
    a. As the liquid mixture enters the flash drum, it undergoes partial vaporization due to the sudden pressure drop or temperature increase.
    b. The more volatile components vaporize quickly, while the less volatile components remain in the liquid phase.
4. **Vapor-Liquid Separation:**
    a. Inside the flash drum, the vapor and liquid phases separate. The vapor, enriched with the more volatile components, rises to the top,

while the liquid, containing the less volatile components, settles at the bottom.

5. **Vapor Recovery:**
    a. The vapor phase, containing the more volatile components, is recovered from the top of the flash drum through the vapor outlet.
    b. The vapor may be condensed back into liquid form using a condenser and collected as the distillate.
6. **Liquid Product Withdrawal:**
    a. The liquid phase, which remains in the bottom of the flash drum, contains the less volatile components of the original mixture.
    b. This liquid product is withdrawn from the bottom of the flash drum through the liquid outlet and may undergo further separation or processing if necessary.

Applications of Flash Distillation:

1. **Petroleum Refining:**
    a. Flash distillation is commonly used in petroleum refineries to separate crude oil into fractions such as gasoline, diesel, and kerosene based on their boiling points.
2. **Chemical Process Industries:**
    a. It finds applications in various chemical processes for separating binary or multicomponent mixtures, such as solvent recovery and product purification.
3. **Food and Beverage Industry:**
    a. Flash distillation is used in food and beverage processing for separating volatile flavor compounds from liquid mixtures, such as in the production of essential oils and alcoholic beverages.
4. **Wastewater Treatment:**

Flash distillation is utilized in wastewater treatment plants for separating volatile organic compounds (VOCs) from water, contributing to environmental protection efforts.

5. Desalination:

a. Flash distillation is also used in desalination processes to separate fresh water from saltwater by exploiting the differences in their boiling points.

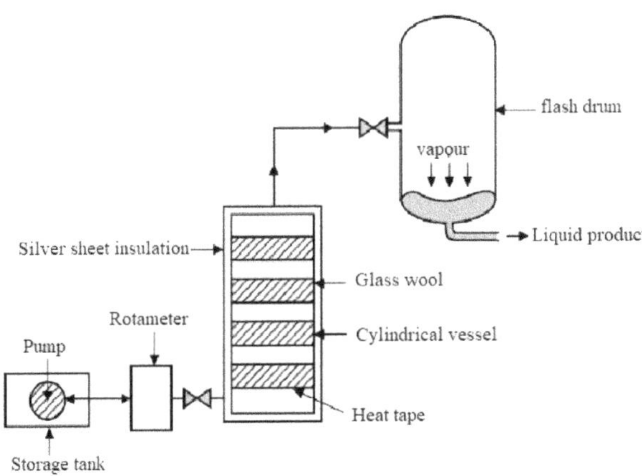

CHAPTER – 10

DISTILLATION – II

Mr. Satyendra Garg

Assistant Professor, Rajiv Gandhi Institute of Pharmacy, Faculty of Pharmaceutical Science & Technology, AKS University Satna, MP-India

---

ABSTRACT:

Fractional distillation is a sophisticated technique used to separate liquid mixtures with closely spaced boiling points. It involves the use of a fractionating column, which provides multiple vaporization-condensation cycles, allowing for more precise separation of components. This method is crucial in refining crude oil into its various fractions, such as gasoline, diesel, and kerosene. Distillation under reduced pressure, or vacuum distillation, is employed for heat-sensitive substances that decompose at high temperatures. By reducing the pressure, the boiling points of the components are lowered, enabling distillation at much gentler temperatures and preserving the integrity of the compounds. Steam distillation is another specialized technique, particularly useful for extracting essential oils from plant materials. In this process, steam is passed through the material, vaporizing the volatile compounds, which are then condensed and collected. Molecular distillation, an advanced form of distillation, operates under extremely low pressures, facilitating the separation of molecules with very high boiling points or those that are thermally unstable. This method is often used in the pharmaceutical and food industries for purifying heat-sensitive compounds. Each of these distillation techniques is tailored to specific applications, ensuring the efficient and effective separation of complex mixtures while maintaining the quality and purity of the desired components.

FRACTIONAL DISTILLATION

Fractional distillation is a powerful technique used for separating a mixture of liquids with similar boiling points. It's an extension of simple distillation, employing a fractionating column to achieve better separation. Here's a detailed explanation of its basic principles and methodology:

Fractional distillation is a separation technique used to separate a mixture of liquids into its individual components based on differences in their boiling points. It's an extension of simple distillation, incorporating a fractionating column to achieve better separation of components with closer boiling points. Here's a detailed explanation of the basic principles, methodology, and applications of fractional distillation:

Basic Principles:

Fractional distillation is a separation process used to separate a mixture of liquids into its individual components based on differences in their boiling points. It's an extension of simple distillation that incorporates a fractionating column to achieve better separation of components with closely spaced boiling points. Here's a detailed explanation of the basic principles involved in fractional distillation:

1. Differential Boiling Points:

Fractional distillation relies on the principle that different components of a liquid mixture have different boiling points. Each component will vaporize and condense at a temperature specific to its boiling point. By exploiting these differences, it's possible to separate the components from one another.

2. Vapor-Liquid Equilibrium:

At a given temperature and pressure, a liquid mixture reaches a state of vapor-liquid equilibrium. This equilibrium is governed by Raoult's law, which states that the vapor pressure of each component in the mixture is proportional to its mole fraction in the liquid phase. In fractional distillation, this equilibrium is maintained throughout the fractionating column.

3. Fractionating Column:

The key component of fractional distillation is the fractionating column, which provides multiple vaporization-condensation stages. The fractionating column consists of trays or packing material, providing a large surface area for vaporization and condensation. As vapor rises through the column, it encounters a temperature gradient, with cooler temperatures at the top and hotter temperatures at the bottom.

4. Differential Condensation:

As vapor rises through the fractionating column, it encounters trays or packing material where it condenses. The more volatile components with lower boiling points condense at higher points in the column, while the less volatile components with higher boiling points remain in the vapor phase and continue to rise.

5. Enrichment of Components:

Each vaporization-condensation cycle in the fractionating column results in enrichment of the more volatile components in the vapor phase and depletion of these components in the liquid phase. This process allows for better separation of components with closely spaced boiling points.

6. Temperature Gradient:

The temperature gradient in the fractionating column is maintained by applying heat at the bottom and providing cooling at the top. This gradient ensures that components condense at different heights in the column based on their boiling points, facilitating separation.

Methodology of Fractional Distillation:

1. **Setup:**
    a. Assemble the fractional distillation apparatus, including a distillation flask, a fractionating column, a condenser, and a receiver flask.
    b. The mixture to be separated is placed in the distillation flask.

2. **Fractionating Column:**
    a. The fractionating column provides multiple vaporization-condensation stages. It consists of trays or packing material, providing a large surface area for vaporization and condensation.
    b. The column is attached to the top of the distillation flask, and the vapor rises through the column.
3. **Heating:**
    a. Apply heat to the distillation flask, typically using a heating mantle or a water bath. The heat causes the mixture to vaporize, and the vapors rise into the fractionating column.
4. **Temperature Gradient:**
    a. Maintain a temperature gradient along the fractionating column by controlling the heat input. The temperature is typically highest at the bottom of the column and decreases towards the top.
    b. This gradient ensures that components condense at different heights in the column based on their boiling points.
5. **Vaporization and Condensation:**
    a. As vapor rises through the fractionating column, it encounters trays or packing material where it condenses. The more volatile components condense at higher points in the column, while the less volatile components remain in the vapor phase and continue to rise.
6. **Fraction Collection:**
    a. Different fractions of the mixture are collected at different heights in the fractionating column. Each fraction represents a mixture of components with similar boiling points.
    b. The temperature is monitored throughout the distillation process to ensure proper separation and collection of fractions.
7. **Product Withdrawal:**

a. Collect the fractions in separate receiver flasks. Each fraction contains components with similar boiling points and can be further processed or analyzed depending on the desired application.

Applications of Fractional Distillation:

1. **Petroleum Refining:**

   Fractional distillation is widely used in petroleum refineries to separate crude oil into fractions such as gasoline, diesel, and kerosene based on their boiling points.

2. **Chemical Industry:**

   a. It is employed in the chemical industry for the separation and purification of various chemicals, including solvents, intermediates, and final products.

3. **Pharmaceuticals:**

   a. Fractional distillation is used in the pharmaceutical industry for the purification of drug compounds, isolation of active pharmaceutical ingredients (APIs), and production of pharmaceutical intermediates.

4. **Alcohol Production:**

   a. It is utilized in the production of alcoholic beverages to separate and purify ethanol from fermentation mixtures.

5. **Essential Oils:**

   a. Fractional distillation is commonly used in the extraction of essential oils from aromatic plants, enabling the separation of volatile aromatic compounds.

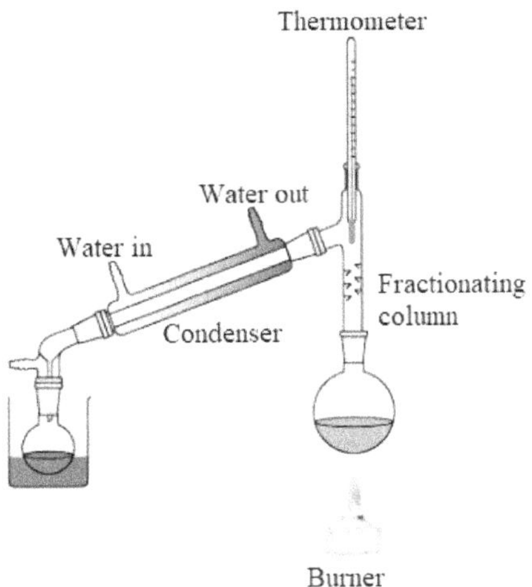

DISTILLATION UNDER REDUCED PRESSURE

Distillation under reduced pressure, also known as vacuum distillation, is a method used to separate substances that are sensitive to high temperatures or undergo decomposition at atmospheric pressure. By lowering the pressure in the distillation apparatus, the boiling points of the components are reduced, allowing for separation at lower temperatures. Here's a detailed explanation of the basic principles and methodology of distillation under reduced pressure:

Basic Principles:

Distillation under reduced pressure, also known as vacuum distillation, is a method used to separate and purify substances that are sensitive to high temperatures or undergo decomposition at atmospheric pressure. The basic principle of distillation under reduced pressure involves lowering the pressure in the distillation apparatus, which lowers the boiling points of the components, allowing for separation at lower temperatures. Here's a detailed explanation of the basic principle of distillation under reduced pressure:

1. Boiling Point Elevation:

In standard distillation, the boiling point of a liquid is the temperature at which its vapor pressure equals the atmospheric pressure. However, in distillation under reduced pressure, the atmospheric pressure is lowered, causing a corresponding decrease in the boiling points of the components. This phenomenon is described by the Clausius-Clapeyron equation.

2. Lowered Vapor Pressure:

As the pressure in the distillation apparatus decreases, the vapor pressure required for boiling is reached at a lower temperature. This allows for the vaporization of the components at temperatures below their normal boiling points at atmospheric pressure.

3. Vapor-Liquid Equilibrium:

Despite the reduced pressure, distillation under reduced pressure still operates based on the principle of vapor-liquid equilibrium. As the mixture is heated, the more volatile components vaporize and are collected, while the less volatile components remain in the liquid phase. However, the equilibrium conditions occur at lower temperatures due to the reduced pressure.

4. Preservation of Temperature-Sensitive Compounds:

Distillation under reduced pressure is particularly useful for separating substances that are sensitive to high temperatures or undergo thermal decomposition. By operating at lower temperatures, it minimizes thermal degradation and allows for the isolation of temperature-sensitive compounds.

5. Pressure Control:

The pressure in the distillation apparatus is controlled using a vacuum pump or other vacuum sources. By adjusting the pressure, the boiling points of the components can be precisely controlled, allowing for efficient separation.

6. Application of Heat:

Heat is applied to the distillation apparatus to raise the temperature of the mixture and promote vaporization. The temperature is carefully controlled to ensure that it is sufficient to vaporize the components but not so high as to cause thermal degradation.

Methodology of Distillation under Reduced Pressure:

1. **Setup:**
   a. Assemble the distillation apparatus, including a distillation flask, a fractionating column (if necessary), a condenser, and a receiver flask.
   b. Connect the vacuum pump to the system to lower the pressure inside the apparatus.
2. **Vacuum Operation:**
   a. Start the vacuum pump to create a vacuum inside the apparatus. The vacuum pump removes air and other gases, lowering the pressure.
   b. Monitor and control the pressure using a vacuum gauge or pressure transducer to achieve the desired level of vacuum.
3. **Heat Application:**
   a. Apply heat to the distillation flask using a heating mantle, hot plate, or other heating source. The heat causes the mixture to vaporize.
   b. Control the temperature carefully to ensure that it is sufficient to vaporize the components but not so high as to cause thermal degradation.
4. **Vaporization and Condensation:**
   a. As the mixture vaporizes, the vapor rises through the fractionating column (if present) or directly into the condenser.
   b. In the condenser, the vapor is cooled and condenses back into liquid form. The condensed liquid, enriched with the more volatile components, is collected in the receiver flask.

5. **Fraction Collection:**
    a. Different fractions of the mixture may be collected at different stages of the distillation process, depending on the components' boiling points.
    b. Each fraction represents a mixture of components with similar boiling points and can be further processed or analyzed as needed.

Applications of Distillation under Reduced Pressure:

1. **Pharmaceutical Industry:**
    a. Distillation under reduced pressure is used in the pharmaceutical industry for the purification of temperature-sensitive drugs and intermediates.
    b. It is particularly useful for the isolation of high-purity compounds without thermal degradation.
2. **Chemical Industry:**
    a. It is employed in the chemical industry for the separation and purification of various chemicals, including solvents, intermediates, and final products.
    b. Distillation under reduced pressure allows for the separation of components with closely spaced boiling points, improving product purity.
3. **Food and Beverage Industry:**
    a. It finds applications in the food and beverage industry for the purification of flavorings, essential oils, and other temperature-sensitive compounds.
    b. Vacuum distillation preserves the delicate flavors and aromas of natural products during the distillation process.
4. **Petroleum Refining:**

a. In petroleum refining, distillation under reduced pressure is used for the separation of crude oil fractions into various petroleum products, such as gasoline, diesel, and jet fuel.
b. It allows for the separation of high-boiling-point fractions at lower temperatures, reducing energy consumption and thermal stress on the components.

5. **Environmental Remediation:**
   a. Distillation under reduced pressure is utilized in environmental remediation for the removal of volatile organic compounds (VOCs) from contaminated soil, water, and air.
   b. It enables the recovery and purification of VOCs for reuse or safe disposal, contributing to environmental protection efforts.

STEAM DISTILLATION

Steam distillation is a specialized form of distillation used to separate heat-sensitive compounds from natural products or mixtures that are insoluble or immiscible in water. It's particularly useful for extracting essential oils from plants, as well as for purifying volatile compounds. Here's a detailed explanation of the basic principles and methodology of steam distillation:

Basic Principles:

Steam distillation is a special type of distillation used to separate heat-sensitive substances, such as natural aromatic compounds and essential oils, from non-volatile components. The basic principle of steam distillation involves passing steam through a mixture of the substance to be distilled, causing the volatile compounds to vaporize along with the steam. Here's a detailed explanation of the basic principle of steam distillation:

1. Introduction of Steam:

a. **Water and Heat Source**: Water is heated in a boiler or flask to generate steam. The steam carries heat and moisture, facilitating the vaporization of volatile compounds in the mixture.

b. **Mixture Introduction**: The steam is passed through the mixture containing the substance to be distilled. The mixture can be placed in a separate flask or directly into the distillation apparatus.

2. Vaporization of Volatile Compounds:

a. **Heat Transfer**: As the steam passes through the mixture, it transfers heat to the mixture, causing the volatile compounds to vaporize.

b. **Volatility Difference**: The volatile compounds vaporize along with the steam, while the non-volatile components remain in the liquid phase.

3. Formation of Vapor Mixture:

a. **Steam and Volatile Compounds**: The vaporized volatile compounds mix with the steam, forming a vapor mixture.

b. **Entrainment:** The volatile compounds are carried along with the steam due to entrainment, effectively separating them from the non-volatile components.

4. Condensation:

a. **Cooling:** The vapor mixture is then passed through a condenser, where it is cooled and condensed back into liquid form.

b. **Separation**: The condensed liquid consists of water and the volatile compounds, which do not mix due to differences in density and solubility.

5. Liquid Collection:

a. **Separation**: The condensed liquid forms two layers, with the essential oil or volatile compounds floating on top of the water layer.

b. **Separation**: The essential oil or volatile compounds are then collected separately from the water layer.

6. Application:

a. **Essential Oils:** Steam distillation is commonly used in the extraction of essential oils from aromatic plants. It allows for the isolation of volatile aromatic compounds without subjecting them to high temperatures that may cause degradation.

b. **Flavorings and Fragrances**: It is employed in the production of natural flavorings, fragrances, and perfumes, where the delicate aromatic compounds need to be preserved.

c. **Pharmaceuticals:** Steam distillation is used in the pharmaceutical industry for the extraction of medicinal compounds and natural products, such as herbal extracts and active pharmaceutical ingredients (APIs).

d. **Food and Beverages**: It finds applications in the food and beverage industry for the extraction of natural flavors and aromas from fruits, herbs, and spices, used in the production of beverages, confectionery, and culinary products.

Methodology of Steam Distillation:

1. **Water Boiling and Steam Generation:**
    a. Water is boiled in a separate flask or boiler to generate steam. The steam carries heat and moisture, which will facilitate the vaporization of the volatile compounds in the mixture.
2. **Mixture Introduction:**
    a. The mixture containing the substance to be distilled is placed in a flask or vessel. The mixture can consist of plant material, aromatic compounds, or other substances containing volatile compounds.
3. **Steam Passage:**
    a. The steam is passed through the mixture using a steam inlet tube or other apparatus. The steam heats the mixture, causing the volatile compounds to vaporize.
4. **Vaporization of Volatile Compounds:**
    a. As the steam passes through the mixture, it transfers heat to the mixture, causing the volatile compounds to vaporize. These

volatile compounds have lower boiling points than water and are carried along with the steam.

5. **Formation of Vapor Mixture:**
   a. The vaporized volatile compounds mix with the steam, forming a vapor mixture. This vapor mixture is then carried out of the mixture vessel and into the condensation apparatus.
6. **Condensation:**
   a. The vapor mixture is passed through a condenser, which cools the mixture and causes it to condense back into liquid form. The condensation releases heat, which is typically removed through a cooling system or water circulation.
7. **Liquid Collection:**
   a. The condensed liquid mixture is collected in a receiver flask. The liquid consists of water and the volatile compounds, which are immiscible with water and form a separate layer.
8. **Separation of Layers:**
   a. The collected liquid forms two distinct layers in the receiver flask: an upper layer containing the essential oil or volatile compounds and a lower layer containing water. The layers are separated, and the essential oil or volatile compounds are collected separately.

Applications of Steam Distillation:

1. **Essential Oils Extraction:**

   Steam distillation is commonly used to extract essential oils from aromatic plants. It allows for the isolation of volatile aromatic compounds without subjecting them to high temperatures that may cause degradation.
2. **Flavorings and Fragrances:**

a. It is employed in the production of natural flavorings, fragrances, and perfumes, where the delicate aromatic compounds need to be preserved.

3. **Pharmaceuticals:**

   a. Steam distillation is used in the pharmaceutical industry for the extraction of medicinal compounds and natural products, such as herbal extracts and active pharmaceutical ingredients (APIs).

4. **Food and Beverages:**

   a. It finds applications in the food and beverage industry for the extraction of natural flavors and aromas from fruits, herbs, and spices, used in the production of beverages, confectionery, and culinary products.

5. **Environmental Remediation:**

   a. Steam distillation is utilized in environmental remediation for the removal of volatile organic compounds (VOCs) from contaminated soil, water, and air.

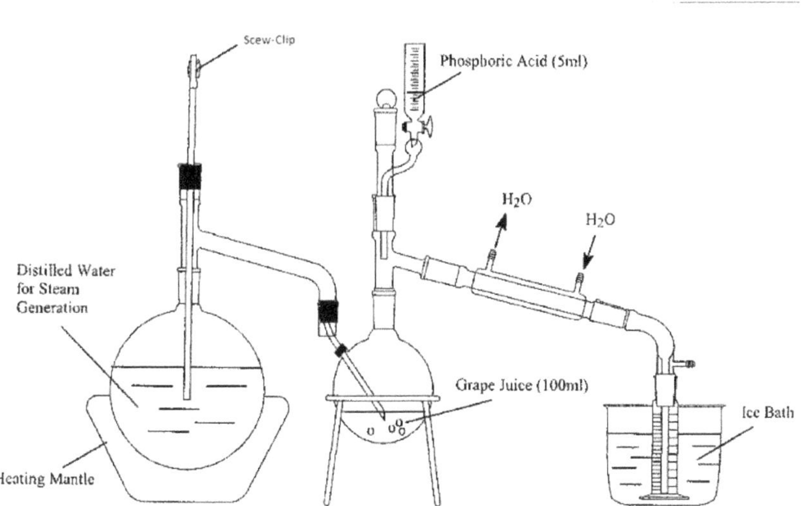

MOLECULAR DISTILLATION

Molecular distillation, also known as short-path distillation, is an advanced separation technique used to separate and purify heat-sensitive and high-boiling-point substances. It's particularly useful for purifying compounds with very close boiling points or those prone to decomposition at high temperatures. Here's a detailed explanation of the basic principles and methodology of molecular distillation:

Basic Principles:

1. **Short Path Distillation**: Molecular distillation operates under high vacuum conditions with very short distances between the evaporator and the condenser, typically on the order of a few millimeters to a few centimeters. This short path minimizes the distance traveled by the vapor molecules, reducing the chance of thermal decomposition or loss of volatile compounds.
2. **Thin Film Evaporation**: In molecular distillation, the mixture is fed onto a heated surface called the evaporator or wiped film evaporator. The mixture forms a thin film on the evaporator surface, where it is rapidly heated under vacuum. The volatile components vaporize quickly and rise to the condenser.
3. **High Vacuum Conditions**: Molecular distillation is carried out under high vacuum conditions to lower the boiling points of the components and minimize the risk of thermal degradation. The reduced pressure allows for separation at lower temperatures, even below the boiling points of the components.
4. **Fractional Separation**: Molecular distillation separates components based on differences in their volatility and molecular weights. Lighter molecules with lower boiling points vaporize more readily and are collected first, while heavier molecules with higher boiling points remain in the residue.

Methodology:

1. **Setup:** The molecular distillation apparatus consists of a heated evaporator, a condenser, a vacuum pump, and a receiver flask. The mixture to be distilled is fed onto the evaporator surface.
2. **Evaporation**: The mixture forms a thin film on the heated surface of the evaporator. The surface is heated under vacuum conditions, causing the volatile components to vaporize rapidly.
3. **Vapor Flow**: The vaporized components rise from the evaporator and enter the condenser. The condenser is typically cooled using a circulating coolant, such as cold water, to condense the vapor back into liquid form.
4. **Collection**: The condensed liquid, enriched with the desired volatile components, is collected in the receiver flask. This liquid is referred to as the distillate or fraction.
5. **Residue Removal:** The non-volatile or heavier components that remain in the evaporator are collected separately as the residue or bottom fraction.
6. **Controlled Operation**: Molecular distillation requires precise control of temperature, pressure, and flow rates to ensure efficient separation and prevent thermal degradation. Automated systems and monitoring equipment are often used to maintain optimal conditions.

Applications:

1. **Oils and Fats Refining**: Molecular distillation is used to refine oils and fats, removing impurities and undesirable components such as free fatty acids and contaminants.
2. **Pharmaceutical Purification**: It is employed in the purification of pharmaceutical compounds, including vitamins, antibiotics, and active pharmaceutical ingredients (APIs).

3. **CBD and Cannabis Concentrates**: Molecular distillation is used to refine and concentrate cannabinoids such as CBD and THC from cannabis extracts.

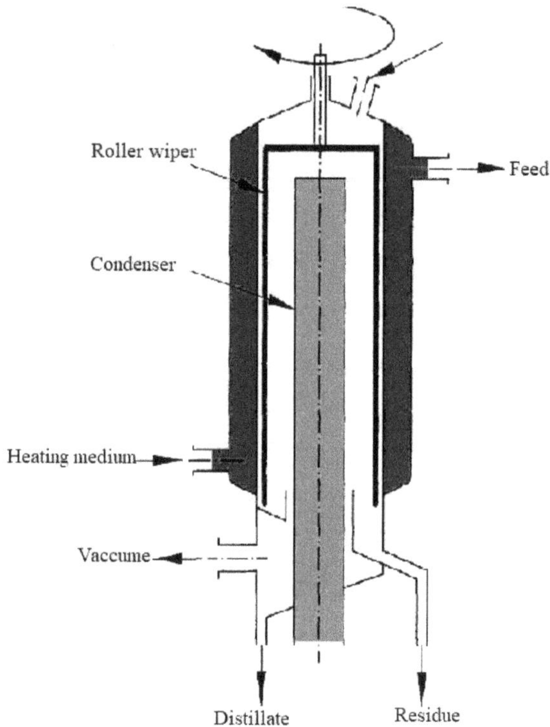

CHAPTER – 11

DRYING – I

Mrs. Neelam Singh

Assistant Professor, Rajiv Gandhi Institute of Pharmacy, Faculty of Pharmaceutical Science & Technology, AKS University Satna, MP-India

---

ABSTRACT:

Drying is an essential process in various industries, involving the removal of moisture from materials to achieve desired properties and stability. It is widely used in food processing, pharmaceuticals, and manufacturing to extend shelf life, enhance product quality, and facilitate handling and storage. Drying can be accomplished through several methods, including convection, conduction, radiation, and microwave drying. Convection drying uses hot air to evaporate moisture, while conduction drying transfers heat through direct contact with heated surfaces. Radiation drying employs electromagnetic waves, and microwave drying uses microwave energy to heat and evaporate water within the material. Factors such as temperature, humidity, airflow, and material properties influence drying efficiency. By optimizing these parameters, industries can achieve uniform drying, prevent spoilage, and maintain the integrity of heat-sensitive products, making drying a critical step in many production processes.

INTRODUCTION

Drying is a process used to remove moisture or water content from a substance, typically a solid material or a liquid mixture, to preserve it, enhance its shelf life, or prepare it for further processing. It's a common technique employed in various industries including food processing, pharmaceuticals, textiles, agriculture, and chemicals. Here's a detailed introduction to the process of drying:

Principles of Drying:

1. **Evaporation**: Drying involves the transfer of moisture from the material to the surrounding air through evaporation. This occurs due to the difference in vapor pressure between the surface of the material and the surrounding air.
2. **Mass Transfer**: Mass transfer mechanisms such as diffusion, capillary action, and convective airflow facilitate the movement of moisture from the interior of the material to its surface.
3. **Heat Transfer**: Heat is typically applied to the material to increase the rate of evaporation. This can be achieved through convection, conduction, or radiation, depending on the drying method used.

Factors Affecting Drying Process:

1. T**emperature**: Higher temperatures generally accelerate the drying process by increasing the rate of evaporation. However, excessive heat can cause damage to the material or alter its properties.
2. **Airflow**: Adequate airflow is crucial for carrying away the moisture released during drying. Proper ventilation prevents the formation of a boundary layer of saturated air around the material, which can impede drying.
3. **Humidity**: The humidity of the drying air affects its capacity to absorb moisture. Lower humidity gradients between the material and the air promote faster drying.
4. **Material Characteristics**: The composition, size, shape, and initial moisture content of the material influence the drying time and efficiency. Porous materials dry more rapidly than dense ones due to increased surface area.

5. **Drying Method**: Various drying methods such as air drying, sun drying, freeze drying, spray drying, and vacuum drying exist, each suitable for specific materials and applications.

Common Drying Techniques:

1. **Air Drying:** Involves exposing the material to ambient air to allow moisture to evaporate naturally. Commonly used for food products like fruits, vegetables, and herbs.
2. **Sun Drying**: Utilizes solar energy to evaporate moisture from the material. Widely practiced in agriculture for drying crops such as grains, nuts, and spices.
3. **Mechanical Drying**: Involves the use of mechanical equipment like dryers, ovens, or kilns to expedite the drying process. Often used in industrial settings for drying bulk materials.
4. **Freeze Drying**: Involves freezing the material and then subjecting it to vacuum conditions to remove moisture in the form of ice crystals. This method preserves the quality and nutritional value of sensitive materials like food and pharmaceuticals.
5. **Spray Drying**: Atomizes a liquid material into fine droplets, which are then dried rapidly by hot air or gas. Widely employed in the food and dairy industries to produce powdered products like milk powder and instant coffee.

Applications of Drying:

1. **Food Processing**: Drying is used to preserve food products, reduce weight and volume for transportation, and create value-added products like dried fruits, jerky, and instant noodles.
2. **Pharmaceuticals**: Drying is critical for preserving the stability and efficacy of drugs, vaccines, and herbal supplements by removing moisture and preventing degradation.

3. **Textiles:** Drying is an essential step in the manufacturing of textiles and garments, ensuring proper moisture levels and enhancing product quality.
4. **Chemicals:** Drying is employed in the production of chemicals, catalysts, and polymers to remove solvents or moisture and achieve specific product characteristics.
5. **Agriculture**: Drying is used in the post-harvest processing of crops to reduce moisture content and prevent spoilage during storage and transport.

OBJECTIVES, APPLICATIONS & MECHANISM OF DRYING PROCESS

Objectives of Drying:

1. **Moisture Removal:** The primary objective of drying is to remove moisture or water content from a material to a desired level. This helps in preserving the material, preventing microbial growth, and extending its shelf life.
2. **Preservation:** Drying is employed to preserve perishable materials such as food products, herbs, and pharmaceuticals by reducing their moisture content to levels where spoilage is inhibited.
3. **Quality Retention**: Proper drying can help maintain the quality attributes of materials, including color, texture, flavor, and nutritional value. Controlled drying conditions minimize undesirable changes and preserve the sensory and functional properties of the material.
4. **Size Reduction**: Drying often leads to a reduction in the size and weight of materials, making them more compact and easier to store, transport, and handle.
5. **Value Addition**: Drying can add value to raw materials by creating new products with enhanced shelf life, convenience, and marketability. Examples include dried fruits, powdered spices, and instant beverages.

Applications of Drying:

1. **Food Processing**: Drying is extensively used in the food industry for preserving a wide range of products, including fruits, vegetables, meats, grains, herbs, and spices. It enables the production of shelf-stable foods with prolonged storage life, such as dried fruits, jerky, pasta, and cereal.
2. **Pharmaceuticals**: Drying plays a crucial role in pharmaceutical manufacturing for removing moisture from drug substances, excipients, and finished dosage forms. It helps maintain the stability, efficacy, and quality of pharmaceutical products, including tablets, capsules, powders, and herbal extracts.
3. **Textiles and Apparel**: Drying is an essential step in textile manufacturing processes such as spinning, weaving, and finishing. It removes moisture introduced during wet processing operations and ensures proper moisture content in fabrics and garments for improved handling, dyeing, and finishing.
4. **Chemical Industry**: Drying is employed in the chemical industry for removing solvents, water, or other liquids from chemical compounds, intermediates, and finished products. It facilitates the production of powders, granules, and solid forms of chemicals, catalysts, and polymers.
5. **Agriculture**: Drying is utilized in agriculture for post-harvest processing of crops to reduce moisture content and prevent spoilage during storage and transport. It is commonly applied to grains, seeds, nuts, and fruits to maintain quality and market value.

Mechanism of Drying:

1. **Evaporation**: Drying involves the transfer of moisture from the surface and interior of the material to the surrounding air through evaporation. This occurs due to the difference in vapor pressure between the material and the drying medium.

2. **Mass Transfer**: Mass transfer mechanisms such as diffusion, capillary action, and convective airflow facilitate the movement of moisture within the material towards its surface, where it evaporates into the surrounding air.
3. **Heat Transfer**: Heat is applied to the material to increase the rate of evaporation and accelerate the drying process. Heat transfer mechanisms including convection, conduction, and radiation transfer thermal energy to the material, promoting the conversion of liquid water into vapor.
4. **Airflow**: Adequate airflow is essential for carrying away the moisture released during drying and maintaining a low-humidity environment around the material. Proper ventilation prevents the formation of a boundary layer of saturated air, which can impede drying.
5. **Humidity Control**: Controlling the humidity of the drying air influences its capacity to absorb moisture from the material. Lower humidity gradients between the material and the air promote faster drying rates.

MEASUREMENTS & APPLICATIONS OF EQUILIBRIUM

Equilibrium moisture content (EMC) plays a crucial role in drying processes, particularly in understanding the behavior of materials during drying and determining when the drying process is complete. Let's explore the measurements and applications of equilibrium in drying in detail:

Measurements of Equilibrium Moisture Content (EMC):

1. **Experimental Methods**: EMC can be determined experimentally using various techniques such as gravimetric analysis, moisture sorption isotherms, or moisture content analysis. These methods involve exposing the material to controlled humidity conditions until it reaches equilibrium and then measuring its moisture content.
2. **Sorption Isotherms**: Sorption isotherms depict the relationship between the equilibrium moisture content of a material and the relative humidity of the surrounding air at a constant temperature. These isotherms provide

valuable data for predicting moisture uptake or release behavior under different environmental conditions.

3. **Drying Kinetics**: Equilibrium moisture content is often used in conjunction with drying kinetics to characterize the drying behavior of materials. By measuring the moisture content of the material over time during drying, one can analyze the drying rate and determine when the material reaches equilibrium moisture content.

Applications of Equilibrium in Drying:

1. **Drying Endpoint Determination**: Equilibrium moisture content serves as a criterion for determining when the drying process is complete. When the moisture content of the material stabilizes at its equilibrium value, it indicates that drying is finished, and the material is sufficiently dry for storage or further processing.
2. **Quality Control**: Monitoring equilibrium moisture content during drying helps ensure product quality and consistency. Maintaining the material within a specified moisture content range can prevent over-drying or under-drying, which may adversely affect product properties such as texture, flavor, and shelf life.
3. **Process Optimization**: Equilibrium moisture content data are used in the optimization of drying processes to achieve desired drying outcomes efficiently. By understanding the relationship between drying parameters (e.g., temperature, airflow, humidity) and equilibrium moisture content, one can adjust process conditions to minimize drying time and energy consumption while maximizing product quality.
4. **Storage Stability**: Knowledge of equilibrium moisture content is essential for determining the appropriate storage conditions for dried products. Storing materials at or below their equilibrium moisture content helps prevent moisture reabsorption and maintains product stability during storage, reducing the risk of spoilage or degradation.

5. **Material Selection**: Equilibrium moisture content data are valuable for selecting suitable materials for specific applications based on their moisture sensitivity. Materials with low equilibrium moisture content are preferred for applications requiring low moisture content, such as pharmaceuticals, while materials with higher equilibrium moisture content may be suitable for applications where moisture content variability is acceptable.
6. **Packaging Design**: Equilibrium moisture content information is used in the design of packaging materials and storage containers to prevent moisture ingress or egress. Packaging materials with barrier properties that limit moisture transmission help maintain the material at its desired equilibrium moisture content, preserving product quality and shelf life.

MOISTURE CONTENT

Moisture content is a critical parameter in drying processes, influencing the quality, efficiency, and effectiveness of the drying operation. Understanding moisture content and its behavior during drying is essential for achieving desired drying outcomes. Let's explore moisture content in drying in detail:

Definition of Moisture Content:

Moisture content, often denoted as *MC*, refers to the amount of water present in a material expressed as a percentage of the material's total mass or volume. It represents the ratio of the mass of water in the material to the mass of the dry solid material, including any dissolved or bound water.

Importance of Moisture Content in Drying:

1. **Quality Control**: Moisture content directly affects the quality attributes of dried products, including texture, color, flavor, and shelf life. Controlling moisture content within specified limits is essential for ensuring product consistency and meeting quality standards.
2. **Process Efficiency**: Monitoring moisture content enables the optimization of drying processes for maximum efficiency and energy

savings. By adjusting drying parameters based on moisture content measurements, such as temperature, airflow, and humidity, one can minimize drying time and energy consumption.

3. **Storage Stability**: Moisture content influences the stability and shelf life of dried products during storage. Excessive moisture can lead to microbial growth, spoilage, and quality deterioration, while insufficient moisture can result in product brittleness, caking, or rehydration.
4. **Product Uniformity**: Maintaining uniform moisture content throughout the material ensures consistent drying and prevents variations in product quality. Uniform drying minimizes the risk of over-drying or under-drying, which may result in uneven texture, color variation, or moisture gradients within the product.
5. **Material Handling**: Moisture content affects the handling properties of materials, including flowability, stickiness, and agglomeration tendencies. Properly dried materials with optimal moisture content are easier to handle, transport, and process downstream.

Measurement of Moisture Content:

1. **Gravimetric Method**: The most common technique for measuring moisture content involves weighing a sample of the material before and after drying to determine the mass loss due to moisture removal. The moisture content is calculated as the ratio of the mass of water lost to the initial mass of the sample, expressed as a percentage.
2. **Instrumental Methods**: Various instrumental techniques such as moisture analyzers, infrared moisture meters, and capacitance sensors are available for rapid and accurate moisture content determination. These methods utilize principles such as heat absorption, electromagnetic radiation absorption, or electrical conductivity to measure moisture levels in the material.

3. **Sorption Isotherms**: Moisture sorption isotherms depict the relationship between the equilibrium moisture content of the material and the relative humidity of the surrounding environment at a constant temperature. By analyzing sorption isotherm data, one can predict moisture uptake or release behavior under different environmental conditions.

Behavior of Moisture Content During Drying:

1. **Initial Moisture Content:** The moisture content of the material at the beginning of the drying process determines the amount of water that needs to be removed to achieve the desired moisture content.
2. **Drying Rate:** Moisture content decreases over time as water is removed from the material through evaporation or other drying mechanisms. The drying rate initially decreases as moisture is drawn from the surface of the material, followed by a period of constant drying rate as moisture migrates from the interior to the surface. The drying rate eventually decreases as the material approaches equilibrium moisture content.
3. **Equilibrium Moisture Content**: Equilibrium moisture content represents the moisture content of the material when it reaches a steady state with the surrounding environment, indicating that drying is complete. Materials with hygroscopic properties may regain moisture over time if exposed to humid conditions, leading to changes in equilibrium moisture content.

RATE OF DRYING CURVE

The rate of drying curve, also known as the drying curve or drying profile, is a graphical representation that illustrates the rate at which moisture content changes over time during the drying process. It provides valuable insights into the behavior of materials undergoing drying and helps in understanding and optimizing the drying operation. Let's explore the rate of drying curve in detail:

Components of the Rate of Drying Curve:

1. **Moisture Content vs. Time:** The x-axis of the curve represents time, typically measured in hours or minutes, while the y-axis represents moisture content, usually expressed as a percentage of the material's dry weight. The curve shows how moisture content changes over the course of the drying process.
2. **Drying Rate:** The slope or gradient of the drying curve indicates the rate at which moisture content decreases over time. The steepness of the curve reflects the intensity of drying, with steeper slopes corresponding to faster drying rates.
3. **Phases of Drying**: The drying curve often consists of distinct phases that characterize different stages of the drying process:
    a. **Initial Constant-Rate Period**: In this phase, moisture is rapidly removed from the surface of the material, and the drying rate is relatively constant. The curve exhibits a steep slope during this period.
    b. **Falling-Rate Period**: As moisture migrates from the interior to the surface of the material, the drying rate gradually decreases. The curve slopes downwards at a decreasing rate during this phase.
    c. **Final Equilibrium Period**: Eventually, the material reaches equilibrium moisture content, where the rate of moisture removal equals the rate of moisture uptake from the surrounding environment. The curve levels off, indicating that drying is complete.

Factors Influencing the Rate of Drying Curve:

1. **Material Properties**: The composition, structure, and physical characteristics of the material significantly influence its drying behavior.

Porous materials with high surface area typically exhibit faster drying rates compared to dense or non-porous materials.

2. **Initial Moisture Content**: The moisture content of the material at the beginning of the drying process affects the rate of drying. Materials with higher initial moisture content require more time and energy to dry completely.
3. **Drying Conditions**: Parameters such as temperature, airflow velocity, humidity, and pressure play a crucial role in determining the rate of drying. Higher temperatures and airflow velocities generally accelerate drying rates, while low humidity gradients promote faster moisture removal.
4. **Equipment and Process Parameters**: The type of drying equipment used, as well as process parameters such as drying time, batch size, and agitation, impact the rate of drying. Proper equipment selection and process optimization are essential for achieving efficient and uniform drying.

Applications of the Rate of Drying Curve:

1. **Process Optimization**: Analysis of the rate of drying curve helps in optimizing drying processes by identifying critical parameters and determining the most effective operating conditions to achieve desired drying outcomes.
2. **Quality Control**: Monitoring the rate of drying enables real-time assessment of product quality and consistency. Deviations from expected drying curves may indicate issues such as uneven drying, equipment malfunction, or material variability.
3. **Energy Efficiency**: Understanding the rate of drying curve helps in minimizing energy consumption by optimizing drying parameters and reducing drying time without compromising product quality.

4. **Scale-Up and Production Planning**: Scaling up drying processes from laboratory or pilot-scale to industrial production requires knowledge of the rate of drying curve to ensure consistent and efficient operation at larger scales.
5. **Product Development**: Studying the rate of drying curve aids in the development of new products or formulations by predicting drying behavior and determining optimal processing conditions for desired product attributes.

TRAY DRYER

Principles of Tray Dryer:

Tray dryer operates based on the principle of convection drying. It utilizes heated air to remove moisture from the material placed on trays or shelves inside the dryer. The hot air circulates around the material, absorbing moisture and carrying it away, thus facilitating drying. The trays are stacked vertically or horizontally within the dryer, allowing efficient airflow and uniform drying.

Construction of Tray Dryer:

1. **Outer Shell**: The outer shell of the tray dryer is typically made of stainless steel or mild steel to provide structural support and insulation.
2. **Internal Chambers**: Tray dryers consist of one or more internal chambers where trays or shelves are placed. These chambers are equipped with air circulation systems, heating elements, and fans for uniform heat distribution and airflow.
3. **Trays or Shelves**: The trays or shelves inside the dryer are made of perforated metal or wire mesh to allow airflow and facilitate even drying of the material.
4. **Heating System**: Tray dryers are equipped with electric or steam heating systems, which generate the heat required for drying. Heating elements or steam coils are located either at the bottom or the sides of the dryer chamber.

5. **Air Circulation System**: Tray dryers feature fans or blowers that circulate heated air throughout the drying chamber, ensuring efficient moisture removal and uniform drying.
6. **Control Panel**: A control panel is installed on the dryer for monitoring and controlling temperature, airflow, and drying time. It may include temperature controllers, timers, and safety features.

Working of Tray Dryer:

1. **Loading**: The material to be dried is spread evenly on the trays or shelves inside the dryer.
2. **Heating**: The heating system of the tray dryer is activated, raising the temperature inside the drying chamber to the desired level.
3. **Air Circulation**: The fans or blowers circulate hot air throughout the drying chamber, creating a convection current. The hot air passes over the material on the trays, absorbing moisture and carrying it away.
4. **Moisture Removal**: As the heated air comes into contact with the moist material, it evaporates the moisture, which is then expelled from the dryer through vents or exhausts.
5. **Drying Process**: The material continues to dry as it is exposed to the circulating hot air. The drying process progresses until the desired moisture content is achieved.
6. **Cooling and Unloading**: Once drying is complete, the heating system is turned off, and the material is allowed to cool before being unloaded from the trays.

Uses of Tray Dryer:

1. **Food Processing**: Tray dryers are commonly used in the food industry for drying fruits, vegetables, herbs, grains, and other food products.
2. **Pharmaceuticals**: Tray dryers are utilized in pharmaceutical manufacturing for drying powders, granules, tablets, and other drug products.

3. **Chemicals**: Tray dryers find applications in the chemical industry for drying chemicals, catalysts, and intermediates.
4. **Textiles:** Tray dryers are employed in textile manufacturing for drying dyed fabrics, yarns, and garments.
5. **Research and Development**: Tray dryers are used in laboratories and research facilities for drying samples, prototypes, and experimental materials.

Merits of Tray Dryer:

1. **Uniform Drying**: Tray dryers provide uniform drying of materials due to efficient air circulation and heat distribution.
2. **Batch Processing**: Tray dryers allow batch processing, making them suitable for small-scale production and research applications.
3. **Versatility**: Tray dryers can handle a wide range of materials, including solids, powders, granules, and liquids.
4. **Ease of Operation**: Tray dryers are relatively simple to operate and require minimal maintenance.
5. **Cost-Effectiveness**: Tray dryers are cost-effective drying solutions, especially for small to medium-scale production.

Demerits of Tray Dryer:

1. **Limited Capacity:** Tray dryers have limited capacity compared to continuous drying systems, which may be a limitation for large-scale production.
2. **Longer Drying Times**: Drying times in tray dryers may be longer compared to other drying methods, especially for materials with high moisture content.
3. **Energy Consumption**: Tray dryers may consume significant energy, especially if not properly insulated or if operated at high temperatures.
4. **Space Requirements**: Tray dryers require sufficient floor space for installation, which may be a constraint in some facilities.

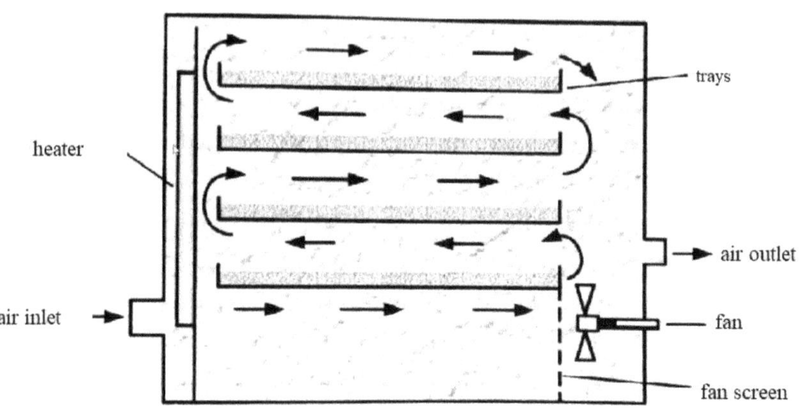
trays
heater
air outlet
air inlet
fan
fan screen

CHAPTER – 12

DRYING – II

Mr. Abu Tahir

Assistant Professor, Rajiv Gandhi Institute of Pharmacy, Faculty of Pharmaceutical Science & Technology, AKS University Satna, MP-India

---

ABSTRACT:

Dryers are essential equipment used across industries to remove moisture from materials efficiently, ensuring product quality and extending shelf life. The drum dryer is a common type, where materials are heated and rotated on a drum's surface, allowing moisture to evaporate and be removed via a stream of hot gas. Fluidized bed dryers suspend particles in a bed of hot air, enhancing drying efficiency by ensuring uniform heat distribution and rapid moisture removal. Vacuum dryers operate under reduced pressure, lowering the boiling point of water and facilitating drying at lower temperatures, ideal for heat-sensitive materials. Freeze dryers, or lyophilizers, freeze materials and then subject them to vacuum conditions, allowing water to sublime directly from solid to vapor phase, preserving the material's structure and nutrients. Each dryer type offers distinct advantages based on material properties and processing requirements. Optimizing dryer parameters such as temperature, airflow, and residence time is crucial for achieving desired moisture levels and product characteristics. Industries ranging from food and pharmaceuticals to chemicals rely on these dryers to enhance product stability, quality, and marketability, underscoring their importance in modern manufacturing processes.

DRUM DRYER

Principles of Tray Dryer:

Tray dryer operates based on the principle of convection drying. It utilizes heated air to remove moisture from the material placed on trays or shelves inside the dryer. The hot air circulates around the material, absorbing moisture and carrying it away, thus facilitating drying. The trays are stacked vertically or horizontally within the dryer, allowing efficient airflow and uniform drying.

Construction of Tray Dryer:

1. **Outer Shell**: The outer shell of the tray dryer is typically made of stainless steel or mild steel to provide structural support and insulation.
2. **Internal Chambers**: Tray dryers consist of one or more internal chambers where trays or shelves are placed. These chambers are equipped with air circulation systems, heating elements, and fans for uniform heat distribution and airflow.
3. **Trays or Shelves**: The trays or shelves inside the dryer are made of perforated metal or wire mesh to allow airflow and facilitate even drying of the material.
4. **Heating System**: Tray dryers are equipped with electric or steam heating systems, which generate the heat required for drying. Heating elements or steam coils are located either at the bottom or the sides of the dryer chamber.
5. **Air Circulation System**: Tray dryers feature fans or blowers that circulate heated air throughout the drying chamber, ensuring efficient moisture removal and uniform drying.
6. **Control Panel**: A control panel is installed on the dryer for monitoring and controlling temperature, airflow, and drying time. It may include temperature controllers, timers, and safety features.

Working of Tray Dryer:

1. **Loading**: The material to be dried is spread evenly on the trays or shelves inside the dryer.
2. **Heating:** The heating system of the tray dryer is activated, raising the temperature inside the drying chamber to the desired level.
3. **Air Circulation**: The fans or blowers circulate hot air throughout the drying chamber, creating a convection current. The hot air passes over the material on the trays, absorbing moisture and carrying it away.
4. **Moisture Removal**: As the heated air comes into contact with the moist material, it evaporates the moisture, which is then expelled from the dryer through vents or exhausts.
5. **Drying Process**: The material continues to dry as it is exposed to the circulating hot air. The drying process progresses until the desired moisture content is achieved.
6. Cooling and Unloading: Once drying is complete, the heating system is turned off, and the material is allowed to cool before being unloaded from the trays.

Uses of Tray Dryer:

1. **Food Processing**: Tray dryers are commonly used in the food industry for drying fruits, vegetables, herbs, grains, and other food products.
2. **Pharmaceutica**ls: Tray dryers are utilized in pharmaceutical manufacturing for drying powders, granules, tablets, and other drug products.
3. **Chemicals**: Tray dryers find applications in the chemical industry for drying chemicals, catalysts, and intermediates.
4. **Textiles:** Tray dryers are employed in textile manufacturing for drying dyed fabrics, yarns, and garments.

5. **Research and Development**: Tray dryers are used in laboratories and research facilities for drying samples, prototypes, and experimental materials.

Merits of Tray Dryer:

1. **Uniform Drying**: Tray dryers provide uniform drying of materials due to efficient air circulation and heat distribution.
2. **Batch Processing**: Tray dryers allow batch processing, making them suitable for small-scale production and research applications.
3. **Versatility**: Tray dryers can handle a wide range of materials, including solids, powders, granules, and liquids.
4. **Ease of Operation**: Tray dryers are relatively simple to operate and require minimal maintenance.
5. **Cost-Effectiveness**: Tray dryers are cost-effective drying solutions, especially for small to medium-scale production.

Demerits of Tray Dryer:

1. **Limited Capacity**: Tray dryers have limited capacity compared to continuous drying systems, which may be a limitation for large-scale production.
2. **Longer Drying Times**: Drying times in tray dryers may be longer compared to other drying methods, especially for materials with high moisture content.
3. **Energy Consumption**: Tray dryers may consume significant energy, especially if not properly insulated or if operated at high temperatures.
4. **Space Requirements**: Tray dryers require sufficient floor space for installation, which may be a constraint in some facilities.

FLUIDIZED BED DRYER

Principles of Fluidized Bed Dryer:

A fluidized bed dryer operates on the principle of fluidization, where a bed of solid particles is suspended and fluidized by passing a stream of gas (usually air or nitrogen) through it. The fluidization process creates a fluid-like behavior in the bed of particles, allowing for efficient heat and mass transfer. In a fluidized bed dryer, hot air is introduced into the bed of solid particles, causing them to behave like a fluidized mass. This promotes uniform drying and prevents particle agglomeration, resulting in fast and efficient drying.

Construction of Fluidized Bed Dryer:

1. **Drying Chamber**: The drying chamber of a fluidized bed dryer is typically cylindrical in shape and is made of stainless steel or other corrosion-resistant materials. It houses the bed of solid particles and is equipped with inlet and outlet ports for gas flow.
2. **Air Distribution System**: An air distribution system consisting of perforated plates or distributors is located at the bottom of the drying chamber. These distributors evenly distribute the incoming air throughout the bed of solid particles, ensuring uniform fluidization.
3. **Heating System**: Fluidized bed dryers are equipped with heating systems such as electric heaters or steam coils. These systems heat the incoming air to the desired temperature before it enters the drying chamber.
4. **Gas Handling System**: A fan or blower is used to supply the gas (usually air or nitrogen) into the drying chamber. The gas may be preheated before entering the chamber to enhance drying efficiency.
5. **Control Panel**: A control panel is installed on the dryer for monitoring and controlling various parameters such as temperature, airflow, and drying time. It may include temperature controllers, flow meters, and timers.

Working of Fluidized Bed Dryer:

1. **Fluidization**: The bed of solid particles is fluidized by passing a stream of gas (usually air) through it. As the gas flows upward through the bed, it lifts and suspends the solid particles, creating a fluid-like behavior.

2. **Heating and Drying**: Hot air is introduced into the fluidized bed through the air distribution system. The heated air comes into contact with the wet solid particles, causing moisture to evaporate. The fluidized bed provides excellent heat and mass transfer, ensuring rapid and uniform drying of the particles.
3. **Moisture Removal**: As moisture evaporates from the solid particles, it is carried away by the flowing air stream. The moisture-laden air is then discharged from the drying chamber through an exhaust port.
4. **Cooling and Unloading**: Once drying is complete, the heating system is turned off, and the flow of gas is stopped. The fluidized bed cools down, and the dried particles settle at the bottom of the drying chamber. The dried product is then discharged from the dryer for further processing or packaging.

Uses of Fluidized Bed Dryer:

1. **Pharmaceuticals**: Fluidized bed dryers are widely used in the pharmaceutical industry for drying granules, powders, and pellets. They are particularly suitable for heat-sensitive materials and for producing uniform, free-flowing products.
2. **Food Processing**: Fluidized bed dryers are employed in the food industry for drying various food products such as grains, cereals, nuts, and snacks. They are valued for their ability to achieve rapid and uniform drying without damaging the product.
3. **Chemicals**: Fluidized bed dryers find applications in the chemical industry for drying chemical powders, catalysts, and granular materials. They are capable of handling a wide range of materials and can be customized to meet specific process requirements.
4. **Agrochemicals**: Fluidized bed dryers are used in the agrochemical industry for drying pesticides, fertilizers, and agricultural chemicals.

They provide efficient and controlled drying, ensuring product quality and consistency.

Merits of Fluidized Bed Dryer:

1. **Uniform Drying**: Fluidized bed dryers offer excellent heat and mass transfer, resulting in uniform drying of the product particles.
2. **Fast Drying:** The fluidized bed provides a large surface area for heat transfer, allowing for rapid evaporation of moisture and shorter drying times.
3. **Gentle Handling**: Fluidized bed dryers gently handle delicate or heat-sensitive materials, minimizing the risk of product degradation or damage.
4. **Energy Efficiency**: Fluidized bed dryers are energy-efficient due to their rapid drying capabilities and effective heat transfer.
5. **Versatility**: Fluidized bed dryers can handle a wide range of materials, particle sizes, and moisture contents, making them versatile for various applications.

Demerits of Fluidized Bed Dryer:

1. **Initial Investment**: Fluidized bed dryers may require a higher initial investment compared to some other drying methods due to their complex design and construction.
2. **Particle Attrition**: Intense fluidization in fluidized bed dryers may cause particle attrition or breakage, particularly for fragile materials.
3. **Dust Emission**: Fluidized bed dryers may generate dust or fines during operation, which can be a concern for certain applications or environments.
4. **Maintenance Requirements**: Fluidized bed dryers require regular maintenance to ensure proper operation and prevent issues such as fouling or plugging of air distribution systems.

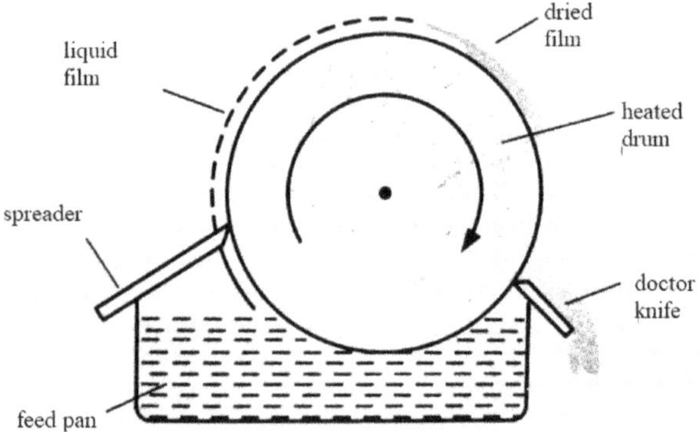

VACUUM DRYER

Principles of Vacuum Dryer:

A vacuum dryer operates on the principle of reducing the pressure inside the drying chamber to lower the boiling point of water or other solvents, thus facilitating the removal of moisture from the material at lower temperatures. By creating a vacuum, the dryer reduces the partial pressure of the vapor above the material, allowing moisture to evaporate more easily. This enables gentle and efficient drying of heat-sensitive materials while minimizing the risk of thermal degradation or product loss.

Construction of Vacuum Dryer:

1. **Drying Chamber**: The drying chamber of a vacuum dryer is typically cylindrical or rectangular in shape and is constructed of stainless steel or other corrosion-resistant materials. It is designed to withstand vacuum conditions and may be insulated to minimize heat loss.
2. **Vacuum System**: The vacuum system consists of vacuum pumps, vacuum lines, and valves, which create and control the vacuum inside the drying chamber. Vacuum pumps may be of various types, including rotary vane pumps, diaphragm pumps, or liquid ring pumps.

3. **Heating System**: Vacuum dryers may be equipped with heating elements, steam coils, or hot water jackets to provide the heat required for drying. These heating systems are often designed to operate at lower temperatures to prevent thermal damage to the material.
4. **Agitation System**: Some vacuum dryers feature agitation systems such as stirrers, paddles, or tumblers to promote uniform mixing and drying of the material inside the chamber.
5. **Control Panel**: A control panel is installed on the vacuum dryer for monitoring and controlling various parameters such as temperature, pressure, and drying time. It may include vacuum gauges, temperature controllers, and timers.

Working of Vacuum Dryer:

1. **Loading**: The material to be dried is loaded into the drying chamber of the vacuum dryer.
2. **Evacuation**: The vacuum system is activated, and air is removed from the drying chamber to create a vacuum. As the pressure decreases, the boiling point of water or other solvents in the material decreases, facilitating evaporation.
3. **Heating**: The heating system of the vacuum dryer is activated, providing the heat necessary for drying. The low-pressure environment allows moisture to evaporate from the material at lower temperatures than atmospheric drying.
4. **Moisture Removal**: As moisture evaporates from the material, it is carried away by the vacuum pump and expelled from the drying chamber. The drying process continues until the desired moisture content is achieved.
5. **Cooling and Unloading**: Once drying is complete, the heating system is turned off, and the vacuum is released. The dried material is cooled down before being unloaded from the dryer for further processing or packaging.

Uses of Vacuum Dryer:

1. **Pharmaceuticals**: Vacuum dryers are commonly used in the pharmaceutical industry for drying heat-sensitive materials such as powders, granules, and active pharmaceutical ingredients (APIs).
2. **Food Processing**: Vacuum dryers find applications in the food industry for drying fruits, vegetables, herbs, and other food products. They are valued for their ability to preserve the color, flavor, and nutritional value of the dried products.
3. **Chemicals**: Vacuum dryers are utilized in the chemical industry for drying solvents, catalysts, and fine chemicals. They offer efficient and gentle drying, making them suitable for sensitive or high-value materials.
4. **Plastics and Polymers**: Vacuum dryers are used in the plastics and polymer industry for drying resins, pellets, and plastic powders. They help remove moisture from hygroscopic materials, preventing defects in the final products.

Merits of Vacuum Dryer:

1. **Gentle Drying**: Vacuum dryers provide gentle drying at lower temperatures, minimizing the risk of thermal degradation or product loss.
2. **Preservation of Product Quality**: Vacuum drying helps preserve the color, flavor, and nutritional value of sensitive materials, making it suitable for high-quality products.
3. **Energy Efficiency**: Vacuum drying requires less energy compared to conventional drying methods due to lower operating temperatures and reduced drying times.
4. **Versatility:** Vacuum dryers can handle a wide range of materials, including heat-sensitive, hygroscopic, and delicate materials.

Demerits of Vacuum Dryer:

1. **Higher Initial Investment**: Vacuum dryers may require a higher initial investment compared to some other drying methods due to their complex design and vacuum system.
2. **Limited Capacity**: Vacuum dryers may have limited capacity compared to some other drying methods, which may be a constraint for large-scale production.
3. **Complex Operation**: Operating and maintaining a vacuum dryer requires specialized knowledge and skills, which may increase operational complexity and training requirements.
4. **Longer Drying Times**: Vacuum drying may result in longer drying times compared to some other drying methods, especially for materials with high moisture content.

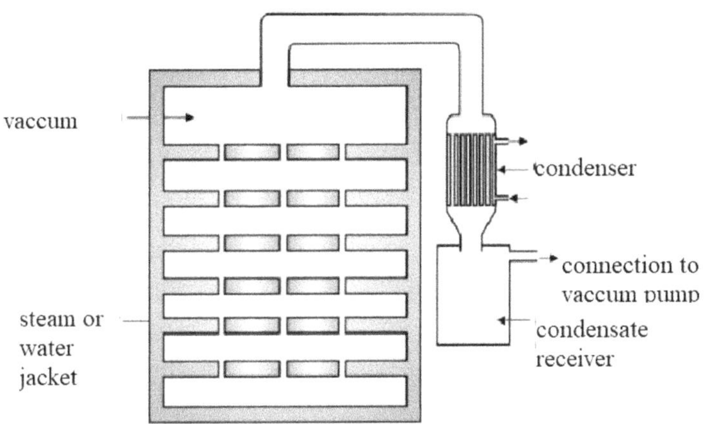

FREEZE DRYER

Principles of Freeze Dryer:

A freeze dryer operates on the principle of sublimation, which is the process of transforming a substance directly from a solid to a gaseous state without passing through the liquid phase. In freeze drying, also known as lyophilization, the material to be dried is frozen at low temperatures, and then a vacuum is applied to remove the frozen water (ice) through sublimation. This preserves the structure, shape, and properties of the dried material, making freeze drying particularly suitable for heat-sensitive and delicate substances.

Construction of Freeze Dryer:

1. **Freezing Chamber**: The freezing chamber of a freeze dryer is where the material is frozen before drying. It is typically equipped with shelves or trays to hold the material and may have a temperature control system to maintain precise freezing conditions.
2. **Drying Chamber**: The drying chamber is where the frozen material undergoes sublimation to remove moisture. It is connected to a vacuum system to create the low-pressure environment necessary for sublimation.
3. **Vacuum System**: The vacuum system consists of vacuum pumps, valves, and vacuum lines, which create and control the vacuum inside the drying chamber. This allows for the removal of water vapor during sublimation.
4. **Condenser**: The condenser is a critical component of the freeze dryer that captures the water vapor sublimated from the frozen material. It is typically cooled to low temperatures, causing the water vapor to condense into ice and preventing it from contaminating the vacuum pump.
5. **Heating System**: Some freeze dryers may be equipped with a heating system to provide gentle heat to the material during drying, which can help improve drying efficiency and reduce drying times.
6. **Control Panel**: A control panel is installed on the freeze dryer for monitoring and controlling various parameters such as temperature, vacuum level, and drying time. It may include temperature controllers, pressure gauges, and timers.

Working of Freeze Dryer:

1. **Freezing:** The material to be dried is first frozen at low temperatures, typically below its eutectic point, in the freezing chamber of the freeze

dryer. Freezing immobilizes the water molecules in the material, preparing it for sublimation.

2. **Primary Drying (Sublimation)**: Once the material is frozen, the drying chamber is evacuated to create a low-pressure environment. Heat is applied to the material, causing the frozen water (ice) to sublimate directly into vapor without passing through the liquid phase. The water vapor is then captured by the condenser and removed from the system.
3. **Secondary Drying (Desorption)**: After primary drying, the material may undergo a secondary drying process to remove any residual moisture that remains bound to the material. This is typically done by applying slight heat and maintaining a vacuum to desorb the remaining moisture.
4. **Cooling and Unloading**: Once drying is complete, the freeze dryer is cooled down, and the vacuum is released. The dried material is then unloaded from the dryer and can be stored or packaged for further use.

Uses of Freeze Dryer:

1. **Pharmaceuticals:** Freeze dryers are widely used in the pharmaceutical industry for drying vaccines, antibodies, proteins, and other biopharmaceuticals. Freeze drying preserves the activity and stability of sensitive pharmaceutical compounds.
2. **Food Processing**: Freeze dryers find applications in the food industry for drying fruits, vegetables, herbs, and dairy products. Freeze-dried foods have a longer shelf life and retain their color, flavor, and nutritional value.
3. **Biotechnology**: Freeze dryers are used in biotechnology for drying enzymes, cell cultures, antibodies, and other biological samples. Freeze drying allows for long-term preservation of biological materials without compromising their integrity.
4. **Cosmetics:** Freeze dryers are employed in the cosmetics industry for drying botanical extracts, essential oils, and other natural ingredients used

in skincare and beauty products. Freeze drying helps retain the potency and efficacy of active ingredients.

Merits of Freeze Dryer:

1. **Preservation of Product Quality**: Freeze drying preserves the structure, shape, and properties of the dried material, making it ideal for heat-sensitive and delicate substances.
2. **Long Shelf Life**: Freeze-dried products have a longer shelf life compared to products dried using other methods, as they are less prone to degradation and spoilage.
3. R**ehydratio**n: Freeze-dried products can be easily rehydrated by adding water, restoring them to their original state with minimal loss of quality.
4. **Versatility:** Freeze dryers can handle a wide range of materials, including pharmaceuticals, foods, biologics, and cosmetics.

Demerits of Freeze Dryer:

1. **High Cost**: Freeze dryers tend to be more expensive than other drying methods due to their complex design, construction, and energy requirements.
2. **Longer Drying Times**: Freeze drying typically requires longer drying times compared to other methods, which may be a limitation for large-scale production.
3. **Energy Consumption**: Freeze dryers consume significant energy, especially during the freezing and condensation phases, which may increase operational costs.
4. **Complex Operation**: Operating a freeze dryer requires specialized knowledge and skills, and the process may be more complex compared to other drying methods.

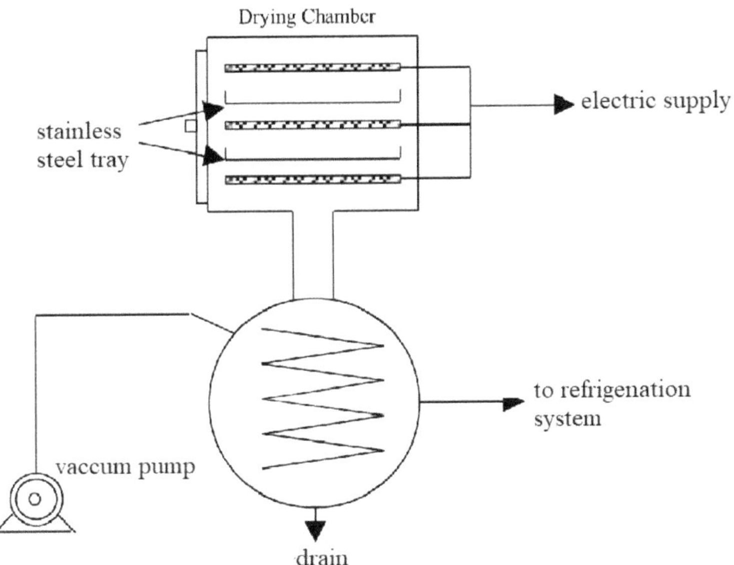
Drying Chamber
electric supply
stainless
steel tray
to refrigenation
system
vaccum pump
drain

CHAPTER – 13

MIXING – I

Ms. Shikha Singh

Assistant Professor, Rajiv Gandhi Institute of Pharmacy, Faculty of Pharmaceutical Science & Technology, AKS University Satna, MP-India

---

Abstract:

Mixing is a fundamental process used in various industries to blend materials homogeneously, ensuring consistent product quality and performance. It involves combining two or more substances to achieve a uniform distribution of components. Different mixing techniques are employed based on the nature of the materials and the desired end product. For instance, mechanical agitation, such as stirring or kneading, is commonly used in food processing, pharmaceuticals, and cosmetics to mix ingredients thoroughly. High-shear mixing involves intense agitation to disperse particles finely and create stable emulsions or suspensions. Fluid mixing utilizes the flow of liquids or gases to achieve uniformity in large-scale industrial processes like chemical manufacturing and wastewater treatment. Factors such as mixing speed, viscosity, temperature, and the geometry of the mixing vessel influence the efficiency and effectiveness of mixing operations. Properly designed mixing processes ensure product consistency, minimize batch variability, and optimize production yields, making it a critical step in manufacturing and industrial processes worldwide.

INTRODUCTION

Mixing, in the context of music production, is the process of combining individual audio tracks (such as vocals, instruments, and effects) into a cohesive and balanced stereo or multichannel mix. It's a crucial step that can make or break the final quality of a recording. Here's a detailed introduction to mixing:

1. **Preparation:**
   a. **Organizing Tracks**: Before diving into mixing, it's essential to organize your project by labeling and arranging tracks logically. Group related tracks together (e.g., drums, guitars, vocals) to streamline the mixing process.
   b. **Gain Staging**: Ensure that the levels of individual tracks are balanced. Use volume faders to adjust the relative loudness of each track, aiming for consistency and clarity.
2. **Setting Up the Mix Environment:**
   a. **Room Acoustics**: Ideally, mix in a well-treated room with balanced acoustics to accurately hear the audio without coloration.
   b. **Monitoring**: Use high-quality studio monitors or headphones to accurately listen to your mix. It's crucial to understand how your monitoring system represents the audio.
3. **Basic Mixing Techniques:**
   a. **Panning:** Positioning audio sources in the stereo field. For example, drums might be centered, while guitars could be panned slightly left and right for width.
   b. **EQ (Equalization)**: Adjusting the frequency balance of each track to carve out space for other instruments and enhance clarity. Cut unwanted frequencies and boost desired ones.
   c. **Compression**: Controlling the dynamic range of audio signals by reducing the volume of loud sounds and boosting softer ones. This helps to balance levels and add consistency to the mix.
   d. **Reverb and Delay**: Adding spatial effects to create depth and ambiance. Use reverb to simulate room acoustics and delay for echo effects.

4. **Advanced Techniques:**
    a. **Automation:** Dynamically adjusting parameters such as volume, panning, and effects over time to add movement and emotion to the mix.
    b. **Parallel Processing**: Processing a copy of a track (e.g., parallel compression) to blend the processed and unprocessed signals for enhanced control and impact.
    c. **Bus Processing**: Grouping tracks together (via bus routing) and applying processing effects to the entire group. This can help create a cohesive sound and streamline workflow.
5. **Listening and Iteration:**
    a. **Critical Listening**: Continuously listen to your mix on various playback systems (e.g., car stereo, headphones, consumer speakers) to ensure it translates well across different environments.
    b. **Iterative Process**: Mixing is often an iterative process. Take breaks to rest your ears, and revisit your mix with fresh perspectives.
6. **Final Touches:**
    a. **Mastering**: Once you're satisfied with the mix, consider mastering to prepare the final stereo mixdown for distribution. Mastering involves optimizing the overall sound quality, adjusting levels, applying final EQ and compression, and preparing for different formats (e.g., streaming, CD).

OBJECTIVES, APPLICATIONS & FACTORS AFFECTING MIXING

Objectives of Mixing:

1. **Balancing**: Achieving a balanced mix where each element (instruments, vocals, effects) occupies its own space in the stereo field, ensuring that no single track dominates the mix excessively.

2. **Clarity**: Enhancing the intelligibility of individual elements by using techniques like EQ to carve out space for each instrument or voice, ensuring they are audible and distinguishable.
3. **Depth and Dimension**: Creating a sense of depth and space in the mix by using techniques such as panning, reverb, and delay to place elements in a three-dimensional sonic landscape.
4. **Emotion and Impact**: Evoking the desired emotional response from the listener by manipulating dynamics, tonal balance, and effects to enhance the impact of the music.
5. **Consistency**: Ensuring a consistent sonic experience across different playback systems by carefully monitoring and adjusting the mix to translate well on various devices.

Applications of Mixing:

1. **Music Production**: Mixing is fundamental to the music production process, whether for recorded tracks in a studio environment or electronic music created entirely in a digital audio workstation (DAW).
2. **Film and TV Soundtracks**: Mixing is crucial in post-production for films, television shows, and other visual media, where it helps to blend dialogue, music, sound effects, and ambient noise seamlessly.
3. **Live Sound**: In live concert settings, mixing is performed in real-time by sound engineers to balance the levels of instruments and vocals, adjust tonal balance, and apply effects for optimal sound quality.
4. **Podcasts and Radio**: Mixing is essential for podcasts, radio shows, and other spoken-word content to ensure clear and intelligible speech, as well as to enhance the overall listening experience with appropriate background music and sound effects.

Factors Affecting Mixing:

1. **Recording Quality**: The quality of the recorded tracks significantly impacts the mixing process. Well-recorded tracks with minimal noise and

distortion provide a solid foundation for achieving a clean and professional mix.

2. **Arrangement**: The arrangement of the music, including the instrumentation, dynamics, and structure, influences the mixing process. A well-arranged composition allows for easier separation of individual elements and better overall balance.
3. **Genre and Style**: Different musical genres and styles may require different mixing approaches. For example, a heavy metal mix might emphasize aggressive dynamics and powerful low-end, while a jazz mix might prioritize clarity and warmth.
4. **Creative Vision**: The artistic vision of the producer, artist, or client guides the mixing process. Understanding their preferences, goals, and intended emotional impact of the music is crucial for achieving a successful mix.
5. **Monitoring Environment**: The acoustics of the mixing room and the quality of monitoring equipment (speakers or headphones) significantly influence the mixing decisions. A well-treated room and accurate monitoring setup enable more precise judgments about the mix.
6. **Experience and Skill**: The experience and skill level of the mixing engineer play a significant role in the final outcome. Experienced engineers are adept at using various mixing techniques and tools to achieve professional results.

DIFFERENCE BETWEEN SOLID AND LIQUID MIXING

Solid mixing and liquid mixing are two distinct processes, each with its own set of challenges, techniques, and considerations. Let's explore the key differences between them:

Solid Mixing:

1. **Physical State**: In solid mixing, the materials being mixed are typically in a solid state, such as powders, granules, or particles.

2. **Mechanical Agitation**: Solid mixing often involves mechanical agitation to blend the materials together. This can be achieved through various equipment such as tumbling mixers, ribbon blenders, or paddle mixers.
3. **Particle Size and Distribution**: Achieving uniformity in solid mixing requires careful attention to particle size and distribution. Proper mixing ensures that each particle is evenly distributed throughout the mixture.
4. **Segregation**: Solid mixtures are prone to segregation, where particles of different sizes or densities separate during handling and mixing. Preventing segregation requires selecting appropriate mixing techniques and equipment, as well as optimizing material properties.
5. **Homogeneity**: The goal of solid mixing is to achieve homogeneity, where the composition of the mixture is consistent throughout. This ensures that each portion of the mixture contains a uniform distribution of all components.
6. **Mixing Time**: Solid mixing may require longer mixing times compared to liquid mixing, especially for cohesive materials or mixtures with large particle sizes. Longer mixing times help ensure thorough blending and homogenization.

Liquid Mixing:

1. **Physical State**: Liquid mixing involves materials that are in a liquid state, such as water-based solutions, suspensions, or emulsions.
2. **Agitation Methods**: Liquid mixing employs various agitation methods, including mechanical stirring, ultrasonic agitation, or air sparging, to promote mixing and dispersion of components.
3. **Viscosity**: The viscosity of liquids plays a significant role in liquid mixing. High-viscosity liquids require more energy and specialized equipment to achieve thorough mixing compared to low-viscosity liquids.
4. **Phase Separation**: Liquid mixtures may undergo phase separation, where immiscible components separate over time. Effective mixing

techniques and additives (such as emulsifiers) are used to stabilize emulsions and prevent phase separation.

5. **Blending and Dissolution**: Liquid mixing often involves blending multiple components or dissolving solids into a liquid solvent. Achieving complete dissolution or dispersion may require optimizing factors such as temperature, agitation speed, and mixing time.
6. **Shear Forces**: Liquid mixing can generate shear forces that may impact the stability and quality of the mixture. Careful control of shear rates and mixing conditions is necessary, particularly for sensitive materials or delicate emulsions.

MECHANISM OF SOLID MIXING

Solid mixing involves blending materials that are in a solid state, such as powders, granules, or particles. The mechanism of solid mixing depends on various factors including the properties of the materials being mixed, the mixing equipment used, and the desired outcome. Here's a detailed explanation of the mechanisms involved in solid mixing:

1. **Convective Mixing:**
   a. **Description:** Convective mixing occurs when solid particles are transported within a mixture due to mechanical agitation or fluid flow. It involves the movement of particles from one location to another within the mixing vessel.
   b. **Mechanism:** As the mixing equipment (e.g., tumbling mixers, ribbon blenders, or paddle mixers) agitates the mixture, solid particles are displaced and transported throughout the bulk material. This movement promotes the intermingling of particles and facilitates blending.
   c. **Applications**: Convective mixing is commonly used in industrial processes where uniformity and homogeneity are essential, such as

pharmaceutical manufacturing, food processing, and chemical production.

2. **Diffusive Mixing:**
    a. **Description**: Diffusive mixing involves the gradual dispersal and redistribution of particles within a mixture through random molecular motion. It relies on the inherent kinetic energy of particles to promote mixing.
    b. **Mechanism**: In diffusive mixing, particles move randomly within the mixing vessel due to Brownian motion or other molecular forces. Over time, this random movement leads to the dispersion of particles and the eventual homogenization of the mixture.
    c. **Applications**: Diffusive mixing is particularly relevant for fine powders or particles with high surface area-to-volume ratios. It is commonly observed in processes such as blending pharmaceutical excipients, mixing pigment powders for paints, and preparing composite materials.
3. **Shear Mixing:**
    a. **Description**: Shear mixing involves the application of shear forces to deform and reorient solid particles within a mixture. It relies on the mechanical energy transferred to the material to induce mixing.
    b. **Mechanism**: In shear mixing, the mixing equipment applies shear forces that cause particles to slide past each other, deform, and undergo interparticle collisions. This action breaks down particle agglomerates and promotes uniform distribution.
    c. **Applications**: Shear mixing is prevalent in processes requiring the breakdown of agglomerates or the dispersion of additives within a matrix. Examples include mixing polymer melts, preparing ceramic slurries, and homogenizing metal powders for additive manufacturing.

4. **Fluidization:**

    a. **Description**: Fluidization involves suspending solid particles within a fluid medium, allowing them to behave like a fluidized bed. It facilitates intimate contact between particles and promotes mixing and heat transfer.

    b. **Mechanism**: In fluidization, a gas or liquid is passed through a bed of solid particles at a sufficient velocity to overcome gravitational forces and suspend the particles. This creates a dynamic system where particles exhibit fluid-like behavior, enhancing mixing efficiency.

    c. **Applications**: Fluidization is widely used in processes such as granulation, coating, and drying in industries such as pharmaceuticals, chemicals, and food processing.

MECHANISM OF LIQUIDS MIXING

Liquid mixing involves blending materials that are in a liquid state, such as water-based solutions, suspensions, or emulsions. The mechanism of liquid mixing depends on various factors including the properties of the liquids being mixed, the mixing equipment used, and the desired outcome. Here's a detailed explanation of the mechanisms involved in liquid mixing:

1. **Agitation:**

    a. **Description**: Agitation is the primary mechanism of liquid mixing, involving the application of mechanical energy to the liquid to induce movement and promote dispersion of components.

    b. **Mechanism**: Agitation can be achieved through various methods such as mechanical stirring, ultrasonic agitation, or air sparging. These techniques create turbulent flow patterns within the liquid, causing intermixing of components and enhancing mass transfer.

    c. **Applications:** Agitation is widely used in industrial processes such as chemical reactions, fermentation, wastewater treatment, and pharmaceutical manufacturing to promote mixing, dissolution, and dispersion of substances.

2. **Turbulence:**
   a. **Description:** Turbulence refers to the chaotic and irregular flow patterns that occur within a liquid when subjected to agitation or fluid motion.
   b. **Mechanism**: Turbulence results from the interaction of fluid layers with different velocities, leading to the formation of eddies, swirls, and vortices. These turbulent flow patterns enhance mixing by promoting intermingling of fluid streams and disrupting boundary layers.
   c. **Application**s: Turbulence plays a critical role in processes such as chemical mixing, heat transfer, and emulsification, where efficient mixing and dispersion of components are essential for achieving desired product characteristics.
3. **Shear Mixing:**
   a. **Description**: Shear mixing involves the application of shear forces to deform and reorient liquid streams within a mixture, promoting mixing and dispersion of components.
   b. **Mechanism**: Shear mixing occurs when adjacent fluid layers slide past each other at different velocities, generating shear stress along their interface. This shear stress causes fluid deformation and induces mixing by breaking down large-scale flow structures and promoting interfacial contact.
   c. **Applications**: Shear mixing is commonly used in processes such as emulsification, dispersion of additives, and blending of viscous liquids in industries such as food processing, cosmetics, and pharmaceuticals.

4. **Diffusion:**
   a. **Description**: Diffusion is the process by which molecules move from regions of higher concentration to regions of lower concentration, resulting in the gradual dispersion of components within a liquid.
   b. **Mechanism:** Diffusion occurs due to random thermal motion of molecules, leading to net movement along a concentration gradient. In liquid mixing, diffusion contributes to the homogenization of concentration gradients and the redistribution of solutes within the mixture.
   c. **Applications:** Diffusion plays a role in processes such as mixing of solutions, dyeing of textiles, and flavor blending in food and beverage production, where achieving uniformity and consistency is important.

MECHANISM OF SEMISOLIDS MIXING

Semisolid mixing involves blending materials that are in a partially solid and partially liquid state, such as creams, pastes, gels, or ointments. The mechanism of semisolid mixing is influenced by the rheological properties of the materials being mixed, as well as the desired texture and consistency of the final product. Here's a detailed explanation of the mechanisms involved in semisolid mixing:

1. **Shear Mixing:**
   a. **Description:** Shear mixing is a fundamental mechanism in semisolid mixing, involving the application of shear forces to deform and blend the materials.
   b. **Mechanism**: Shear mixing occurs when adjacent layers of the semisolid material slide past each other, resulting in deformation and reorientation of the material. This action promotes intermixing of components and homogenization of the mixture.

c. **Applications**: Shear mixing is commonly used in the production of creams, gels, and ointments in industries such as cosmetics, pharmaceuticals, and food processing.

2. **Kneading:**
   a. **Description:** Kneading involves the repetitive folding, stretching, and pressing of the semisolid material to achieve thorough mixing and blending.
   b. **Mechanism:** During kneading, the material is subjected to compressive and shear forces, causing it to deform and redistribute. This process facilitates the dispersion of components and ensures uniformity in the mixture.
   c. **Applications:** Kneading is commonly employed in the preparation of dough for baking, as well as in the manufacturing of cosmetic products and pharmaceutical formulations.

3. **Rolling and Compaction:**
   a. **Description**: Rolling and compaction involve the compression and rolling of the semisolid material between rollers or surfaces to achieve mixing and homogenization.
   b. **Mechanism**: As the material passes between rollers or surfaces, it undergoes compression and shearing, leading to deformation and redistribution of components. This action promotes blending and uniformity in the mixture.
   c. **Applications**: Rolling and compaction are utilized in processes such as the production of solid dosage forms (e.g., tablets), as well as in the manufacturing of cosmetic products and confectionery items.

4. **Extrusion:**

a. **Description:** Extrusion involves forcing the semisolid material through a die or nozzle to produce a uniform and continuous stream.

b. **Mechanism**: During extrusion, the material undergoes shearing and stretching as it passes through the die or nozzle, resulting in thorough mixing and dispersion of components. This process also helps in achieving the desired texture and consistency of the final product.

c. **Applications**: Extrusion is commonly used in the production of food products (e.g., pasta, snacks), as well as in pharmaceutical manufacturing (e.g., extrusion of tablets or pellets) and the processing of plastic materials.

DOUBLE CONE BLENDER

Principles of Double Cone Blender:

The double cone blender operates on the principle of gentle tumbling and diffusion. It consists of two conical-shaped vessels joined at their bases. When the blender is in operation, the vessel rotates slowly around its axis, causing the material inside to tumble and move in a gentle, cascading motion. This movement promotes the intermixing of components and facilitates blending without causing excessive shear or degradation of the materials.

Construction of Double Cone Blender:

A typical double cone blender consists of the following components:

1. **Conical Vessels**: The blender features two conical-shaped vessels made of stainless steel or other suitable materials. These vessels are joined at their bases and are supported by a sturdy frame.
2. **Drive Mechanism**: The blender is equipped with a motor and drive mechanism to rotate the vessel slowly around its axis. The rotation speed can usually be controlled to suit the mixing requirements.

3. **Loading and Discharge Ports**: The blender has ports for loading materials into the vessel and discharging the blended mixture. These ports are typically equipped with covers or valves to prevent spillage during operation.
4. **Sealing Arrangement**: To ensure a dust-free operation, the blender may feature sealing arrangements such as gaskets or mechanical seals at the loading and discharge ports.

Working of Double Cone Blender:

The working principle of a double cone blender involves the following steps:

1. **Loading**: The materials to be mixed are loaded into the conical vessel through the loading port. Care should be taken to distribute the materials evenly to ensure uniform blending.
2. **Rotation:** Once the vessel is loaded, the blender is started, and the vessel begins to rotate slowly around its axis. The rotation causes the material inside to tumble and move in a cascading motion, promoting mixing and blending.
3. **Blending:** As the vessel continues to rotate, the materials inside undergo gentle tumbling and diffusion, allowing for thorough blending without causing excessive shear or degradation. The duration of blending can be adjusted based on the desired level of homogeneity.
4. **Discharge**: After the blending process is complete, the blended mixture is discharged from the blender through the discharge port. The discharge port is typically positioned at the lowest point of the vessel to ensure complete emptying.

Uses of Double Cone Blender:

Double cone blenders are widely used in various industries for blending dry powders and granules. Some common applications include:

1. **Pharmaceutical industry**: Mixing of powders for tablet formulations, granulation processes, and blending of excipients.

2. **Food industry**: Blending of powdered ingredients for bakery products, spices, food supplements, and dry mixes.
3. **Chemical industry**: Homogenization of powdered chemicals, blending of pigments, dyes, and catalysts.
4. **Cosmetic industry:** Mixing of powdered ingredients for cosmetics, personal care products, and toiletries.

Merits of Double Cone Blender:

1. **Gentle Mixing**: The gentle tumbling motion of the double cone blender ensures thorough mixing without causing degradation or alteration of the materials.
2. **Versatility:** It can handle a wide range of materials, including powders, granules, and fragile particles.
3. **Easy to Clean**: The conical shape of the vessel allows for easy cleaning and discharge of the blended mixture.
4. **Uniform Blending**: The cascading motion of the materials promotes uniform blending and homogeneity of the mixture.

Demerits of Double Cone Blender:

1. **Limited Mixing Capacity**: Double cone blenders are typically available in smaller capacities and may not be suitable for large-scale production.
2. **Longer Blending Times**: Compared to some other mixing techniques, such as high-shear mixing, double cone blending may require longer blending times to achieve the desired level of homogeneity.
3. **Not Suitable for Liquid Mixing**: Double cone blenders are primarily designed for dry blending applications and may not be suitable for mixing liquids or viscous materials.

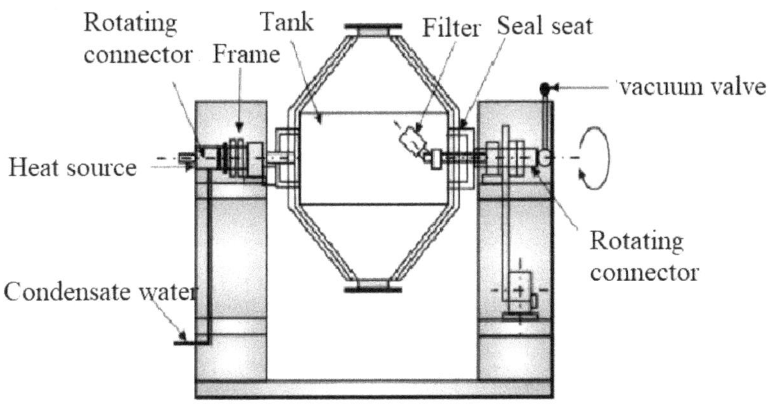
Rotating connector
Tank
Filter
Seal seat
Frame
vacuum valve
Heat source
Rotating connector
Condensate water

CHAPTER – 14

MIXING – II

Mrs. Evneet Kaur Bhatia

Assistant Professor, Rajiv Gandhi Institute of Pharmacy, Faculty of Pharmaceutical Science & Technology, AKS University Satna, MP-India

---

Abstract:

Mixing technology encompasses various equipment designed to blend materials effectively across different industries. The twin shell blender, also known as a double cone blender, features a shell with two connected cones that rotate to gently tumble and mix powders and granular materials. This design ensures thorough blending without damaging fragile particles, making it suitable for pharmaceutical and food applications. Ribbon blenders utilize a horizontal, ribbon-shaped agitator that moves materials in multiple directions, ensuring even distribution and consistent mixing of dry and semi-dry materials in industries such as agriculture and chemicals. Sigma blade mixers are robust machines with two sigma-shaped blades that rotate and knead materials against a trough or bowl, ideal for mixing high-viscosity materials like adhesives, rubber compounds, and doughs in the food industry. Planetary mixers feature a rotating, planetary-like agitator that moves around a central axis while simultaneously rotating on its own axis, providing intense mixing action for products like cosmetics, pharmaceuticals, and pastes. Each type of mixer offers distinct advantages depending on the application's requirements for mixing speed, intensity, and material properties. Optimizing the choice of mixer and operational parameters ensures efficient blending, uniform product quality, and adherence to industry standards, making mixing technology indispensable in modern manufacturing processes.

TWIN SHELL BLENDER

Principles of Twin Shell Blender:

The twin shell blender operates on the principle of gentle tumbling and diffusion, similar to the double cone blender. It consists of two cylindrical-shaped shells joined at their ends, forming a V-shaped chamber. When the blender is in operation, the shells rotate slowly in opposite directions, causing the material inside to tumble and move in a gentle, cascading motion. This movement promotes the intermixing of components and facilitates blending without causing excessive shear or degradation of the materials.

Construction of Twin Shell Blender:

A typical twin shell blender consists of the following components:

1. **Cylindrical Shells**: The blender features two cylindrical-shaped shells made of stainless steel or other suitable materials. These shells are joined at their ends to form a V-shaped chamber.
2. **Drive Mechanism**: The blender is equipped with a motor and drive mechanism to rotate the shells slowly in opposite directions. The rotation speed can usually be controlled to suit the mixing requirements.
3. **Loading and Discharge Ports**: The blender has ports for loading materials into the chamber and discharging the blended mixture. These ports are typically equipped with covers or valves to prevent spillage during operation.
4. **Sealing Arrangement**: To ensure a dust-free operation, the blender may feature sealing arrangements such as gaskets or mechanical seals at the loading and discharge ports.

Working of Twin Shell Blender:

The working principle of a twin shell blender is similar to that of a double cone blender and involves the following steps:

1. **Loading**: The materials to be mixed are loaded into the chamber through the loading port. Care should be taken to distribute the materials evenly to ensure uniform blending.
2. **Rotation**: Once the chamber is loaded, the blender is started, and the shells begin to rotate slowly in opposite directions. The rotation causes the material inside to tumble and move in a cascading motion, promoting mixing and blending.
3. **Blending:** As the shells continue to rotate, the materials inside undergo gentle tumbling and diffusion, allowing for thorough blending without causing excessive shear or degradation. The duration of blending can be adjusted based on the desired level of homogeneity.
4. **Discharge**: After the blending process is complete, the blended mixture is discharged from the blender through the discharge port. The discharge port is typically positioned at the lowest point of the chamber to ensure complete emptying.

Uses of Twin Shell Blender:

Twin shell blenders are used in various industries for blending dry powders, granules, and fragile particles. Some common applications include:

1. **Pharmaceutical industry**: Mixing of powders for tablet formulations, granulation processes, and blending of excipients.
2. **Food industry:** Blending of powdered ingredients for bakery products, spices, food supplements, and dry mixes.
3. **Chemical industry**: Homogenization of powdered chemicals, blending of pigments, dyes, and catalysts.
4. **Cosmetic industry**: Mixing of powdered ingredients for cosmetics, personal care products, and toiletries.

Merits of Twin Shell Blender:

1. **Gentle Mixing**: The gentle tumbling motion of the twin shell blender ensures thorough mixing without causing degradation or alteration of the materials.
2. **Versatility**: It can handle a wide range of materials, including powders, granules, and fragile particles.
3. **Uniform Blending**: The cascading motion of the materials promotes uniform blending and homogeneity of the mixture.
4. **Easy to Clean**: The design of the blender allows for easy cleaning and discharge of the blended mixture.

Demerits of Twin Shell Blender:

1. **Limited Mixing Capacity**: Twin shell blenders are typically available in smaller capacities and may not be suitable for large-scale production.
2. **Longer Blending Times**: Compared to some other mixing techniques, such as high-shear mixing, twin shell blending may require longer blending times to achieve the desired level of homogeneity.
3. **Not Suitable for Liquid Mixing**: Twin shell blenders are primarily designed for dry blending applications and may not be suitable for mixing liquids or viscous materials.

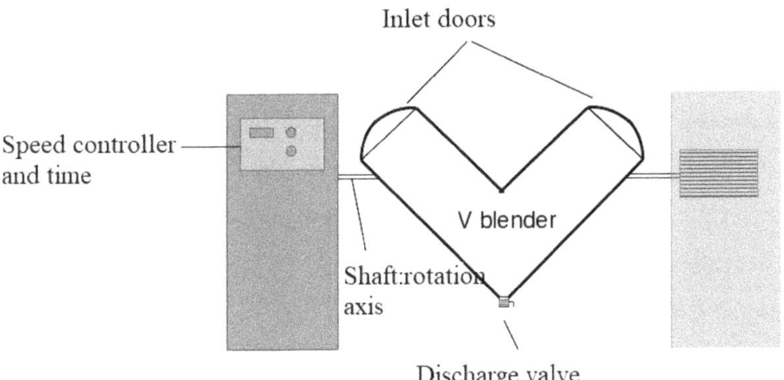

RIBBON BLENDER

Principles of Ribbon Blender:

The ribbon blender operates on the principle of convective mixing and diffusion. It consists of a horizontal trough with a ribbon-like agitator that rotates on a central shaft. The ribbon agitator moves the materials in both radial and axial directions, creating a fluidized mixing zone. This movement promotes intermixing of components and facilitates blending without causing excessive shear or degradation of the materials.

Construction of Ribbon Blender:

A typical ribbon blender consists of the following components:

1. **Horizontal Trough**: The blender features a horizontal trough made of stainless steel or other suitable materials. The trough has a U-shaped cross-section and is equipped with covers to prevent spillage during operation.
2. **Ribbon Agitator**: The blender is equipped with a ribbon-like agitator that is mounted on a central shaft inside the trough. The ribbon agitator consists of helical blades that extend along the length of the shaft and are designed to move the materials in both radial and axial directions.
3. **Drive Mechanism**: The blender is powered by a motor and drive mechanism that rotates the central shaft and the ribbon agitator. The rotation speed can usually be controlled to suit the mixing requirements.
4. **Loading and Discharge Ports**: The blender has ports for loading materials into the trough and discharging the blended mixture. These ports are typically equipped with covers or valves to ensure a dust-free operation.

Working of Ribbon Blender:

The working principle of a ribbon blender involves the following steps:

1. **Loading**: The materials to be mixed are loaded into the trough through the loading port. Care should be taken to distribute the materials evenly to ensure uniform blending.
2. **Rotation:** Once the trough is loaded, the blender is started, and the central shaft and ribbon agitator begin to rotate. The rotation causes the ribbon agitator to move the materials in both radial and axial directions, creating a fluidized mixing zone.
3. **Blending:** As the ribbon agitator continues to rotate, the materials inside the trough undergo convective mixing and diffusion, allowing for thorough blending without causing excessive shear or degradation. The helical blades of the ribbon agitator ensure that all components are uniformly mixed.
4. **Discharge**: After the blending process is complete, the blended mixture is discharged from the blender through the discharge port. The discharge port is typically positioned at the lowest point of the trough to ensure complete emptying.

Uses of Ribbon Blender:

Ribbon blenders are used in various industries for blending dry powders, granules, and fragile particles. Some common applications include:

1. **Food industry**: Mixing of powdered ingredients for bakery products, spices, food supplements, and dry mixes.
2. **Pharmaceutical industry**: Blending of powders for tablet formulations, granulation processes, and blending of excipients.
3. **Chemical industry**: Homogenization of powdered chemicals, blending of pigments, dyes, and catalysts.
4. **Cosmetic industry**: Mixing of powdered ingredients for cosmetics, personal care products, and toiletries.

Merits of Ribbon Blender:

1. **Uniform Blending**: The convective mixing action of the ribbon blender ensures uniform blending and homogeneity of the mixture.
2. **Versatility**: It can handle a wide range of materials, including powders, granules, and fragile particles.
3. **Gentle Mixing**: The ribbon agitator moves the materials in a gentle manner, minimizing the risk of degradation or alteration of the materials.
4. **Easy to Clean:** The design of the blender allows for easy cleaning and discharge of the blended mixture.

Demerits of Ribbon Blender:

1. **Limited Mixing Capacity**: Ribbon blenders are typically available in smaller capacities and may not be suitable for large-scale production.
2. **Longer Blending Times**: Compared to some other mixing techniques, ribbon blending may require longer blending times to achieve the desired level of homogeneity.
3. **Not Suitable for Viscous Materials**: Ribbon blenders are primarily designed for dry blending applications and may not be suitable for mixing highly viscous materials or liquids.

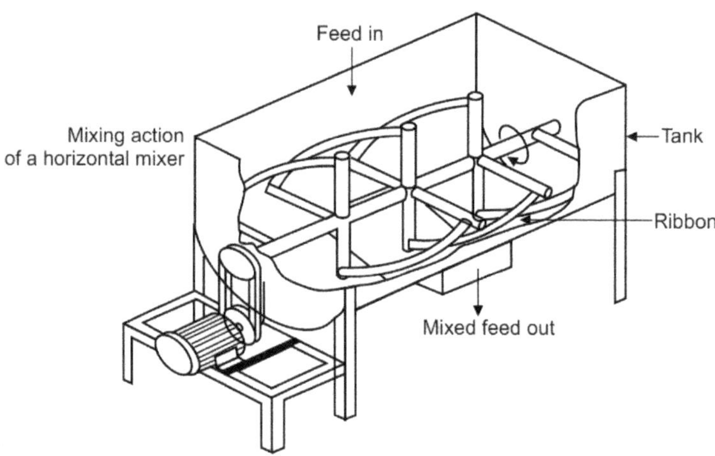

SIGMA BLADE MIXER

Principles of Sigma Blade Mixer:

The sigma blade mixer operates on the principle of kneading and shearing. It consists of two sigma-shaped blades that rotate on parallel shafts inside a trough-shaped container. The blades are designed to intermesh closely, creating a shearing and kneading action as they rotate. This movement effectively mixes and blends viscous materials, pastes, and dough-like substances by folding, stretching, and compressing the material.

Construction of Sigma Blade Mixer:

A typical sigma blade mixer consists of the following components:

1. **Trough-shaped Container**: The mixer features a trough-shaped container made of stainless steel or other suitable materials. The container has a jacket for heating or cooling the material if required.
2. **Sigma Blades**: The mixer is equipped with two sigma-shaped blades mounted on parallel shafts inside the container. The blades are designed to intermesh closely and rotate in opposite directions, creating a shearing and kneading action.
3. **Drive Mechanism**: The mixer is powered by a motor and drive mechanism that rotates the shafts and sigma blades. The rotation speed and direction can usually be controlled to suit the mixing requirements.
4. **Heating or Cooling System**: Some sigma blade mixers are equipped with a jacketed trough and internal heating or cooling coils to control the temperature of the material during mixing.

Working of Sigma Blade Mixer:

The working principle of a sigma blade mixer involves the following steps:

1. **Loading**: The materials to be mixed are loaded into the trough-shaped container of the mixer. The container may be equipped with a tilting mechanism or a removable lid for easy loading and unloading of materials.

2. **Rotation**: Once the container is loaded, the mixer is started, and the sigma blades begin to rotate in opposite directions. The closely intermeshing blades create a shearing and kneading action, folding, stretching, and compressing the material.
3. **Mixing**: As the sigma blades continue to rotate, the material undergoes thorough mixing and blending. The shearing and kneading action of the blades effectively homogenizes viscous materials, pastes, and dough-like substances, ensuring uniformity in the mixture.
4. **Discharge**: After the mixing process is complete, the mixed material is discharged from the mixer through a discharge port located at the bottom of the container. The discharge port is typically equipped with a valve or gate to control the flow of the material.

Uses of Sigma Blade Mixer:

Sigma blade mixers are used in various industries for mixing and blending viscous materials, pastes, and dough-like substances. Some common applications include:

1. **Food industry**: Mixing of dough for bread, cookies, and pastries, blending of chocolate, confectionery, and sauces.
2. **Chemical industry**: Mixing of adhesives, sealants, rubber compounds, and polymers.
3. **Pharmaceutical industry**: Mixing of ointments, creams, gels, and dental materials.
4. **Cosmetic industry**: Mixing of cosmetic creams, lotions, and emulsions.

Merits of Sigma Blade Mixer:

1. **Effective Mixing**: The shearing and kneading action of the sigma blades ensure thorough mixing and blending of viscous materials, pastes, and dough-like substances.
2. **Uniformity**: The mixer provides excellent uniformity in the mixture, resulting in consistent product quality.

3. **Versatility**: It can handle a wide range of materials, including food products, chemicals, pharmaceuticals, and cosmetics.
4. **Controlled Temperature**: Some sigma blade mixers are equipped with a heating or cooling system to control the temperature of the material during mixing.

Demerits of Sigma Blade Mixer:

1. **High Energy Consumption**: Sigma blade mixers may consume more energy compared to some other mixing techniques, especially when mixing highly viscous materials.
2. **Complex Cleaning Process**: Cleaning and maintenance of sigma blade mixers can be complex, especially due to the intricate design of the sigma blades and the trough-shaped container.
3. **Not Suitable for Dry Mixing**: Sigma blade mixers are primarily designed for mixing viscous materials, pastes, and dough-like substances and may not be suitable for dry mixing applications.

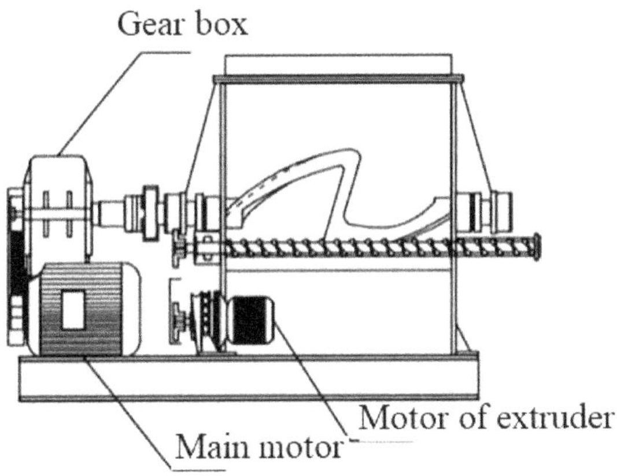

PLANETARY MIXERS

Principles of Planetary Mixers:

Planetary mixers operate on the principle of planetary motion, where the mixing elements rotate around a central axis while simultaneously orbiting the mixing vessel. This dual motion creates a highly efficient mixing action by combining rotational and orbital movements. The mixing elements, typically blades or paddles, sweep through the entire volume of the mixing vessel, ensuring thorough blending and homogenization of the materials.

Construction of Planetary Mixers:

A typical planetary mixer consists of the following components:

1. **Mixing Vessel**: The mixer features a bowl-shaped mixing vessel made of stainless steel or other suitable materials. The vessel is securely mounted on a stand or frame and is equipped with a locking mechanism to prevent movement during operation.
2. **Planetary Mixing Head**: The mixer is equipped with a planetary mixing head that contains the mixing elements (blades or paddles). The mixing head is mounted on a vertical shaft connected to the drive mechanism.
3. **Drive Mechanism**: The mixer is powered by a motor and drive mechanism that rotates the mixing head and drives the orbital motion. The rotation speed and direction can usually be controlled to suit the mixing requirements.
4. **Control Panel:** The mixer may have a control panel with switches, knobs, or digital controls for adjusting the mixing speed, time, and other parameters.

Working of Planetary Mixers:

The working principle of a planetary mixer involves the following steps:

1. **Loading:** The materials to be mixed are loaded into the mixing vessel. The vessel may have a tilting mechanism or a removable bowl for easy loading and unloading of materials.

2. **Rotation**: Once the vessel is loaded, the mixer is started, and the mixing head begins to rotate around its central axis. At the same time, the mixing head orbits the mixing vessel, creating a dual motion.
3. **Mixing**: As the mixing head rotates and orbits, the mixing elements sweep through the entire volume of the mixing vessel, ensuring thorough blending and homogenization of the materials. The combination of rotational and orbital movements promotes efficient mixing without dead zones.
4. **Discharge**: After the mixing process is complete, the mixed material is discharged from the mixer through a discharge port located at the bottom of the mixing vessel. The discharge port is typically equipped with a valve or gate to control the flow of the material.

Uses of Planetary Mixers:

Planetary mixers are used in various industries for mixing and blending a wide range of materials. Some common applications include:

1. **Food industry**: Mixing of dough for bread, cookies, and pastries, blending of cake batters, sauces, and dressings.
2. **Pharmaceutical industry**: Mixing of powders for tablet formulations, blending of granules, and preparation of ointments and creams.
3. **Chemical industry**: Mixing of adhesives, sealants, polymers, and rubber compounds.
4. **Cosmetic industry**: Mixing of cosmetic creams, lotions, and emulsions, blending of fragrances and colorants.

Merits of Planetary Mixers:

1. **High Mixing Efficiency**: The dual motion of rotational and orbital movements ensures thorough blending and homogenization of the materials.

2. **Versatility**: Planetary mixers can handle a wide range of materials, viscosities, and batch sizes, making them suitable for various applications.
3. **Uniform Mixing**: The mixing elements sweep through the entire volume of the mixing vessel, resulting in uniform mixing and consistent product quality.
4. **Controlled Mixing Parameters**: Planetary mixers typically offer control over mixing speed, time, and other parameters, allowing for precise adjustment of the mixing process.

Demerits of Planetary Mixers:

1. **High Cost**: Planetary mixers may be more expensive compared to some other mixing techniques, especially for larger capacities and more advanced features.
2. **Complex Cleaning Process**: Cleaning and maintenance of planetary mixers can be complex due to the intricate design of the mixing head and the mixing vessel.
3. **Limited Mixing Capacity**: Planetary mixers may have limitations in terms of mixing capacity, especially for very large batch sizes.

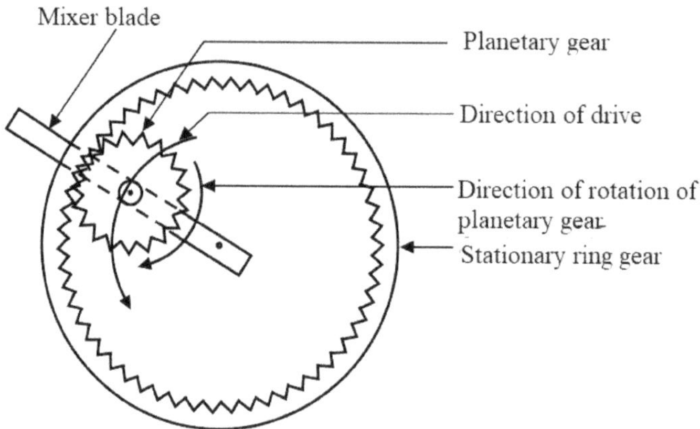

PROPELLERS

Principles of Propellers in Mixing:

Propellers in mixing operate on the principle of fluid dynamics, where the rotation of the propeller blades generates a flow field within the mixing vessel. The propeller blades are designed to create axial flow, pushing the material along the axis of rotation. This movement promotes mixing by inducing fluid circulation and intermixing of the materials.

Construction of Propellers:

A typical propeller mixer consists of the following components:

1. **Propeller Blades**: The mixer features a set of propeller blades mounted on a central shaft. The propeller blades may have various designs, including pitched, flat, or curved blades, depending on the desired mixing characteristics.
2. **Shaft**: The propeller blades are mounted on a shaft, which is connected to the drive mechanism. The shaft is typically made of stainless steel or other corrosion-resistant materials.
3. **Drive Mechanism**: The mixer is powered by a motor and drive mechanism that rotates the shaft and propeller blades. The rotation speed and direction can usually be controlled to suit the mixing requirements.
4. **Mounting Assembly**: The mixer may be mounted on a stand or frame to support the mixing vessel and provide stability during operation.

Working of Propellers:

The working principle of a propeller mixer involves the following steps:

1. **Loading**: The materials to be mixed are loaded into the mixing vessel. The vessel may have a lid or cover to prevent spillage during mixing.
2. **Rotation**: Once the vessel is loaded, the mixer is started, and the motor rotates the shaft and propeller blades. The rotation of the blades generates

fluid flow within the mixing vessel, inducing mixing and blending of the materials.

3. **Mixing**: As the propeller blades rotate, they create axial flow, pushing the material along the axis of rotation. This movement promotes fluid circulation and intermixing of the materials, ensuring thorough blending and homogenization.
4. **Discharge**: After the mixing process is complete, the mixed material is discharged from the mixer through a discharge port located at the bottom of the vessel. The discharge port is typically equipped with a valve or gate to control the flow of the material.

Uses of Propellers in Mixing:

Propellers are used in various industries for mixing and blending a wide range of materials. Some common applications include:

1. **Chemical industry**: Mixing of liquid-liquid, liquid-solid, and gas-liquid systems in chemical reactions, polymerization processes, and wastewater treatment.
2. **Pharmaceutical industry:** Blending of solutions, suspensions, and emulsions in drug formulations, compounding processes, and API manufacturing.
3. **Food industry**: Mixing of ingredients for beverages, sauces, soups, and dressings, homogenization of dairy products, and emulsification of fats and oils.
4. **Water treatment**: Mixing of chemicals for water and wastewater treatment processes, including coagulation, flocculation, and disinfection.

Merits of Propellers in Mixing:

1. **Simple Design**: Propeller mixers have a simple and robust design, making them easy to operate and maintain.
2. **Cost-Effective**: Propeller mixers are generally cost-effective compared to some other mixing techniques, especially for smaller-scale applications.

3. **High Mixing Efficiency**: Propeller mixers can achieve high mixing efficiency, especially for liquid-liquid and gas-liquid systems.
4. **Versatility**: Propeller mixers can handle a wide range of materials, viscosities, and batch sizes, making them suitable for various applications.

Demerits of Propellers in Mixing:

1. **Limited Shear**: Propeller mixers may provide limited shear compared to some other mixing techniques, such as high-shear mixers, which may be required for certain applications.
2. **Non-Uniform Mixing**: In some cases, propeller mixers may not provide uniform mixing, especially for materials with high viscosity or non-homogeneous properties.
3. **Cavitation Risk**: Propeller mixers operating at high speeds may be prone to cavitation, leading to reduced mixing efficiency and potential equipment damage.

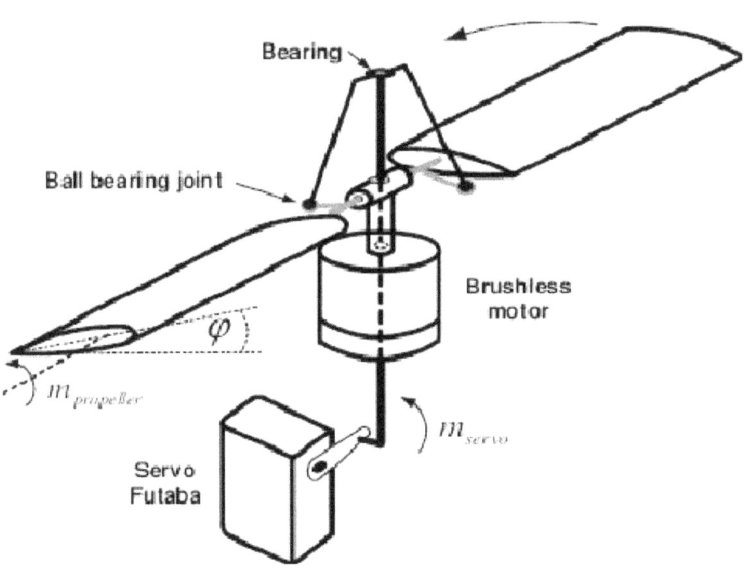

DOUBLE TURBINES

Principles of Double Turbines in Mixing:

Double turbines in mixing operate on the principle of creating intense fluid movement within a mixing vessel. They consist of two sets of turbine blades mounted on a central shaft, rotating in opposite directions. This configuration generates complex fluid flow patterns, including both axial and radial flow, resulting in thorough mixing and blending of materials.

Construction of Double Turbines:

A typical double turbine mixer consists of the following components:

1. **Turbine Blades**: The mixer features two sets of turbine blades mounted on a central shaft. The blades are designed to create fluid movement and promote mixing by inducing both axial and radial flow.
2. **Shaft:** The turbine blades are mounted on a shaft, which is connected to the drive mechanism. The shaft is typically made of stainless steel or other corrosion-resistant materials.
3. **Drive Mechanism**: The mixer is powered by a motor and drive mechanism that rotates the shaft and turbine blades. The rotation speed and direction can usually be controlled to suit the mixing requirements.
4. **Mounting Assembly**: The mixer may be mounted on a stand or frame to support the mixing vessel and provide stability during operation.

Working of Double Turbines:

The working principle of a double turbine mixer involves the following steps:

1. **Loading**: The materials to be mixed are loaded into the mixing vessel. The vessel may have a lid or cover to prevent spillage during mixing.
2. **Rotation**: Once the vessel is loaded, the mixer is started, and the motor rotates the shaft and turbine blades. The rotation of the blades generates intense fluid movement within the mixing vessel, inducing both axial and radial flow.

3. **Mixing:** As the turbine blades rotate, they create complex fluid flow patterns, promoting thorough mixing and blending of the materials. The combination of axial and radial flow ensures efficient mixing, even for highly viscous or difficult-to-mix materials.
4. **Discharge**: After the mixing process is complete, the mixed material is discharged from the mixer through a discharge port located at the bottom of the vessel. The discharge port is typically equipped with a valve or gate to control the flow of the material.

Uses of Double Turbines in Mixing:

Double turbines are used in various industries for mixing and blending a wide range of materials. Some common applications include:

1. **Chemical industry**: Mixing of viscous liquids, dispersion of powders, and emulsification of immiscible liquids in chemical reactions, polymerization processes, and wastewater treatment.
2. **Pharmaceutical industry**: Blending of suspensions, emulsions, and APIs in drug formulations, compounding processes, and API manufacturing.
3. **Food industry**: Mixing of sauces, dressings, beverages, and dairy products, emulsification of fats and oils, and dispersion of additives in food processing.
4. **Water treatment**: Mixing of chemicals for water and wastewater treatment processes, including coagulation, flocculation, and disinfection.

Merits of Double Turbines in Mixing:

1. **Intense Mixing Action**: Double turbines create intense fluid movement within the mixing vessel, ensuring thorough mixing and blending of materials.
2. **Efficient Mixing:** The combination of axial and radial flow patterns promotes efficient mixing, even for highly viscous or difficult-to-mix materials.

3. **Versatility**: Double turbine mixers can handle a wide range of materials, viscosities, and batch sizes, making them suitable for various applications.
4. **Uniformity**: The intense mixing action of double turbines results in uniform mixing and consistent product quality.

Demerits of Double Turbines in Mixing:

1. **High Power Consumption**: Double turbine mixers may consume more power compared to some other mixing techniques, especially for larger-scale applications.
2. **Complex Design**: The design of double turbine mixers can be complex, requiring careful engineering to optimize fluid flow patterns and mixing efficiency.
3. **Maintenance Requirements**: Double turbine mixers may require regular maintenance to ensure proper functioning of the blades, shaft, and drive mechanism.

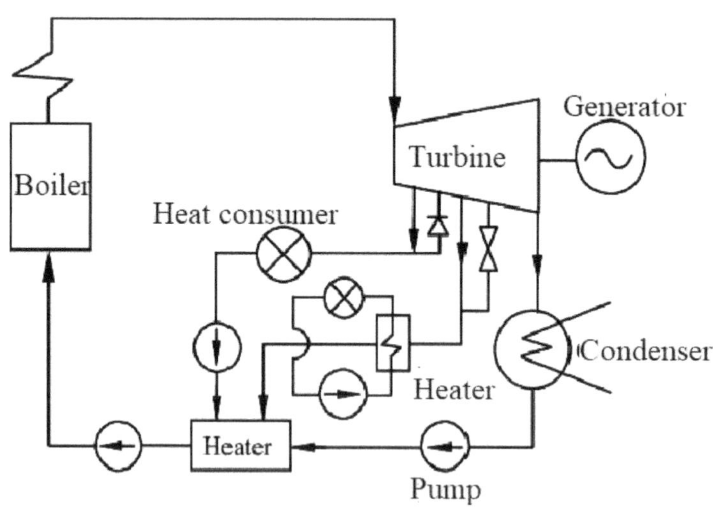

PADDLES & SILVERSON EMULSIFIER

Principles of Paddles in Mixing:

Paddles in mixing operate on the principle of creating fluid movement within a mixing vessel through the rotation of paddle blades. The paddle blades are designed to generate both axial and radial flow, promoting mixing by inducing fluid circulation and intermixing of materials. Paddles are typically used for low to medium viscosity mixing applications where gentle agitation is required.

Construction of Paddles:

A typical paddle mixer consists of the following components:

1. **Paddle Blades**: The mixer features paddle blades mounted on a central shaft. The paddle blades may have various designs, including flat, curved, or angled blades, depending on the desired mixing characteristics.
2. **Shaft**: The paddle blades are mounted on a shaft, which is connected to the drive mechanism. The shaft is typically made of stainless steel or other corrosion-resistant materials.
3. **Drive Mechanism**: The mixer is powered by a motor and drive mechanism that rotates the shaft and paddle blades. The rotation speed and direction can usually be controlled to suit the mixing requirements.
4. **Mounting Assembly**: The mixer may be mounted on a stand or frame to support the mixing vessel and provide stability during operation.

Working of Paddles:

The working principle of a paddle mixer involves the following steps:

1. **Loading**: The materials to be mixed are loaded into the mixing vessel. The vessel may have a lid or cover to prevent spillage during mixing.
2. **Rotation:** Once the vessel is loaded, the mixer is started, and the motor rotates the shaft and paddle blades. The rotation of the blades generates fluid movement within the mixing vessel, inducing both axial and radial flow.

3. **Mixing**: As the paddle blades rotate, they create fluid circulation and intermixing of the materials, ensuring thorough blending and homogenization.
4. **Discharge:** After the mixing process is complete, the mixed material is discharged from the mixer through a discharge port located at the bottom of the vessel. The discharge port is typically equipped with a valve or gate to control the flow of the material.

Uses of Paddles:

Paddle mixers are used in various industries for mixing and blending materials with low to medium viscosity. Some common applications include:

1. **Food industry**: Mixing of batters, doughs, sauces, dressings, and marinades.
2. **Chemical industry**: Mixing of powders, granules, and liquids in chemical reactions and manufacturing processes.
3. **Pharmaceutical industry**: Blending of powders, granules, and APIs in drug formulations and compounding processes.
4. **Cosmetics industry**: Mixing of creams, lotions, and emulsions in cosmetic manufacturing.

Merits of Paddles:

1. **Gentle Mixing**: Paddle mixers provide gentle agitation, making them suitable for delicate materials and sensitive processes.
2. **Versatility:** Paddle mixers can handle a wide range of materials and batch sizes, making them suitable for various applications.
3. **Ease of Operation**: Paddle mixers have a simple and straightforward design, making them easy to operate and maintain.
4. **Uniform Mixing**: Paddle mixers promote uniform mixing and consistent product quality.

Demerits of Paddles:

1. **Limited Shear**: Paddle mixers may provide limited shear compared to some other mixing techniques, which may be required for certain applications.
2. **Longer Mixing Times**: Paddle mixers may require longer mixing times to achieve thorough blending, especially for larger batch sizes or more viscous materials.
3. **Not Suitable for High Viscosity**: Paddle mixers may not be suitable for mixing highly viscous materials or materials with very different viscosities.

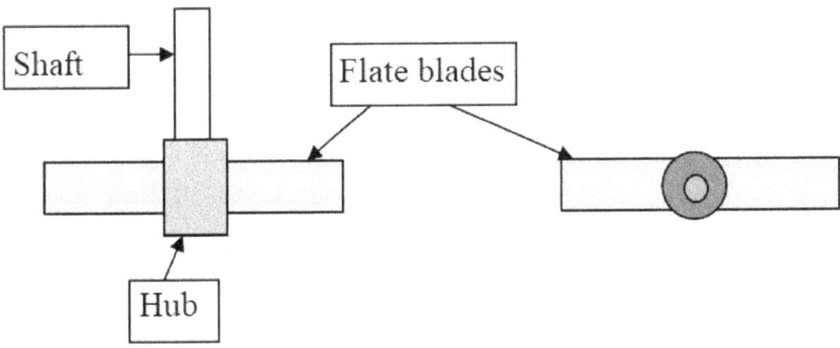

Principles of Silverson Emulsifier in Mixing:

Silverson emulsifiers operate on the principle of high shear mixing to create stable emulsions and dispersions. They consist of a rotor-stator system, where a rotor spins at high speeds within a fixed stator. This configuration creates intense shear forces and turbulence, effectively breaking down particles and droplets to create fine emulsions and dispersions.

Construction of Silverson Emulsifier:

A typical Silverson emulsifier consists of the following components:

1. **Rotor**: The emulsifier features a rotor mounted on a high-speed motor shaft. The rotor typically has several blades or teeth designed to create intense shear forces and turbulence.
2. **Stator**: The emulsifier has a fixed stator surrounding the rotor. The stator may have grooves, channels, or teeth that work in conjunction with the rotor to create shear forces and turbulence.
3. **Drive Mechanism**: The emulsifier is powered by a high-speed motor that rotates the rotor at high speeds. The rotation speed can usually be controlled to suit the mixing requirements.
4. **Mounting Assembly**: The emulsifier may be mounted on a stand or frame to support the mixing vessel and provide stability during operation.

Working of Silverson Emulsifier:

The working principle of a Silverson emulsifier involves the following steps:

1. **Loading:** The materials to be mixed are loaded into the mixing vessel. The vessel may have a lid or cover to prevent spillage during mixing.
2. **Rotation**: Once the vessel is loaded, the emulsifier is started, and the high-speed motor rotates the rotor at high speeds. The rotation of the rotor creates intense shear forces and turbulence within the mixing vessel.
3. **Emulsification:** As the rotor spins, it creates shear forces that break down particles and droplets, dispersing them evenly throughout the liquid. This process results in the formation of stable emulsions and dispersions with fine particle or droplet sizes.
4. **Discharge:** After the mixing process is complete, the emulsified mixture is discharged from the mixer through a discharge port located at the bottom of the vessel. The discharge port is typically equipped with a valve or gate to control the flow of the mixture.

Uses of Silverson Emulsifier:

Silverson emulsifiers are used in various industries for creating stable emulsions and dispersions. Some common applications include:

1. **Food industry**: Production of mayonnaise, sauces, dressings, dairy products, and beverage emulsions.
2. **Pharmaceutical industry**: Preparation of creams, lotions, ointments, suspensions, and emulsions for drug formulations.
3. **Cosmetic industry**: Manufacturing of cosmetic creams, lotions, serums, and emulsions for skincare and haircare products.
4. **Chemical industry**: Production of emulsions, dispersions, and suspensions for paints, coatings, adhesives, and lubricants.

Merits of Silverson Emulsifier:

1. **High Shear Mixing**: Silverson emulsifiers provide intense shear forces and turbulence, resulting in rapid and efficient emulsification and dispersion.
2. **Fine Particle Size**: The high shear mixing action of Silverson emulsifiers produces stable emulsions and dispersions with fine particle or droplet sizes.
3. **Fast Processing**: Silverson emulsifiers are capable of processing large volumes of material in a relatively short amount of time, improving productivity.
4. **Versatility**: Silverson emulsifiers can handle a wide range of materials, viscosities, and batch sizes, making them suitable for various applications.

Demerits of Silverson Emulsifier:

1. **High Cost:** Silverson emulsifiers may be more expensive compared to some other mixing techniques, especially for larger-scale applications.
2. **Complex Design**: The design of Silverson emulsifiers can be complex, requiring careful engineering and maintenance to ensure optimal performance.

3. **Risk of Overmixing**: Silverson emulsifiers provide intense shear forces, which may lead to overmixing and degradation of sensitive materials if not properly controlled.

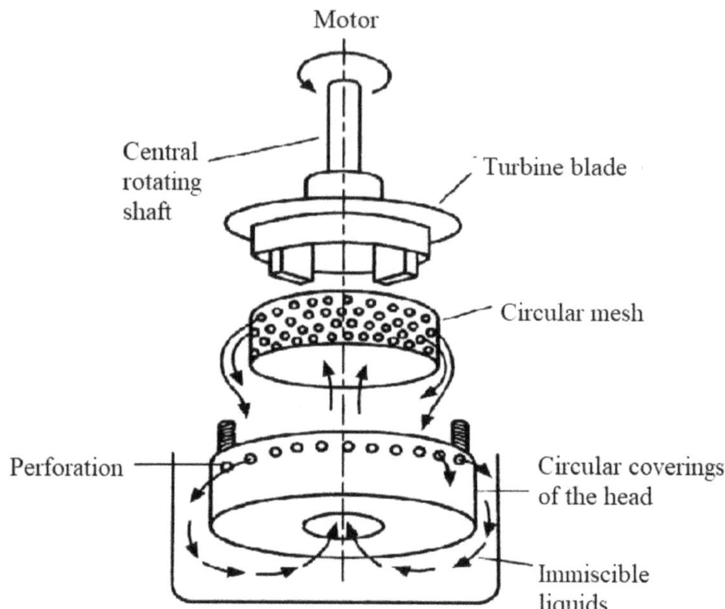

CHAPTER – 15

FILTRATION – I

Mrs. Neha Soni

Assistant Professor, Rajiv Gandhi Institute of Pharmacy, Faculty of Pharmaceutical Science & Technology, AKS University Satna, MP-India

---

ABSTRACT:

Filtration is a crucial separation process used across various industries to separate solids from liquids or gases through a porous medium, known as a filter. This process is essential for purifying liquids, capturing particulate matter, and ensuring product quality in sectors such as pharmaceuticals, food and beverage, wastewater treatment, and manufacturing. Filtration techniques include gravity filtration, where a liquid passes through a filter under the force of gravity, and pressure filtration, which uses pressure to drive the liquid through the filter medium, allowing for faster separation and higher throughput. In addition to liquid filtration, gas filtration is vital in applications such as air purification, industrial processes, and cleanroom environments. Filters used in gas filtration range from simple mesh screens to advanced membranes and electrostatic precipitators, depending on the particulate size and filtration efficiency required. Filtration media vary widely and may include materials like cellulose, activated carbon, ceramic, or synthetic polymers, each tailored to specific filtration needs. Filtration efficiency is influenced by factors such as pore size, flow rate, pressure differential, and the properties of the filtered material. Proper selection and maintenance of filtration systems are crucial to achieving desired separation outcomes, maintaining production efficiency, and meeting regulatory standards for product purity and environmental protection. As industries continue to innovate, filtration technology evolves to meet increasingly stringent requirements for cleanliness, efficiency, and sustainability in manufacturing processes globally.

INTRODUCTION

Filtration is a process used to separate solids from fluids (liquids or gases) by passing the mixture through a medium that retains the solid particles while allowing the fluid to pass through. This process finds extensive applications across various industries, including water treatment, pharmaceuticals, food and beverage, oil and gas, and many others. Let's delve into the details of filtration:

Principles of Filtration:

1. **Mechanism**: Filtration operates on the principle of size exclusion. The filter medium, often called the filter media, has pores of a specific size that allows only particles smaller than the pore size to pass through. Larger particles are retained on the surface or within the pores of the filter medium.
2. **Types of Filtration**: Filtration can be categorized into several types based on various factors such as the nature of the fluid, the size of particles, and the mechanism of filtration. Some common types include:
   a. **Gravity Filtration**: Relies on the force of gravity to pull the liquid through the filter medium.
   b. **Vacuum Filtration**: Uses a vacuum to increase the pressure differential across the filter medium, speeding up the filtration process.
   c. **Pressure Filtration:** Applies pressure to the fluid to force it through the filter medium.
   d. **Centrifugal Filtration**: Utilizes centrifugal force to separate particles from the fluid.
   e. **Membrane Filtration**: Involves the use of a semi-permeable membrane to separate particles based on size or molecular weight.

f. **Depth Filtration:** Involves a thick layer of filter media where particles are trapped throughout the depth of the medium.

3. **Filter Medium**: The effectiveness of filtration depends largely on the characteristics of the filter medium. Common filter media include:
   a. **Sand:** Used in sand filters for water treatment.
   b. **Activated Carbon**: Effective in removing organic contaminants and improving taste and odor in water and air filtration.
   c. **Membranes**: Such as microfiltration, ultrafiltration, nanofiltration, and reverse osmosis membranes, which are used for precise separation based on size or molecular weight.
   d. **Filter Paper**: Used in laboratory settings and for fine particle filtration in various industries.
4. **Particle Size and Distribution**: The efficiency of filtration is influenced by the size and distribution of particles in the fluid. Smaller particles may pass through the filter medium, especially if the pores are large or if the particles can deform to fit through the pores.

Applications of Filtration:

1. **Water Treatment**: Filtration is essential in removing suspended solids, microorganisms, and other impurities from water to make it safe for drinking, industrial processes, and recreational use.
2. **Pharmaceuticals**: Filtration is used in pharmaceutical manufacturing to separate solids from liquids, clarify solutions, sterilize liquids, and ensure product purity.
3. **Food and Beverage Industry**: Filtration is employed to clarify juices, remove particles and impurities from beverages, purify oils, and sterilize food and beverage products.
4. **Chemical Processing**: Filtration plays a critical role in chemical processing for separating solids from liquids or gases, purifying chemical solutions, and recovering valuable products.

5. **Air Filtration**: Air filtration is essential for removing particulate matter, dust, allergens, and other contaminants from indoor and outdoor air, improving air quality and protecting respiratory health.

Factors Affecting Filtration Efficiency:

1. **Pore Size**: The size of the filter pores determines the size of particles that can be retained. Proper selection of filter media with the appropriate pore size is crucial for achieving the desired level of filtration.
2. **Pressure and Flow Rate**: Pressure differentials across the filter medium and flow rates of the fluid affect filtration efficiency. Higher pressure differentials and slower flow rates generally result in better filtration.
3. **Filter Media Characteristics**: Properties such as porosity, surface area, and material composition of the filter medium influence its filtration efficiency and capacity.
4. **Particle Characteristics**: The size, shape, density, and concentration of particles in the fluid affect their ability to be retained by the filter medium.
5. **Operating Conditions**: Factors such as temperature, pH, and chemical composition of the fluid can impact filtration efficiency and the performance of the filter medium.

OBJECTIVES, APPLICATIONS, THEORIES & FACTORS INFLUENCING FILTRATION

Objectives of Filtration:

1. **Separation**: The primary objective of filtration is to separate solid particles from fluids (liquids or gases) based on the size of the particles. This separation is essential for various purposes such as purification, clarification, and removal of contaminants.
2. **Purification**: Filtration is used to purify fluids by removing suspended solids, impurities, microorganisms, and other unwanted particles, thereby improving the quality of the fluid.

3. **Clarification**: Filtration clarifies fluids by removing turbidity, haze, or cloudiness caused by suspended particles, making the fluid transparent or translucent.
4. **Concentration**: In some cases, filtration is used to concentrate solids from a dilute suspension or solution, resulting in a higher concentration of solids in the filtrate.
5. **Sterilization:** Filtration can be employed for sterilizing fluids by removing microorganisms, bacteria, and viruses, making the fluid microbiologically safe for various applications.

Applications of Filtration:

1. **Water Treatment**: Filtration is extensively used in water treatment processes to remove suspended solids, sediment, bacteria, algae, and other impurities from raw water, making it safe for drinking, industrial use, and recreational purposes.
2. **Pharmaceuticals:** Filtration plays a critical role in pharmaceutical manufacturing for processes such as clarification of solutions, sterilization of liquids, removal of particulates, and separation of solids from liquids.
3. **Food and Beverage Industry**: Filtration is essential in the food and beverage industry for clarifying juices, wines, beers, and other beverages, removing particles, microbes, and contaminants, and improving product quality and shelf life.
4. **Chemical Processing**: Filtration is utilized in chemical processing for separating solids from liquids or gases, recovering valuable products from process streams, purifying chemical solutions, and ensuring product quality and consistency.
5. **Environmental Remediation**: Filtration is employed in environmental remediation efforts to remove pollutants, suspended solids, and

contaminants from air, soil, and water, mitigating environmental pollution and protecting ecosystems.

Theories of Filtration:

1. **Size Exclusion**: Filtration operates on the principle of size exclusion, where the filter medium allows fluid to pass through while retaining particles larger than the pore size of the medium. This theory forms the basis for the separation of solids from fluids during the filtration process.
2. **Cake Filtration**: In cake filtration, as the fluid passes through the filter medium, particles are deposited on the surface, forming a layer known as the filter cake. The filter cake acts as an additional filtration barrier, enhancing the efficiency of particle removal.
3. **Filtration Resistance**: Filtration resistance refers to the combined resistance to fluid flow caused by the filter medium, filter cake, and fluid properties. Understanding filtration resistance is essential for optimizing filtration processes and selecting appropriate filter media.
4. **Flow Dynamics**: Theories of flow dynamics describe the behavior of fluids as they pass through the filter medium, including phenomena such as laminar flow, turbulent flow, and pressure gradients. These principles influence the efficiency and performance of filtration systems.

Factors Influencing Filtration:

1. **Pore Size of Filter Medium**: The pore size of the filter medium determines the size range of particles that can be retained. Proper selection of filter media with the appropriate pore size is crucial for achieving the desired level of filtration.
2. **Pressure Differential**: The pressure differential across the filter medium influences the rate of filtration and the efficiency of particle removal. Higher pressure differentials can enhance filtration rates but may also increase energy consumption and operating costs.

3. **Filter Media Characteristics**: Properties such as porosity, permeability, surface area, material composition, and surface chemistry of the filter medium affect its filtration efficiency, capacity, and compatibility with the fluid being filtered.
4. **Fluid Properties**: The properties of the fluid being filtered, including viscosity, density, pH, temperature, and chemical composition, can impact filtration efficiency, flow dynamics, and the performance of the filter medium.
5. **Particle Characteristics**: The size, shape, density, concentration, and surface properties of particles in the fluid influence their ability to be retained by the filter medium and affect filtration efficiency.
6. **Operating Conditions**: Factors such as temperature, pressure, flow rate, filtration time, and agitation can significantly influence filtration performance and should be optimized to achieve the desired level of particle removal and fluid quality.

FILTER AIDS

Filter aids are substances added to the filtration process to enhance the efficiency of particle removal and improve the performance of the filter medium. They work by modifying the properties of the filter cake formed during the filtration process, thereby reducing resistance to fluid flow and increasing the capacity for particle retention. Let's delve into the details of filter aids:

Types of Filter Aids:

1. **Diatomaceous Earth (DE):**
   a. DE is a naturally occurring, highly porous sedimentary rock composed of the fossilized remains of diatoms, a type of algae.
   b. It is commonly used as a filter aid due to its high porosity, which provides a large surface area for particle capture.

   c. DE filter aids can be classified into two main types: calcined (heat-treated) and non-calcined (raw). Calcined DE has higher porosity and greater filtration efficiency.

2. **Activated Carbon:**
   a. Activated carbon is a highly porous form of carbon with a large internal surface area, characterized by a network of pores and tunnels.
   b. It is widely used as a filter aid in water treatment, wastewater treatment, and gas purification processes.
   c. Activated carbon adsorbs impurities, contaminants, and odors from the fluid, improving the quality of the filtrate.

3. **Cellulose:**
   a. Cellulose-based filter aids, derived from plant fibers, are commonly used in filtration applications where high purity and low extractable content are required.
   b. They are effective in removing fine particles, colloids, and microorganisms from fluids, making them suitable for pharmaceutical, food, and beverage applications.

4. **Perlite:**
   a. Perlite is a volcanic glass that expands when heated, creating a lightweight, highly porous material with excellent filtration properties.
   b. It is used as a filter aid in various industrial processes, including food and beverage processing, pharmaceutical manufacturing, and water treatment.

5. **Bentonite:**
   a. Bentonite is a clay mineral composed primarily of montmorillonite, known for its high swelling capacity and cation exchange properties.

b. It is often used as a filter aid in wine and beer production to remove proteins, colloids, and other haze-forming substances.

Mechanisms of Action:

1. **Pre-coat Filtration:**
   a. In pre-coat filtration, a layer of filter aid is applied to the surface of the filter medium before the filtration process begins.
   b. The filter aid forms a porous pre-coat or cake layer, which serves as an additional filtration barrier to capture particles and impurities from the fluid.
2. **Body-feed Filtration:**
   a. In body-feed filtration, the filter aid is continuously added to the fluid being filtered during the filtration process.
   b. The filter aid particles become incorporated into the filter cake, enhancing its structure and increasing particle retention capacity.

Benefits of Using Filter Aids:

1. **Improved Filtration Efficiency**: Filter aids enhance the efficiency of particle removal by increasing the surface area available for particle capture and reducing resistance to fluid flow.
2. **Extended Filter Life**: By reducing clogging and fouling of the filter medium, filter aids help prolong the operational life of filtration systems, reducing maintenance requirements and downtime.
3. **Enhanced Clarity and Quality of Filtrate:** Filter aids contribute to the production of clearer, higher-quality filtrate by effectively removing fine particles, colloids, and impurities from the fluid.
4. **Cost Savings**: Using filter aids can lead to cost savings by optimizing filtration processes, reducing energy consumption, minimizing product losses, and extending the service life of filtration equipment.

Considerations for Using Filter Aids:

1. **Compatibility**: Selecting the appropriate filter aid depends on factors such as the nature of the fluid, the type of particles to be removed, and the characteristics of the filter medium.
2. **Dosage and Application**: Proper dosing and application of filter aids are crucial to achieving optimal filtration performance. Dosage rates should be carefully controlled to avoid over- or under-treatment.
3. **Regeneration and Disposal**: Some filter aids, such as activated carbon, can be regenerated and reused multiple times, while others may require disposal after use. Proper handling and disposal practices should be followed to minimize environmental impact.
4. **Regulatory Compliance**: Ensure that the use of filter aids complies with relevant regulations and standards governing the specific industry and application, particularly in food, pharmaceutical, and water treatment sectors.

By understanding the types, mechanisms of action, benefits, and considerations associated with filter aids, engineers and operators can effectively integrate these substances into filtration processes to achieve superior particle removal and improve the quality of the filtrate.

FILTER MEDIAS

Filter media are materials used in filtration processes to separate solids from fluids (liquids or gases) by retaining the solid particles while allowing the fluid to pass through. The selection of appropriate filter media is crucial for achieving efficient particle removal, optimizing filtration performance, and meeting the specific requirements of diverse applications. Let's explore filter media in detail:

Types of Filter Media:

1. **Depth Filter Media:**

a. Depth filter media consist of thick, porous materials with a complex network of interconnected pores throughout their thickness.
b. Examples include cellulose fibers, cotton, glass fiber, polyester, and polypropylene.
c. Depth filter media capture particles by a combination of mechanisms, including interception, diffusion, inertial impaction, and electrostatic attraction.

2. **Surface Filter Media:**
   a. Surface filter media have a relatively thin layer of closely spaced pores on their surface, which effectively trap particles larger than the pore size.
   b. Examples include filter paper, membranes (microfiltration, ultrafiltration, nanofiltration, and reverse osmosis), and sintered metal filters.
   c. Surface filter media primarily operate through size exclusion, where particles larger than the pore size are retained on the surface while the fluid passes through.

Characteristics of Filter Media:

1. **Pore Size Distribution:**
   a. Filter media are characterized by their pore size distribution, which determines the range of particle sizes that can be retained.
   b. Filter media with uniform pore size distribution are suitable for precise particle removal, while graded pore size distribution can provide depth filtration capabilities.
2. **Porosity and Permeability:**
   a. Porosity refers to the ratio of void volume to total volume in the filter media, while permeability is a measure of the ease with which fluids can flow through the media.

b. Higher porosity and permeability facilitate fluid flow and increase filtration efficiency by reducing resistance to flow.

3. **Surface Area:**

    a. The surface area of the filter media influences its particle retention capacity and filtration efficiency.

    b. High surface area allows for greater contact between the fluid and the filter media, enhancing particle capture and removal.

4. **Material Composition:**

    a. Filter media can be composed of various materials, including natural fibers (e.g., cellulose, cotton), synthetic polymers (e.g., polyester, polypropylene), metals (e.g., stainless steel), and ceramics.

    b. The material composition affects properties such as chemical compatibility, thermal stability, mechanical strength, and resistance to chemical and biological degradation.

Applications of Filter Media:

1. **Water Treatment:**

    a. Filter media are widely used in water treatment processes for removing suspended solids, sediment, microorganisms, and other impurities from raw water sources.

    b. Applications include municipal water treatment, industrial process water filtration, wastewater treatment, and point-of-use filtration for residential and commercial use.

2. **Air Filtration:**

    a. Filter media are employed in air filtration systems to remove particulate matter, dust, allergens, pollutants, and microorganisms from indoor and outdoor air.

b. Applications include HVAC (heating, ventilation, and air conditioning) systems, industrial air filtration, cleanrooms, automotive cabin air filters, and respiratory protection devices.

3. **Pharmaceuticals:**
   a. Filter media play a critical role in pharmaceutical manufacturing for processes such as clarification of solutions, sterilization of liquids, removal of particulates, and isolation of microorganisms.
   b. Applications include sterile filtration of parenteral drugs, bioburden reduction, virus removal, and protein purification.
4. **Food and Beverage Industry:**
   a. Filter media are essential in the food and beverage industry for clarifying juices, wines, beers, and other beverages, removing particles, microbes, and contaminants, and improving product quality and shelf life.
   b. Applications include filtration of sugar syrups, edible oils, dairy products, fruit juices, and alcoholic beverages.

Factors Influencing Filter Media Selection:

1. **Particle Size and Distribution:**
   a. The size and distribution of particles in the fluid determine the pore size requirements of the filter media.
   b. Fine filtration requires filter media with smaller pore sizes to effectively capture smaller particles, while coarse filtration may utilize media with larger pore sizes.
2. **Fluid Properties:**
   a. The properties of the fluid being filtered, including viscosity, temperature, pH, chemical composition, and particulate concentration, influence the selection of filter media.
   b. Compatibility with the fluid is essential to prevent chemical reactions, degradation, or contamination of the filtrate.

3. **Operating Conditions:**
    a. Factors such as flow rate, pressure, temperature, filtration time, and frequency of filter replacement or regeneration affect the performance and longevity of filter media.
    b. Operating conditions should be optimized to ensure efficient particle removal and minimize fouling or clogging of the media.
4. **Regulatory Requirements:**
    a. Compliance with regulatory standards and industry guidelines governing filtration processes, product quality, safety, and environmental protection is essential.
    b. Filter media selection should consider regulatory requirements related to material purity, biocompatibility, extractables, leachables, and product contact surfaces.

CHAPTER – 16

FILTRATION – II

Mrs. Priyanka Soni

Assistant Professor, Rajiv Gandhi Institute of Pharmacy, Faculty of Pharmaceutical Science & Technology, AKS University Satna, MP-India

---

ABSTRACT:

Filtration technologies encompass a diverse array of equipment designed for separating solids from liquids across various industrial applications. The plate and frame filter press is a widely used device consisting of plates and frames arranged alternately with filter medium, typically cloth, where solids are retained while filtrate passes through. This method is effective for high-solids slurries in industries like pharmaceuticals and chemicals. Filter leaves are another common design, featuring a series of vertical metal frames covered with filter media, used for continuous filtration of large volumes in processes such as sugar refining and edible oil production. Rotary drum filters utilize a rotating drum with internal filter media to separate solids from liquids continuously, suitable for wastewater treatment and food processing. Meta filters and cartridge filters employ replaceable filter elements made of materials like metal, polyester, or ceramic, offering flexibility and efficiency in removing contaminants from liquids in diverse applications such as beverage production and electronics manufacturing. Membrane filters, including microfiltration, ultrafiltration, nanofiltration, and reverse osmosis membranes, employ selective barriers to separate particles and solutes based on size and molecular weight, critical for water purification, pharmaceutical processing, and food and beverage production. Seitz filters, developed by Pall Corporation, are specialized depth filters used in the beverage industry to remove yeast and other fine particles during beer and wine clarification processes. Each filtration method and equipment type offers specific advantages in terms of efficiency, throughput, and purity depending on the application requirements. Advances in filtration technology continue to drive improvements in product quality, process efficiency, and sustainability across industries globally, underscoring the critical role of filtration in modern manufacturing and environmental protection initiatives.

PLATE & FRAME FILTER

Plate and frame filters are a type of batch filtration equipment commonly used for solid-liquid separation in various industries. They consist of a series of plates and frames arranged alternately, with filter media (such as filter cloth or filter paper) placed between each plate and frame. The fluid to be filtered is pumped into the chambers formed by the plates and frames, and solids are retained on the filter media while the filtrate passes through. Let's explore the principle, construction, working, uses, merits, and demerits of plate and frame filters in detail:

Principle:

The principle behind plate and frame filtration is based on the combination of depth and surface filtration mechanisms. As the fluid passes through the filter media, particles larger than the pore size of the media are retained, forming a filter cake on the surface. Additionally, some smaller particles may be captured within the pores of the filter media, contributing to depth filtration. The filter cake acts as an additional filtration barrier, improving particle retention and enhancing filtration efficiency.

Construction:

1. **Plates:**
    a. Plates are flat, rigid structures with holes or recesses around the edges to allow the fluid to flow through.

b. Each plate typically has a raised perimeter or a sealing mechanism to create a sealed chamber when stacked together with frames.

2. **Frames:**
    a. Frames are hollow structures that surround the plates and provide support for the filter media.
    b. Frames often have channels or grooves to facilitate the flow of filtrate to collection points.
3. **Filter Media:**
    a. Filter media, such as filter cloth or filter paper, are placed between each plate and frame.
    b. The filter media trap solid particles while allowing the filtrate to pass through.
4. **Closure Mechanism:**
    a. Plate and frame filters are equipped with a closure mechanism, such as hydraulic or manual clamps, to hold the plates and frames together tightly during operation, preventing leakage.

Working:

1. **Assembly:** Plates and frames are assembled alternately with filter media in between to form a stack.
2. **Pre-coating (Optional)**: In some applications, the filter media may be pre-coated with a filter aid to improve particle retention.
3. **Filtration**: The fluid to be filtered is pumped into the chambers formed by the plates and frames.
4. **Particle Retention**: Solid particles are retained on the surface of the filter media, forming a filter cake, while the filtrate passes through.
5. **Discharge**: Once filtration is complete, the filter cake is removed from the filter media, and the filtrate is collected for further processing or disposal.

6. **Cleaning and Maintenance**: The plates and frames are disassembled, and the filter media are cleaned or replaced as needed. The filter cake may be washed or dried for disposal or further processing.

Uses:

Plate and frame filters are utilized in various industries and applications, including:

1. **Chemical Processing**: Separation of solids from chemical suspensions, catalyst recovery, and purification of process streams.
2. **Pharmaceuticals:** Clarification of pharmaceutical solutions, removal of impurities, and sterile filtration of parenteral drugs.
3. **Food and Beverage Industry**: Filtration of beverages, juices, syrups, oils, and food processing liquids to remove solids and improve clarity.
4. **Water Treatment**: Removal of suspended solids, algae, and microorganisms from raw water sources in municipal and industrial water treatment plants.
5. **Oil and Gas**: Filtration of drilling fluids, removal of contaminants from lubricating oils, and purification of hydrocarbon streams.

Merits:

1. **Versatility:** Plate and frame filters can handle a wide range of particle sizes and concentrations, making them suitable for various applications.
2. **Efficiency**: They offer high filtration efficiency and can achieve fine particle removal with proper filter media selection.
3. **Scalability**: Plate and frame filters are available in different sizes and configurations, allowing for scalability to accommodate varying production capacities.
4. **Easy Maintenance**: They are relatively easy to clean and maintain, with removable plates and frames for access to filter media.
5. **Product Quality**: Plate and frame filters produce high-quality filtrate with minimal product loss or contamination.

Demerits:

1. **Batch Operation**: Plate and frame filters operate in batch mode, which may result in longer processing times and lower throughput compared to continuous filtration systems.
2. **Labor Intensive**: Assembly, disassembly, and cleaning of plate and frame filters can be labor-intensive and time-consuming, especially for large units.
3. **Space Requirement**: Plate and frame filters require adequate space for installation and operation, including space for access during maintenance.
4. **Sealing Issues**: Proper sealing is crucial to prevent leakage and ensure efficient filtration, but sealing mechanisms may deteriorate over time and require maintenance.
5. **Filter Media Replacement**: Regular replacement of filter media is necessary to maintain filtration efficiency, adding to operational costs and downtime.

Despite these limitations, plate and frame filters remain widely used in industries where batch filtration is suitable and where high-quality filtrate is essential for product quality and process efficiency. Proper selection, operation, and maintenance are key to maximizing the performance and longevity of plate and frame filtration systems.

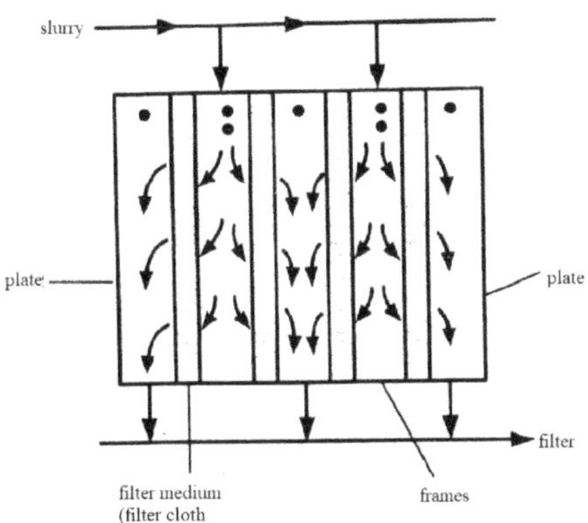

FILTER LEAF FILTER:

Principle:

Filter leaf filters operate on the principle of depth filtration. The fluid to be filtered is pumped into a vessel containing a stack of filter leaves, which are thin, flat, porous structures with filter media. As the fluid passes through the filter media, solid particles are retained on the surface and within the pores of the media, forming a filter cake.

Construction:

1. Filter leaves are typically constructed from a support frame with a filter medium attached, such as filter cloth or filter paper.
2. The leaves are arranged in a vertical stack within a pressure vessel or housing.
3. A manifold system directs the fluid flow through the filter leaves and collects the filtrate.

Working:

1. **Pre-coating (Optional)**: Filter leaves may be pre-coated with a filter aid to improve particle retention.
2. **Filtration**: The fluid is pumped into the vessel, and pressure forces it through the filter leaves.
3. **Particle Retention**: Solid particles are trapped on the surface and within the pores of the filter media, forming a filter cake.
4. **Filtrate Collection**: The filtrate passes through the filter media and is collected in the vessel or directed to a separate outlet.
5. **Cake Removal**: Once filtration is complete, the filter cake is removed from the filter media, typically by backwashing or mechanical scraping.
6. **Cleaning and Maintenance**: The filter leaves may be cleaned or replaced as needed to maintain filtration efficiency.

Uses:

Filter leaf filters are used in various industries and applications, including:

a. Chemical processing
b. Pharmaceutical manufacturing
c. Edible oil refining
d. Beverage production
e. Water and wastewater treatment

Merits:

1. **High Filtration Efficiency**: Filter leaf filters offer high filtration efficiency and can remove fine particles from fluids.
2. **Scalability**: They can be scaled up or down to accommodate different flow rates and production capacities.
3. **Continuous Operation**: Some filter leaf filters can operate continuously, offering higher throughput compared to batch filtration systems.
4. **Versatility:** They can handle a wide range of fluid viscosities and particle sizes.
5. **Low Product Loss**: Filter leaf filters minimize product loss during filtration due to efficient cake formation and removal.

Demerits:

1. **Complex Maintenance**: Cleaning and maintaining filter leaf filters can be complex and time-consuming, especially for large units.
2. **Limited Particle Retention**: The depth filtration mechanism of filter leaf filters may have limitations in retaining very fine particles.
3. **High Initial Cost**: The initial cost of installing filter leaf filters may be higher compared to other filtration systems.
4. **Risk of Filter Media Damage**: Filter leaves are relatively fragile and may be damaged during handling, requiring replacement.

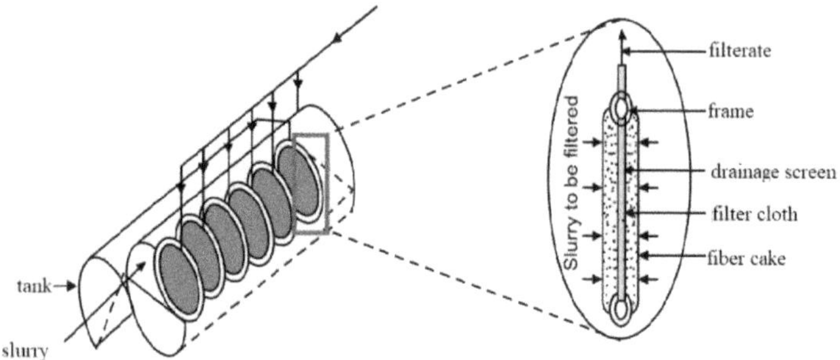

ROTARY DRUM FILTER:

Principle:

Rotary drum filters utilize a rotating drum covered with filter media to separate solids from liquids. As the drum rotates, it partially submerges in the fluid to be filtered, allowing solids to accumulate on the surface of the drum while the filtrate passes through the filter media.

Construction:

- A cylindrical drum with internal partitions and filter media covers its surface.
- The drum is mounted horizontally on a central shaft and rotates continuously.
- A drive mechanism rotates the drum and advances the filter cake through the filtration cycle.

Working:

1. **Submergence:** The drum is partially submerged in the fluid to be filtered, with the filter media facing outward.
2. **Filtration:** As the drum rotates, the fluid flows through the filter media, and solid particles are retained on the surface of the drum, forming a filter cake.
3. **Cake Removal**: As the drum continues to rotate, the filter cake is removed from the surface by a scraper or vacuum system.

4. **Filtrate Collection:** The filtrate passes through the filter media and is collected in a trough or discharged through outlets.
5. **Cleaning and Maintenance**: The filter media may be cleaned or replaced periodically to maintain filtration efficiency.

Uses:

Rotary drum filters find applications in various industries, including:

a. Mining and mineral processing
b. Chemical manufacturing
c. Food and beverage processing
d. Municipal wastewater treatment
e. Environmental remediation

Merits:

1. **Continuous Operation**: Rotary drum filters can operate continuously, offering high throughput and efficiency.
2. **Compact Design**: They have a relatively compact footprint compared to other filtration systems, making them suitable for space-limited installations.
3. **Versatility:** Rotary drum filters can handle a wide range of fluid viscosities, solids concentrations, and particle sizes.
4. **Low Energy Consumption**: They require relatively low energy consumption compared to some other filtration systems.
5. **Automated Operation**: Rotary drum filters can be equipped with automated control systems for efficient operation and maintenance.

Demerits:

1. **Complex Maintenance**: Maintenance of rotary drum filters can be complex, especially for large units, requiring periodic cleaning and replacement of filter media.

2. **Risk of Mechanical Failure:** Mechanical components such as the drive system and scraper may be prone to wear and require regular inspection and maintenance.
3. **High Initial Cost**: The initial cost of installing rotary drum filters may be higher compared to batch filtration systems.
4. **Limited Particle Retention**: The depth filtration mechanism of rotary drum filters may have limitations in retaining very fine particles.
5. **Risk of Filter Media Damage**: The filter media on the drum's surface may be damaged during operation or cleaning, requiring replacement.

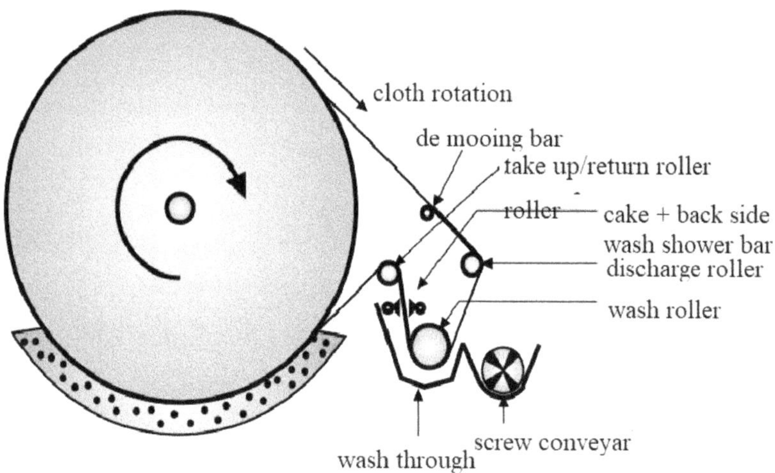

META FILTER:

Principle:

Meta filters operate on the principle of depth filtration, where the fluid to be filtered passes through a porous filter medium. The filter medium captures solid particles based on various mechanisms, including interception, diffusion, and inertial impaction.

Construction:

1. **Filter Medium**: Meta filters use a porous material, such as sintered metal, ceramic, or composite materials, as the filter medium.
2. **Support Structure**: The filter medium is typically supported by a metal or plastic housing, which provides structural support and facilitates fluid flow.

Working:

1. **Filtration**: The fluid to be filtered is passed through the meta filter, allowing solid particles to be captured within the pores or on the surface of the filter medium.
2. **Particle Retention**: Solid particles are retained by the filter medium based on mechanisms such as interception, diffusion, and inertial impaction.
3. **Filtrate Collection**: The filtrate, free of solid particles, passes through the filter medium and is collected for further processing or disposal.

Uses:

Meta filters find applications in various industries, including:

1. **Chemical Processing**: Filtration of chemical suspensions, catalyst recovery, and purification of process streams.
2. **Oil and Gas**: Filtration of drilling fluids, removal of contaminants from lubricating oils, and purification of hydrocarbon streams.
3. **Water Treatment**: Filtration of industrial process water, municipal wastewater, and drinking water to remove suspended solids and impurities.
4. **Pharmaceuticals:** Clarification of pharmaceutical solutions, removal of impurities, and sterile filtration of parenteral drugs.

Merits:

1. **High Temperature and Pressure Resistance**: Meta filters are capable of operating under high temperature and pressure conditions, making them suitable for demanding applications.
2. **Chemical Compatibility**: They are compatible with a wide range of chemicals and fluids, including corrosive and abrasive substances.
3. **Long Service Life**: Meta filters have a long service life and are resistant to degradation, providing reliable filtration performance over time.
4. **High Filtration Efficiency**: They offer high filtration efficiency and can remove fine particles from fluids effectively.
5. **Easy Cleaning and Maintenance**: Meta filters are relatively easy to clean and maintain, with some types being reusable after cleaning.

Demerits:

1. **High Initial Cost:** Meta filters may have a higher initial cost compared to some other filtration systems due to the specialized materials and manufacturing processes involved.
2. **Limited Flexibility**: Meta filters may have limited flexibility in terms of pore size and filtration capacity, depending on the specific material and design.
3. **Potential for Clogging**: Depending on the application, meta filters may be prone to clogging, especially when filtering fluids with high solids concentrations or viscous fluids.
4. **Risk of Damage**: Meta filters may be susceptible to damage from mechanical stress or impact, requiring careful handling and maintenance.

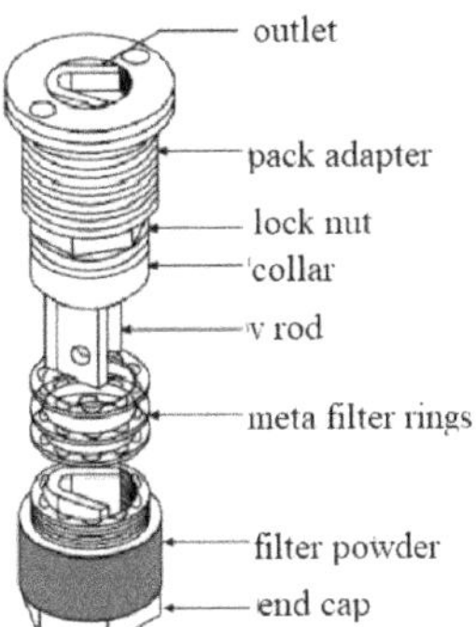

CARTRIDGE FILTER:

Principle:

Cartridge filters operate on the principle of surface filtration, where the fluid to be filtered passes through a filter medium with a defined pore size. Solid particles larger than the pore size are retained on the surface of the filter medium, while the filtrate passes through.

Construction:

1. **Filter Medium**: Cartridge filters use a cylindrical or pleated filter medium made of materials such as paper, polyester, polypropylene, or cellulose.
2. **End Caps**: The filter medium is attached to end caps made of plastic or metal, which provide structural support and sealing.
3. **Outer Casing**: The cartridge filter is housed within an outer casing, which may be made of plastic, metal, or other materials.

Working:

1. **Filtration:** The fluid to be filtered is passed through the cartridge filter, allowing solid particles larger than the pore size to be retained on the surface of the filter medium.
2. **Particle Retention**: Solid particles are captured on the surface of the filter medium as the fluid passes through, forming a filter cake.

3. **Filtrate Collection**: The filtrate, free of solid particles, passes through the filter medium and is collected for further processing or disposal.

Uses:

Cartridge filters have a wide range of applications, including:

1. **Water Filtration**: Filtration of drinking water, process water, and wastewater in residential, commercial, and industrial settings.
2. **HVAC Systems**: Filtration of air in heating, ventilation, and air conditioning (HVAC) systems to remove dust, pollen, and other airborne particles.
3. **Food and Beverage Processing**: Clarification of beverages, filtration of cooking oils, and removal of particulates from food processing liquids.
4. **Pharmaceuticals**: Sterile filtration of pharmaceutical solutions, purification of process streams, and removal of impurities from drug formulations.

Merits:

1. **Wide Range of Pore Sizes**: Cartridge filters are available in a wide range of pore sizes, allowing for precise filtration tailored to specific applications.
2. **Ease of Installation**: They are easy to install and replace, with standardized dimensions and fittings.
3. **Compact Design**: Cartridge filters have a compact design, making them suitable for installations with limited space.
4. **Low Initial Cost**: They generally have a lower initial cost compared to some other filtration systems, making them cost-effective for many applications.
5. **High Filtration Efficiency**: Cartridge filters offer high filtration efficiency and can remove a wide range of solid particles from fluids effectively.

Demerits:

1. **Limited Capacity**: Cartridge filters may have limited filtration capacity compared to some other filtration systems, requiring more frequent replacement.
2. **Risk of Clogging**: Depending on the application, cartridge filters may be prone to clogging, especially when filtering fluids with high solids concentrations.
3. **Disposable Design**: Some cartridge filters are designed for single-use and must be disposed of after reaching their capacity, contributing to waste generation.
4. **Potential for Bypass**: Improper installation or damage to the cartridge filter may result in fluid bypass, reducing filtration efficiency.

Both Meta filters and Cartridge filters offer unique advantages and are suitable for different applications based on their specific characteristics, capabilities, and performance requirements. Careful consideration of the application, operating conditions, and filtration objectives is essential for selecting the most appropriate filter type.

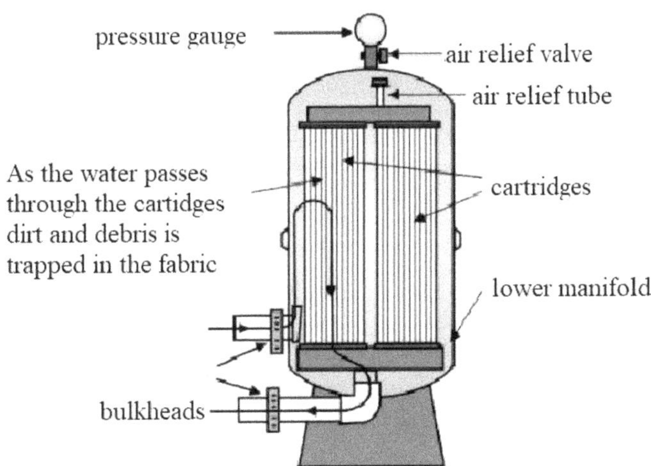

MEMBRANE FILTERS:

Principle:

Membrane filters operate on the principle of size exclusion, where solid particles larger than the pore size of the membrane are retained, while smaller particles and the filtrate pass through. Membrane filtration relies on a semi-permeable membrane with precise pore sizes to separate particles from fluids based on their size and molecular weight.

Construction:

1. **Membrane Material**: Membrane filters are made from materials such as cellulose acetate, polyethersulfone (PES), polyvinylidene difluoride (PVDF), nylon, or mixed esters of cellulose.
2. **Pore Structure**: The membrane has a defined pore structure, with pore sizes ranging from nanometers to micrometers, depending on the application.
3. **Support Structure**: The membrane may be supported by a porous backing material or a support grid to provide mechanical strength and stability.

Working:

1. **Filtration:** The fluid to be filtered is applied to the surface of the membrane filter.
2. **Particle Retention**: Solid particles larger than the pore size of the membrane are retained on the surface or within the pores, forming a filter cake.
3. **Filtrate Collection**: The filtrate, containing particles smaller than the pore size, passes through the membrane and is collected for further processing or disposal.

Uses:

Membrane filters have a wide range of applications, including:

1. **Biopharmaceuticals:** Sterile filtration of pharmaceutical solutions, purification of biologics, and removal of microorganisms from drug formulations.
2. **Water Treatment**: Removal of bacteria, viruses, and particulate matter from drinking water, process water, and wastewater.
3. **Food and Beverage Processing**: Clarification of beverages, removal of microorganisms, and concentration of liquids in the food and beverage industry.
4. **Microelectronic**s: Filtration of ultrapure water and chemicals in semiconductor manufacturing and microelectronics industries.

Merits:

1. **High Filtration Efficiency**: Membrane filters offer high filtration efficiency and can remove particles down to sub-micron sizes.
2. **Precise Pore Sizes**: Membrane filters are available with precise pore sizes, allowing for accurate particle retention tailored to specific applications.
3. **Sterile Filtration**: Some membrane filters are capable of sterile filtration, ensuring the removal of microorganisms and maintaining product integrity.
4. **Chemical Compatibility**: They are compatible with a wide range of chemicals and fluids, making them suitable for diverse applications.

Demerits:

1. **High Operating Pressure**: Membrane filtration may require high operating pressures to overcome resistance and achieve adequate filtration rates.
2. **Limited Flux:** Flux rates (filtration flow rates) may decrease over time due to fouling or clogging of the membrane pores.

3. **Potential for Membrane Fouling**: Membrane filters may be prone to fouling, especially when filtering fluids with high solids concentrations or colloidal suspensions.
4. **Cost:** Membrane filters may have higher initial costs compared to some other filtration systems, particularly for membranes with specialized materials or pore structures.

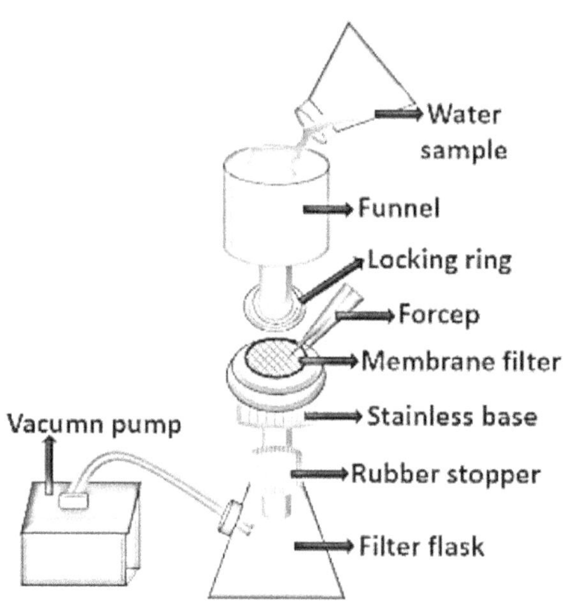

SEITZ FILTER:

Principle:

Seitz filters, also known as plate and frame filters, operate on the principle of depth filtration. They consist of a series of plates and frames arranged alternately, with filter media (such as filter cloth or filter paper) placed between each plate and frame. The fluid to be filtered is pumped into the chambers formed by the plates and frames, and solids are retained on the filter media while the filtrate passes through.

Construction:

1. **Plates and Frames**: Seitz filters comprise flat, rigid plates and frames made of materials such as stainless steel or plastic.
2. **Filter Medium**: Filter media, such as filter cloth or filter paper, are placed between each plate and frame to capture solid particles during filtration.
3. **Closure Mechanism**: Seitz filters are equipped with a closure mechanism, such as hydraulic or manual clamps, to hold the plates and frames together tightly during operation, preventing leakage.

Working:

1. **Assembly**: Plates and frames are assembled alternately with filter media in between to form a stack.
2. **Filtration**: The fluid to be filtered is pumped into the chambers formed by the plates and frames.
3. **Particle Retention**: Solid particles are retained on the surface of the filter media, forming a filter cake, while the filtrate passes through.
4. **Discharge**: Once filtration is complete, the filter cake is removed from the filter media, and the filtrate is collected for further processing or disposal.
5. **Cleaning and Maintenance**: The plates and frames are disassembled, and the filter media are cleaned or replaced as needed. The filter cake may be washed or dried for disposal or further processing.

Uses:

Seitz filters find applications in various industries and applications, including:

1. **Chemical Processing**: Separation of solids from chemical suspensions, catalyst recovery, and purification of process streams.
2. **Pharmaceuticals:** Clarification of pharmaceutical solutions, removal of impurities, and sterile filtration of parenteral drugs.

3. **Food and Beverage Industry**: Filtration of beverages, juices, syrups, oils, and food processing liquids to remove solids and improve clarity.
4. **Water Treatment**: Removal of suspended solids, algae, and microorganisms from raw water sources in municipal and industrial water treatment plants.

Merits:

1. **Versatility:** Seitz filters can handle a wide range of particle sizes and concentrations, making them suitable for various applications.
2. **Efficiency**: They offer high filtration efficiency and can achieve fine particle removal with proper filter media selection.
3. **Scalability:** Seitz filters are available in different sizes and configurations, allowing for scalability to accommodate varying production capacities.
4. **Easy Maintenance**: They are relatively easy to clean and maintain, with removable plates and frames for access to filter media.

Demerits:

1. **Batch Operation**: Seitz filters operate in batch mode, which may result in longer processing times and lower throughput compared to continuous filtration systems.
2. **Labor Intensive**: Assembly, disassembly, and cleaning of Seitz filters can be labor-intensive and time-consuming, especially for large units.
3. **Space Requirement**: Seitz filters require adequate space for installation and operation, including space for access during maintenance.
4. **Sealing Issues**: Proper sealing is crucial to prevent leakage and ensure efficient filtration, but sealing mechanisms may deteriorate over time and require maintenance.
5. **Filter Media Replacement**: Regular replacement of filter media is necessary to maintain filtration efficiency, adding to operational costs and downtime.

Both membrane filters and Seitz filters offer unique advantages and are suitable for different applications based on their specific characteristics, capabilities, and performance requirements. Careful consideration of the application, operating conditions, and filtration objectives is essential for selecting the most appropriate filter type.

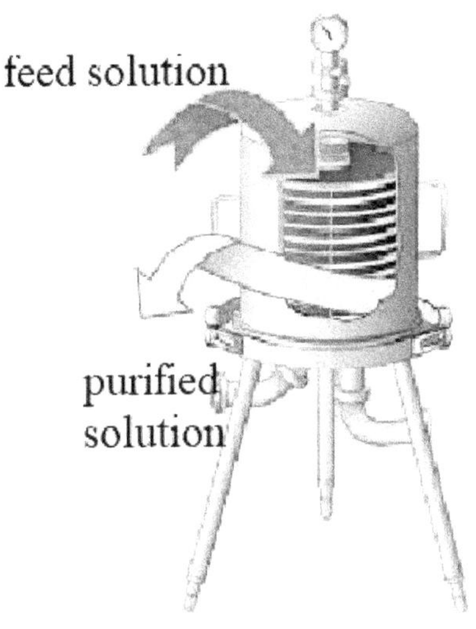

CHAPTER – 17

CENTRIFUGATION – I

Mr. Prabhanshu Vaishya

Assistant Professor, Rajiv Gandhi Institute of Pharmacy, Faculty of Pharmaceutical Science & Technology, AKS University Satna, MP-India

---

ABSTRACT:

Centrifugation is a technique used for separating components of heterogeneous mixtures based on their densities in a rotating container, called a centrifuge. This method applies centrifugal force to rapidly spin the mixture, causing denser particles or components to migrate away from the axis of rotation and settle at the bottom of the container. Centrifugation finds widespread applications in various industries, including biology, chemistry, medicine, and food processing. There are several types of centrifuges designed for specific applications. High-speed or ultracentrifuges operate at very high speeds, often using rotor speeds in excess of 100,000 revolutions per minute (rpm). These are used for separating subcellular components, studying molecular structures, and purifying biomolecules like proteins and DNA. Refrigerated centrifuges include cooling systems to maintain low temperatures during operation, crucial for preserving sample integrity in biochemical and clinical applications. Benchtop centrifuges are smaller and more compact, suitable for routine laboratory tasks such as separating blood components, isolating DNA, or processing small volumes of samples. Industrial centrifuges, such as decanter centrifuges and disk-stack centrifuges, are employed in large-scale applications for processes like wastewater treatment, oil refining, and chemical manufacturing. These machines handle high volumes of material and are designed for continuous operation under demanding conditions.

Centrifugation is preferred for its rapid processing, efficiency in separating particles based on density differences, and versatility across a wide range of industries. Advances in centrifuge technology continue to enhance performance, reliability, and automation, contributing to advancements in research, diagnostics, and industrial processes globally.

INTRODUCTION

Centrifugation is a widely used technique in science and industry to separate particles from a suspension based on their size, shape, density, and viscosity differences. It works on the principle of sedimentation, where denser particles settle faster under the influence of a centrifugal force.

Here's a detailed introduction to centrifugation:

Principle of Centrifugation:

Centrifugation exploits the principle of sedimentation, which is the gravitational force acting on particles in a liquid medium. When a mixture is subjected to centrifugal force, particles with higher density or larger mass experience a greater centrifugal force and sediment more quickly than lighter particles. This process causes the particles to separate based on their sedimentation rate.

Components of a Centrifuge:

1. **Rotor**: This is the central part of a centrifuge where the samples are placed. Rotors come in various sizes and designs to accommodate different sample volumes and types.
2. **Centrifuge Tubes or Bottles**: These are containers that hold the samples during centrifugation. They come in different sizes and materials depending on the application.
3. **Drive System**: The drive system is responsible for rotating the rotor at high speeds to generate the centrifugal force required for sedimentation.
4. **Control Panel**: Centrifuges have control panels where users can set parameters such as speed, time, and temperature for the centrifugation process.

Types of Centrifuges:

1. **Microcentrifuges**: These are small, benchtop centrifuges used for processing small volumes of samples, typically in the range of micro- to milliliters. They are commonly used in molecular biology and biochemistry applications.
2. **Refrigerated Centrifuges**: These centrifuges have built-in cooling systems to maintain low temperatures during centrifugation. They are used for applications where temperature-sensitive samples need to be processed.
3. **Ultracentrifuges**: These are high-speed centrifuges capable of generating extremely high centrifugal forces. They are used for applications such as separating subcellular components, studying macromolecules, and determining molecular weights of large molecules.
4. **Preparative Centrifuges**: Preparative centrifuges are used for large-scale separations and purification of biomolecules, cells, and organelles.

Centrifugation Techniques:

1. **Differential Centrifugation**: This technique involves multiple rounds of centrifugation at increasing speeds to separate particles based on their sedimentation rates. It's often used to isolate subcellular components such as organelles from cell lysates.
2. **Density Gradient Centrifugation**: In this technique, a density gradient medium (such as sucrose or cesium chloride) is formed in the centrifuge tube. When the sample is centrifuged, particles migrate through the medium until they reach a position where their density matches that of the surrounding medium. This technique is used for separating particles with similar densities, such as purifying viruses or isolating cellular components based on buoyant density.
3. **Isopycnic Centrifugation**: Also known as equilibrium density gradient centrifugation, this technique involves centrifuging samples in a density

gradient until the particles reach equilibrium, settling at positions where their density matches that of the gradient medium. It's particularly useful for separating particles solely based on density.

Applications of Centrifugation:

1. **Cell Biology**: Centrifugation is widely used to isolate organelles, separate cellular components, and purify biomolecules such as proteins, nucleic acids, and lipids.
2. **Microbiology**: In microbiology, centrifugation is used to concentrate microorganisms from liquid cultures, separate bacterial and viral particles, and purify biomolecules.
3. **Clinical Diagnostics**: Centrifugation plays a crucial role in clinical diagnostics for separating blood components (e.g., red blood cells, white blood cells, platelets) and isolating pathogens or biomarkers from biological samples.
4. **Industrial Applications**: Centrifugation is used in various industrial processes, including wastewater treatment, food processing, pharmaceutical manufacturing, and chemical production, for separating particles, purifying products, and clarifying liquids.

OBJECTIVES, PRINCIPLE & APPLICATIONS OF CENTRIFUGATION

Objectives of Centrifugation:

The objectives of centrifugation encompass a range of goals aimed at separating, purifying, concentrating, and fractionating particles or substances within a mixture. Here are the detailed objectives:

1. Separation:

Centrifugation aims to separate components within a heterogeneous mixture based on their different physical properties such as size, shape, density, and viscosity. By subjecting the mixture to centrifugal force, denser particles sediment more rapidly than lighter particles, leading to their separation.

2. Purification:

Another key objective is to purify substances by isolating them from impurities or other components in the mixture. Centrifugation facilitates the removal of unwanted particles, contaminants, or undesired phases, resulting in a purified product.

3. Concentration:

Centrifugation helps concentrate particles or solutes in a solution by increasing their density or reducing their volume. This concentration step is essential for further analysis, processing, or characterization of the concentrated material.

4. Fractionation:

Centrifugation allows for the fractionation of complex mixtures into distinct components or fractions based on their physical properties. By adjusting centrifugation parameters such as speed, time, and temperature, different fractions can be separated for specific purposes or analyses.

5. Clarification:

Centrifugation is employed to clarify liquids by removing suspended solids, impurities, or other particulate matter. This objective is common in industries such as food processing, pharmaceuticals, and wastewater treatment, where clear liquids are desired for further processing or consumption.

6. Isolation of Substances:

Centrifugation facilitates the isolation of specific substances or components from a mixture, such as organelles from cell lysates in biological research, viruses from culture supernatants in virology, or nanoparticles from colloidal suspensions in material science.

7. Dewatering:

In applications involving sludges, slurries, or industrial wastewater, centrifugation is used for dewatering by separating water from solid particles. This objective is crucial for reducing the volume and weight of waste materials, facilitating disposal or further treatment.

8. Particle Size Classification:

Centrifugation can be utilized for particle size classification, separating particles into different fractions based on their size and density. This objective is important in industries such as mining, environmental science, and particle technology for analyzing particle size distributions and controlling product quality.

9. Analysis and Characterization:

Centrifugation is often employed as a preparatory step for subsequent analytical or characterization techniques. By separating and concentrating target components, centrifugation enables more accurate and sensitive analysis using methods such as spectroscopy, chromatography, microscopy, and mass spectrometry.

10. Industrial Processing:

Centrifugation plays a crucial role in various industrial processes, including chemical manufacturing, biotechnology, food and beverage production, and pharmaceutical development. Its objectives in these contexts include product purification, separation of reaction components, and optimization of production efficiency.

Principle of Centrifugation:

The principle of centrifugation is based on the concept of sedimentation, where particles in a suspension settle under the influence of gravity. Centrifugation enhances this process by subjecting the mixture to a centrifugal force, which is generated by rotating the sample at high speeds. This force causes denser particles to sediment more rapidly than lighter particles, leading to their separation.

Detailed Explanation of the Principle:

1. **Centrifugal Force:**

a. When a sample is placed in a centrifuge and spun rapidly, it experiences a centrifugal force directed radially outward from the axis of rotation.
b. This force is proportional to the mass of the particle and the square of the angular velocity (rotational speed) of the centrifuge.

b. **Sedimentation:**
   a. The centrifugal force causes particles in the sample to move away from the axis of rotation, similar to the effect of gravity in sedimentation.
   b. Denser particles experience a greater centrifugal force and sediment more rapidly than lighter particles.

c. **Buoyant Force:**
   a. As particles sediment, they encounter resistance from the surrounding medium, resulting in a buoyant force acting in the opposite direction to the centrifugal force.
   b. The equilibrium between the centrifugal force and the buoyant force determines the position at which particles settle within the sample.

d. **Separation:**
   a. By adjusting the rotational speed and duration of centrifugation, it is possible to achieve the separation of particles based on their density, size, shape, and other physical properties.
   b. Denser particles settle closer to the bottom of the centrifuge tube or container, while lighter particles remain suspended or settle at higher positions.

Factors Affecting Centrifugation:

1. **Rotational Speed:**
   a. Increasing the rotational speed of the centrifuge results in higher centrifugal forces, leading to faster sedimentation of particles.

2. **Sample Density:**

   Particles with higher density sediment more rapidly than those with lower **density under the same centrifugal force.**

3. **Particle Size:**

   Larger particles sediment more quickly than smaller particles due to their greater mass and inertia.

4. **Viscosity of the Medium:**

   The viscosity of the medium affects the resistance encountered by particles during sedimentation, influencing the rate of separation.

Applications of Centrifugation based on Principle:

1. **Separation of Components:**

   Centrifugation is used to separate components within heterogeneous mixtures, such as isolating cells from culture media or separating blood components.

2. **Purification:**

   It facilitates the purification of biomolecules, such as proteins and nucleic acids, by separating them from contaminants or other components.

3. **Concentration:**

   Centrifugation concentrates particles or solutes in a solution, enabling the analysis or processing of concentrated samples.

4. **Fractionation:**

   It fractionates complex mixtures into distinct components or fractions for further analysis or characterization.

5. **Dewatering:**

   Centrifugation is utilized for dewatering sludges, slurries, and industrial wastewater by separating water from solid particles.

6. **Analytical Techniques:**

Centrifugation is a preparatory step for various analytical techniques, including spectroscopy, chromatography, and microscopy, by concentrating and separating target components.

Applications of Centrifugation:

Centrifugation finds extensive applications across various fields due to its ability to separate, purify, concentrate, and fractionate components within heterogeneous mixtures. Here are detailed applications of centrifugation:

1. Biochemistry and Molecular Biology:

a. **Isolation of Biomolecules**: Centrifugation is used to isolate biomolecules such as proteins, nucleic acids, and lipids from complex biological samples.

b. **Subcellular Fractionation**: It facilitates the isolation of subcellular components (organelles) for studying cellular structures and functions.

c. **Cell Lysis**: Centrifugation is employed for cell lysis and subsequent separation of cellular debris from the lysate.

2. Clinical Diagnostics:

a. **Blood Component Separation**: Centrifugation separates blood components (red blood cells, white blood cells, platelets, and plasma) for diagnostic purposes and blood banking.

b. **Pathogen Detection**: It aids in the detection and isolation of pathogens (e.g., viruses, bacteria) from clinical specimens such as blood, urine, and cerebrospinal fluid.

c. **Biomarker Analysis**: Centrifugation concentrates biomarkers from bodily fluids (e.g., serum, urine) for diagnostic tests and disease monitoring.

3. Microbiology:

a. **Culture Enrichment**: Centrifugation concentrates microorganisms from culture media for downstream analysis or inoculation.

b. **Viral Purification**: It is used to purify viruses from infected cell cultures for vaccine production and virology research.

c. **Microbial Cell Harvesting**: Centrifugation harvests microbial cells from fermentation broth in bioprocessing and biomanufacturing.

4. Environmental Science:

a. **Wastewater Treatment**: Centrifugation removes solids and sludge from wastewater for treatment and disposal.

b. **Pollutant Analysis**: It concentrates pollutants from environmental samples (e.g., soil, water) for analysis and monitoring.

c. **Environmental Remediation**: Centrifugation separates contaminants from soil or sediment in remediation projects.

5. Pharmaceutical and Biotechnology:

a. **Drug Discovery**: Centrifugation purifies target proteins, enzymes, and drug candidates for pharmaceutical research and development.

b. **Bioprocessing**: It is used in downstream processing of biopharmaceuticals, including cell harvesting, clarification, and purification.

c. **Vaccine Production**: Centrifugation concentrates and purifies vaccine antigens and viral vectors for vaccine manufacturing.

6. Food and Beverage Industry:

a. **Juice Clarification**: Centrifugation clarifies fruit juices by separating pulp and solid particles from the liquid phase.

b. **Brewing and Winemaking**: It separates solids (e.g., yeast, proteins) from beer and wine during fermentation and maturation processes.

c. **Edible Oil Production**: Centrifugation separates oil from solids and water in oilseed processing for edible oil production.

7. Chemistry and Material Sciences:

a. **Particle Size Classification**: Centrifugation fractionates particles based on size and density, aiding in nanoparticle synthesis and material characterization.
b. **Nanomaterial Purification**: It purifies nanoparticles and nanomaterials from colloidal suspensions for research and industrial applications.
c. **Chemical Synthesis**: Centrifugation separates reaction components and purifies chemical products in synthetic chemistry.

8. Forensic Science:

a. **Sample Preparation**: Centrifugation is used for sample preparation in forensic DNA analysis, such as isolating DNA from biological samples (e.g., blood, saliva, hair).
b. **Toxicology**: It aids in the extraction and purification of toxic substances from forensic samples for toxicological analysis and evidence processing.

9. Oil and Gas Industry:

a. **Drilling Fluid Management**: Centrifugation separates solids and contaminants from drilling mud and drilling fluid systems in oil and gas exploration.
b. **Produced Water Treatment**: It removes oil, solids, and contaminants from produced water for reuse or disposal in oil and gas production operations.

10. Academic and Research Laboratories:

a. **Sample Preparation**: Centrifugation is a common technique for sample preparation in various research disciplines, including chemistry, biology, physics, and engineering.
b. **Isotope Separation**: Ultracentrifugation is used for isotope separation in nuclear research and isotopic labeling studies.

Centrifugation's versatility and wide-ranging applications make it a fundamental technique in scientific research, industrial processes, and diagnostic methodologies across diverse fields. Its ability to manipulate and separate components within complex mixtures contributes significantly to advancements in various disciplines.

PERFORATED BASKET CENTRIFUGE

Principles of Perforated Basket Centrifuge:

The principle of a perforated basket centrifuge is rooted in the fundamental concepts of sedimentation and centrifugal force. This type of centrifuge is designed to separate solid particles from a liquid suspension by exploiting the differences in density between the particles and the liquid. Here's a detailed explanation of the principle of a perforated basket centrifuge:

1. Sedimentation:

a. Sedimentation is the process by which particles settle under the influence of gravity when placed in a liquid medium.

b. In a centrifuge, sedimentation is accelerated by applying centrifugal force, which effectively increases the gravitational force acting on the particles.

2. Centrifugal Force:

a. When the perforated basket centrifuge rotates at high speeds, it generates centrifugal force, which is directed radially outward from the axis of rotation.

b. This centrifugal force acts on the particles in the liquid suspension, causing them to move away from the axis of rotation towards the outer wall of the centrifuge basket.

3. Particle Separation:

a. As the centrifuge spins, denser particles in the suspension experience a greater centrifugal force and sediment more rapidly than lighter particles.

b. The perforated basket of the centrifuge serves as a containment vessel, holding the mixture while allowing the liquid phase to pass through the perforations.

4. Liquid Drainage:

a. The centrifugal force drives the liquid phase through the perforations in the basket, allowing it to exit the centrifuge and collect in a separate container.

b. Meanwhile, the denser solid particles accumulate against the inner wall of the basket, forming a compact cake or sediment layer.

5. Solid Discharge:

a. Once centrifugation is complete, the solid particles retained in the perforated basket can be discharged manually or through automated mechanisms.

b. The separated solid phase may require further processing or analysis depending on the application.

6. Continuous Operation:

a. Perforated basket centrifuges are often designed for continuous operation, allowing for continuous feeding of the suspension and continuous discharge of separated components.

b. This feature enables high-throughput processing of materials in industrial applications.

7. Optimization of Parameters:

a. The efficiency of a perforated basket centrifuge depends on various factors such as rotational speed, particle size distribution, and liquid viscosity.

b. Optimal centrifugation parameters are determined based on the specific characteristics of the suspension and the desired separation outcome.

8. Versatility:

a. Perforated basket centrifuges are versatile tools that can handle a wide range of materials, including slurries, pastes, and viscous liquids.

b. They find applications in industries such as chemical processing, pharmaceuticals, food and beverage, wastewater treatment, and more.

Construction of Perforated Basket Centrifuge:

1. **Basket:** The central component of the centrifuge is the perforated basket, typically made of stainless steel or other corrosion-resistant materials. The basket contains perforations or holes of varying sizes, allowing the passage of liquid while retaining solid particles.
2. **Drive System**: The centrifuge is equipped with a motor and drive mechanism that rotates the perforated basket at high speeds to generate centrifugal force.
3. **Housing:** The centrifuge housing encloses the perforated basket and collects the separated components. It may include features such as drainage ports for the liquid phase and discharge mechanisms for the solid phase.
4. **Control Panel**: Modern centrifuges are equipped with control panels for setting parameters such as rotational speed, acceleration, and centrifugation time.

Working of Perforated Basket Centrifuge:

1. **Loading:** The mixture to be separated is loaded into the perforated basket of the centrifuge.
2. **Acceleration**: The centrifuge is started, and the rotational speed is gradually increased, subjecting the mixture to increasing centrifugal force.
3. **Separation**: As the centrifuge spins, denser particles sediment against the basket wall due to centrifugal force, while the liquid phase passes through the perforations and collects in the centrifuge housing.
4. **Discharge:** Once the centrifugation process is complete, the separated components are discharged. The solid particles retained in the basket are typically removed manually, while the liquid phase is drained from the centrifuge housing.

Uses of Perforated Basket Centrifuge:

1. **Solid-Liquid Separation**: It is commonly used for separating solid particles from liquid suspensions in various industries such as chemical, pharmaceutical, and food processing.
2. **Dewatering**: Perforated basket centrifuges are employed for dewatering sludges, slurries, and industrial wastewater by separating water from solid particles.
3. **Clarification**: They are used for clarifying liquids by removing suspended solids or impurities, thus improving product quality.
4. **Size Classification**: Perforated basket centrifuges can also be used for size classification of particles, separating them into different fractions based on their size and density.

Merits of Perforated Basket Centrifuge:

1. **High Efficiency**: Perforated basket centrifuges offer high separation efficiency, making them suitable for a wide range of applications.
2. **Continuous Operation**: They can be operated continuously, allowing for large-scale processing of materials.
3. **Versatility:** Perforated basket centrifuges can handle a variety of materials, including slurries, pastes, and viscous liquids.
4. **Low Maintenance**: They are relatively easy to maintain and clean, with fewer moving parts compared to other types of centrifuges.

Demerits of Perforated Basket Centrifuge:

1. **Limited Particle Size Range**: The effectiveness of perforated basket centrifuges may be limited for particles below a certain size range.
2. **Potential Damage to Fragile Particles**: Fragile particles may be damaged during centrifugation due to the high centrifugal forces involved.
3. **Prone to Clogging**: The perforations in the basket may become clogged with fine particles or debris, requiring frequent cleaning and maintenance.

4. **Limited Separation Efficiency for Small Density Differences**: Perforated basket centrifuges may have limited separation efficiency for materials with small density differences or similar buoyant densities.

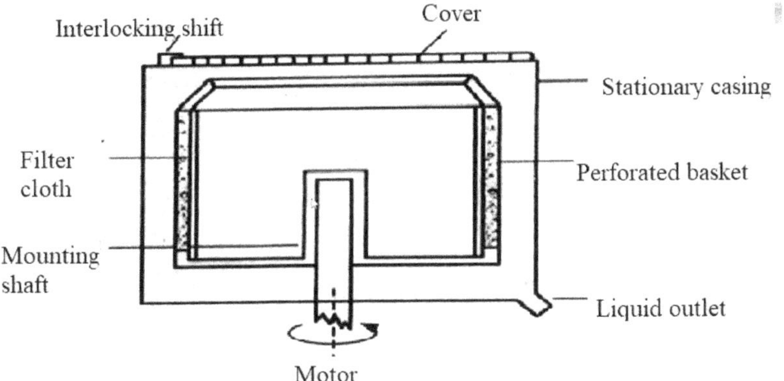

CHAPTER – 18

CENTRIFUGATION – II

Mr. Santosh Kumar

Assistant Professor, Rajiv Gandhi Institute of Pharmacy, Faculty of Pharmaceutical Science & Technology, AKS University Satna, MP-India

----

ABSTRACT:

Centrifugation encompasses a range of specialized equipment tailored for diverse industrial and scientific applications. The non-perforated basket centrifuge, also known as a solid bowl centrifuge, features a solid, impermeable basket that retains solids while allowing liquids to pass through. This type of centrifuge is ideal for separating solids from liquids in applications such as chemical processing, pharmaceutical manufacturing, and wastewater treatment, where high solids recovery and purity are crucial. Semi-continuous centrifuges operate continuously, feeding and discharging materials intermittently. They are employed in industries requiring continuous processing with intermittent product discharge, such as pharmaceuticals, food processing, and mining. This design allows for efficient separation of materials while maintaining continuous operation. Super centrifuges, often referred to as ultracentrifuges, are high-speed centrifuges capable of achieving rotor speeds exceeding 100,000 rpm. They are used in research and biotechnology for separating and purifying biomolecules like proteins, DNA, and viruses based on their sedimentation rates. Ultracentrifugation enables precise separation of particles down to the nanoscale, facilitating advanced studies in molecular biology and materials science. Each type of centrifuge—whether solid bowl, semi-continuous, or ultracentrifuge—offers distinct advantages depending on the specific application requirements, such as throughput, separation efficiency, and scalability. Advances in centrifuge technology continue to expand their capabilities in various industries, driving innovations in product development, research, and process optimization worldwide.

NON-PERFORATED BASKET CENTRIFUGE

Principles of Non-Perforated Basket Centrifuge:

A non-perforated basket centrifuge operates on the same fundamental principles as a perforated basket centrifuge, utilizing centrifugal force to separate components based on their densities. However, instead of relying on perforations for liquid drainage, non-perforated basket centrifuges use a solid basket or liner to contain the mixture during centrifugation. The separation occurs as denser particles are forced outward by centrifugal force, while the liquid phase migrates inward and collects in the center of the basket.

Construction of Non-Perforated Basket Centrifuge:

1. **Basket or Liner:** The central component is a solid basket or liner made of materials such as stainless steel, which holds the mixture during centrifugation without perforations.
2. **Drive System**: Similar to other centrifuges, it includes a motor and drive mechanism to rotate the basket at high speeds.
3. **Housing**: The centrifuge housing encloses the basket and collects the separated components, with features for draining the liquid phase and discharging the solid phase.
4. **Control Panel**: It includes controls for setting parameters such as rotational speed, acceleration, and centrifugation time.

Working of Non-Perforated Basket Centrifuge:

1. **Loading**: The mixture to be separated is loaded into the non-perforated basket or liner of the centrifuge.
2. **Acceleration**: The centrifuge is started, and the rotational speed is gradually increased, subjecting the mixture to increasing centrifugal force.

3. **Separation:** Denser particles migrate outward and accumulate against the basket wall, forming a solid cake, while the liquid phase migrates inward and collects in the center of the basket.
4. **Discharge:** Once centrifugation is complete, the separated components are discharged. The solid cake is typically removed manually, while the liquid phase is drained from the centrifuge housing.

Uses of Non-Perforated Basket Centrifuge:

1. **Solid-Liquid Separation**: It is widely used for separating solid particles from liquid suspensions, particularly in industries such as chemical processing, pharmaceuticals, and wastewater treatment.
2. **Dewatering:** Non-perforated basket centrifuges are utilized for dewatering sludges, slurries, and industrial wastewater by removing water from solid particles.
3. **Clarificatio**n: They are employed for clarifying liquids by removing suspended solids or impurities, improving product quality.
4. **Centrifugal Filtration**: Non-perforated basket centrifuges can also be used for centrifugal filtration, separating particles from a liquid phase using a filter medium within the basket.

Merits of Non-Perforated Basket Centrifuge:

1. **High Separation Efficiency**: Non-perforated basket centrifuges offer high separation efficiency, making them suitable for a wide range of applications.
2. **Versatility**: They can handle various materials, including abrasive or corrosive substances, due to their solid construction.
3. **Continuous Operation**: Non-perforated basket centrifuges can be operated continuously, facilitating large-scale processing of materials.
4. **Reduced Risk of Basket Clogging**: Unlike perforated basket centrifuges, there is no risk of basket clogging with non-perforated designs, simplifying maintenance.

Demerits of Non-Perforated Basket Centrifuge:

1. **Manual Cake Discharge**: Removing the solid cake from the basket typically requires manual intervention, which can be labor-intensive and time-consuming.
2. **Potential Damage to Fragile Particles**: Fragile particles may be damaged during centrifugation due to the high centrifugal forces involved.
3. **Limited Particle Size Range**: The effectiveness of non-perforated basket centrifuges may be limited for particles below a certain size range.
4. **Higher Initial Cost**: Non-perforated basket centrifuges may have a higher initial cost compared to other centrifuge designs due to their solid construction.

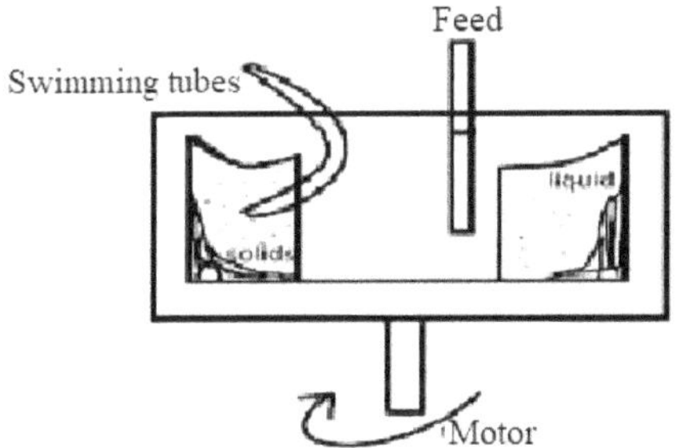

SEMI CONTINUOUS CENTRIFUGE

Principles of Semi-Continuous Centrifuge:

A semi-continuous centrifuge combines features of both batch and continuous centrifuges. It operates on the principles of sedimentation and centrifugal force, similar to other centrifuges, but it allows for continuous feeding of the mixture and continuous discharge of separated components. This allows for a more efficient and continuous separation process compared to batch centrifuges.

Construction of Semi-Continuous Centrifuge:

1. **Rotating Drum or Bowl**: The central component is a rotating drum or bowl, typically made of stainless steel or other corrosion-resistant materials, where the mixture is fed continuously.
2. **Feed System**: Semi-continuous centrifuges are equipped with a feed system that continuously delivers the mixture into the rotating drum or bowl.
3. **Discharge System**: They also feature a discharge system for continuous removal of separated components, such as a scroll or conveyor mechanism.
4. **Drive System**: Like other centrifuges, semi-continuous centrifuges have a motor and drive mechanism to rotate the drum or bowl at high speeds.

Working of Semi-Continuous Centrifuge:

1. **Continuous Feeding**: The mixture to be separated is continuously fed into the rotating drum or bowl through the feed system.
2. **Acceleration:** As the mixture enters the centrifuge, it is subjected to centrifugal force due to the high-speed rotation of the drum or bowl.
3. **Separation**: Denser particles migrate outward and accumulate against the drum or bowl wall, forming a solid cake, while the liquid phase migrates inward and collects in the center.
4. **Continuous Discharge**: Separated components are continuously discharged from the centrifuge using the discharge system, allowing for uninterrupted operation.

Uses of Semi-Continuous Centrifuge:

1. **Continuous Solid-Liquid Separation**: They are widely used for continuous separation of solid particles from liquid suspensions in various industries, including chemical processing, pharmaceuticals, and wastewater treatment.

2. **Continuous Dewatering**: Semi-continuous centrifuges are employed for continuous dewatering of sludges, slurries, and industrial wastewater by removing water from solid particles.
3. **Continuous Clarification**: They are utilized for continuous clarification of liquids by removing suspended solids or impurities, improving product quality.
4. **Continuous Filtration**: Semi-continuous centrifuges can also be used for continuous centrifugal filtration, separating particles from a liquid phase using a filter medium within the centrifuge.

Merits of Semi-Continuous Centrifuge:

1. **Continuous Operation**: Semi-continuous centrifuges offer continuous operation, allowing for efficient and uninterrupted processing of materials.
2. **High Separation Efficiency**: They provide high separation efficiency and throughput compared to batch centrifuges.
3. **Versatility**: Semi-continuous centrifuges can handle a wide range of materials and applications due to their continuous operation and flexible design.
4. **Reduced Labor Requirements:** Continuous feeding and discharge systems reduce the need for manual intervention, leading to lower labor requirements.

Demerits of Semi-Continuous Centrifuge:

1. **Complex Design:** Semi-continuous centrifuges may have a more complex design compared to batch centrifuges, leading to higher initial costs and maintenance requirements.
2. **Higher Energy Consumption**: Continuous operation may result in higher energy consumption compared to batch centrifuges, especially for processes with varying feed compositions.

3. **Potential for Process Upsets**: Continuous operation increases the risk of process upsets or equipment failures affecting the entire process, requiring careful monitoring and control.
4. **Limited Flexibility**: Semi-continuous centrifuges may have limited flexibility in handling changes in feed composition or operating conditions compared to batch centrifuges.

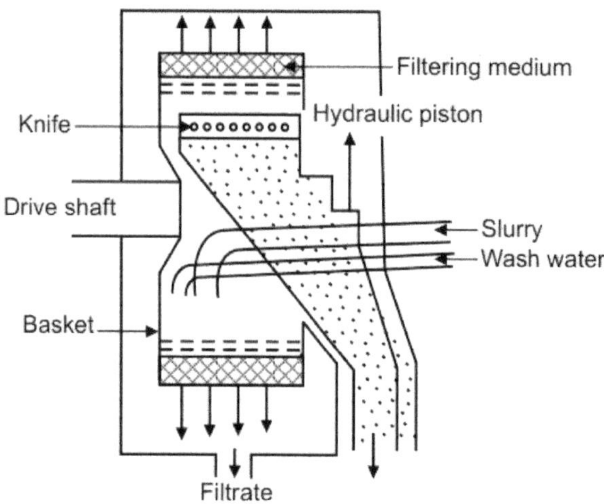

SUPER CENTRIFUGE

Principles of Super Centrifuge:

A super centrifuge, also known as an ultracentrifuge, operates on the principles of sedimentation and centrifugal force, but it is capable of generating much higher centrifugal forces compared to conventional centrifuges. This allows for the separation of particles with very small density or size differences and enables the study of macromolecules, nanoparticles, and subcellular structures with high resolution.

Construction of Super Centrifuge:

1. **Rotor:** The central component is a rotor, typically made of materials such as titanium or carbon fiber, which holds the samples during

centrifugation. The rotor is designed to withstand high speeds and generate extremely high centrifugal forces.

2. **Drive System**: Super centrifuges are equipped with powerful motors and drive mechanisms capable of rotating the rotor at speeds exceeding tens of thousands of revolutions per minute (RPM).
3. **Control Panel**: They feature sophisticated control panels for setting parameters such as rotational speed, acceleration, temperature, and centrifugation time.
4. **Safety Features**: Due to the high speeds and forces involved, super centrifuges incorporate advanced safety features such as automatic rotor imbalance detection, rotor over-speed protection, and containment systems to prevent accidents.

Working of Super Centrifuge:

1. **Sample Loading**: Samples are loaded into specialized centrifuge tubes or rotors designed for use with the super centrifuge.
2. **Acceleration**: The centrifuge is started, and the rotational speed is gradually increased to reach the desired speed, subjecting the samples to extremely high centrifugal forces.
3. **Separation:** As the rotor spins at high speeds, particles in the samples sediment based on their density and size differences. Ultra-high centrifugal forces allow for the separation of particles with exceptional resolution.
4. **Data Collection**: Super centrifuges are often equipped with sensors and detectors for real-time monitoring of parameters such as sedimentation rate, allowing for precise control and data collection during centrifugation.

Uses of Super Centrifuge:

1. **Biological Research:** Super centrifuges are extensively used in molecular biology, biochemistry, and cell biology for isolating subcellular

components, studying macromolecules such as proteins and nucleic acids, and determining molecular weights of biomolecules.

2. **Material Science**: They are employed in material science research for characterizing nanoparticles, studying colloidal systems, and synthesizing nanomaterials with precise control over particle size and distribution.
3. **Pharmaceutical Development**: Super centrifuges play a crucial role in drug discovery and development for purifying recombinant proteins, isolating viruses and viral vectors, and studying drug interactions with biomolecules.
4. **Chemical Analysis**: They are used in analytical chemistry for separating and quantifying analytes in complex mixtures, such as separating isotopes and studying molecular interactions.
5. **Environmental Monitoring**: Super centrifuges are utilized in environmental science for analyzing pollutants, studying sedimentation processes in aquatic ecosystems, and purifying water samples for analysis.

Merits of Super Centrifuge:

1. **High Resolution**: Super centrifuges offer exceptional resolution and separation efficiency, allowing for the study of particles with very small density or size differences.
2. **Versatility**: They are versatile tools suitable for a wide range of applications in biological, chemical, and material sciences.
3. **Precise Control**: Super centrifuges provide precise control over centrifugation parameters, enabling researchers to manipulate and study complex systems with high precision.
4. **Data-rich Results**: Real-time monitoring and data collection capabilities provide researchers with detailed insights into centrifugation processes and sample characteristics.

Demerits of Super Centrifuge:

1. **High Cost**: Super centrifuges are expensive to purchase and maintain due to their advanced technology, specialized materials, and precision engineering.
2. **Complex Operation**: Operating and maintaining super centrifuges requires specialized training and expertise due to the high speeds and forces involved.
3. **Sample Limitations**: Some samples may not withstand the extreme conditions generated by super centrifuges, limiting their applicability in certain cases.
4. **Safety Concerns**: Due to the high speeds and forces, there are inherent safety risks associated with super centrifuges, necessitating strict safety protocols and precautions.

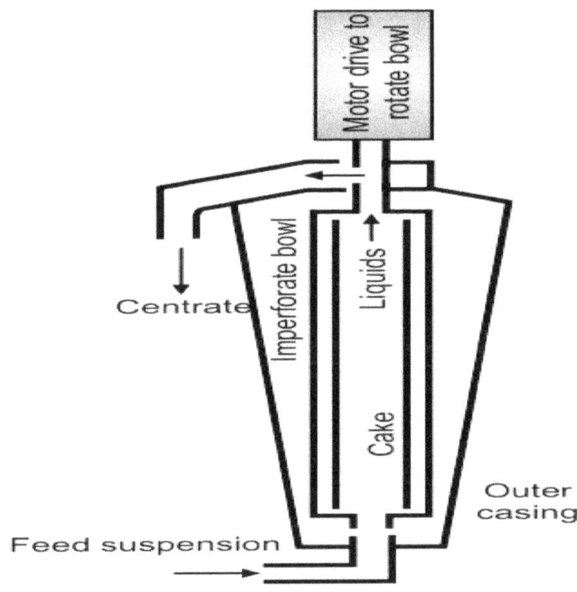

CHAPTER – 19

MATERIALS OF PHARMACEUTICAL PLANT CONSTRUCTION, CORROSION AND ITS PREVENT – I

Mr. Ram Prasad Sahu

Assistant Professor, Rajiv Gandhi Institute of Pharmacy, Faculty of Pharmaceutical Science & Technology, AKS University Satna, MP-India

---

ABSTRACT:

Materials used in pharmaceutical plant construction must meet stringent requirements to ensure safety, hygiene, and compliance with regulatory standards. Stainless steel, particularly grades like 316L, is widely favored due to its excellent corrosion resistance, durability, and ease of cleaning. These qualities make it suitable for equipment such as tanks, piping, and vessels that handle pharmaceutical ingredients and products. Corrosion, a significant concern in pharmaceutical plants, can compromise product quality and pose contamination risks. It occurs when metal surfaces react with chemicals, moisture, or process fluids, leading to deterioration, metal leaching, and potential product contamination. Preventing corrosion involves selecting appropriate materials, surface treatments, and maintenance practices. Preventive measures include using corrosion-resistant alloys like Hastelloy and titanium for handling corrosive chemicals or high-temperature applications. Protective coatings and linings, such as epoxy coatings or glass linings, provide an additional barrier against corrosion for equipment and piping. Regular inspection and maintenance programs, including cleaning procedures and monitoring corrosion rates, help identify and address potential issues before they escalate. Design considerations, such as minimizing crevices and dead spaces where fluids can stagnate, also contribute to corrosion prevention by reducing the accumulation of corrosive agents. Proper material selection, coupled with stringent cleaning and maintenance protocols, ensures pharmaceutical plants operate efficiently and safely, maintaining product integrity and regulatory compliance. Innovations in materials science continue to advance corrosion-resistant materials and protective coatings, enhancing their performance and durability in pharmaceutical manufacturing environments. These advancements play a crucial role in supporting the pharmaceutical industry's commitment to producing safe, effective, and high-quality medications for global healthcare needs.

INTRODUCTION

Materials used in pharmaceutical plant construction must meet stringent requirements to ensure product purity, maintain sanitation standards, and comply with regulatory guidelines. Here's an introduction to materials commonly used and the prevention of corrosion:

Materials Used in Pharmaceutical Plant Construction:

1. **Stainless Steel**: Preferred due to its corrosion resistance, durability, and ease of cleaning. Grades such as 316L, 304, and 316Ti are commonly used. Stainless steel resists corrosion from most chemicals used in pharmaceutical manufacturing processes.
2. **Glass**: Utilized for vessels and equipment requiring visibility or inert surfaces. Borosilicate glass is the most common type used due to its resistance to thermal shock and chemical corrosion.
3. **Plastics**: Certain plastics like polyethylene (PE), polypropylene (PP), and polytetrafluoroethylene (PTFE) are employed in non-critical applications due to their inertness, low cost, and ease of fabrication.
4. **Coatings**: Epoxy coatings are applied to surfaces to enhance resistance to corrosion and facilitate cleaning. They are used in areas where stainless steel alone may not provide adequate protection against corrosion.

Corrosion and Its Prevention:

Corrosion in pharmaceutical plant equipment and infrastructure can lead to contamination of products, equipment failure, and safety hazards. Preventive measures include:

1. **Material Selection**: Choose materials with high corrosion resistance appropriate for the specific chemicals and conditions present in the process. Stainless steel is often the material of choice due to its resistance to corrosion from most pharmaceutical process fluids.
2. **Surface Finish**: Smooth surfaces with minimal imperfections reduce areas where corrosion can initiate and facilitate cleaning, preventing buildup of contaminants that can accelerate corrosion.
3. **Passivation:** Stainless steel surfaces are often passivated to enhance their corrosion resistance. Passivation involves treating the surface with an acid solution to remove impurities and promote the formation of a protective oxide layer.
4. **Proper Design:** Design equipment and infrastructure to minimize stagnant areas where fluids can accumulate and promote corrosion. Proper drainage, sloping surfaces, and avoiding crevices can reduce the risk of corrosion.
5. **Monitoring and Maintenance**: Regular inspection and maintenance of equipment and infrastructure are essential to identify corrosion early and take corrective actions. Monitoring corrosion rates and conditions can help in predicting potential failures and planning maintenance activities.
6. **Chemical Inhibition**: In some cases, adding corrosion inhibitors to process fluids can help mitigate corrosion. These inhibitors form protective films on metal surfaces, reducing the rate of corrosion.
7. **Cathodic Protection**: This method involves connecting the metal to be protected to a sacrificial anode, such as zinc or magnesium, which

corrodes instead of the protected metal. Cathodic protection is often used for buried pipelines and underground structures.

FACTORS AFFECTING DURING MATERIALS SELECTED FOR PHARMACEUTICAL PLANT CONSTRUCTION

Factors Affecting Material Selection:

Material selection in pharmaceutical plant construction is influenced by various factors to ensure compliance with regulatory standards, maintain product quality, and ensure operational efficiency. Let's explore these factors in detail:

1. Chemical Compatibility:

a. **Description:** Materials must be compatible with the chemicals used in pharmaceutical processes to prevent contamination and ensure product purity.

b. **Factors to Consider**:

I. **Chemical Resistance**: Assess the resistance of materials to acids, alkalis, solvents, and other chemicals used in the process.

II. **Compatibility Charts**: Refer to compatibility charts and chemical resistance data to determine the suitability of materials for specific chemicals.

2. Corrosion Resistance:

a. **Description:** Materials must withstand exposure to corrosive substances commonly found in pharmaceutical processes to prevent equipment degradation and contamination.

b. **Factors to Consider**:

I. **Corrosion Rates**: Evaluate the corrosion resistance of materials under the operating conditions of the pharmaceutical plant.

II. **Environment:** Consider factors such as temperature, humidity, and chemical exposure that may affect corrosion rates.

3. Sanitary Requirements:

a. **Description**: Pharmaceutical manufacturing environments demand materials that are easy to clean and sanitize to prevent microbial contamination.

b. **Factors to Consider**:

   I. **Surface Finish**: Select materials with smooth surfaces and minimal crevices to facilitate cleaning and prevent bacterial growth.

   II. **Regulatory Compliance**: Ensure materials comply with regulatory standards such as Good Manufacturing Practices (GMP) regarding cleanliness and sanitation.

4. Mechanical Properties:

a. **Descriptio**n: Materials must possess adequate mechanical strength, durability, and dimensional stability to withstand the stresses and strains encountered during operation.

b. **Factors to Consider**:

   I. **Strength**: Assess the tensile strength, yield strength, and hardness of materials to ensure they can withstand mechanical loads.

   II. **Temperature Resistance**: Consider the temperature range at which materials maintain their mechanical properties without deformation or degradation.

5. Thermal Properties:

a. **Description:** Materials must be capable of withstanding the temperature variations encountered during pharmaceutical processes without deformation or degradation.

b. **Factors to Consider**:

   I. **Thermal Conductivity**: Evaluate the thermal conductivity and heat resistance of materials to ensure they can handle temperature fluctuations.

II. **Thermal Expansion**: Consider the coefficient of thermal expansion to minimize the risk of dimensional changes and thermal stresses.

6. Regulatory Compliance:

a. **Description**: Materials used in pharmaceutical plant construction must comply with regulatory standards such as FDA regulations and GMP guidelines.

b. **Factors to Consider:**

I. **Material Certification**: Ensure materials are certified for use in pharmaceutical applications and comply with relevant standards and regulations.

II. **Documentation**: Maintain documentation of material specifications, certifications, and regulatory compliance for auditing purposes.

7. Cost and Availability:

a. **Description**: Material selection must balance performance requirements with cost-effectiveness and availability.

b. **Factors to Consider:**

I. **Cost Analysis**: Evaluate the lifecycle costs of materials, including initial purchase cost, maintenance, and replacement expenses.

II. **Availability:** Consider the availability of materials from suppliers and potential supply chain disruptions.

8. Environmental Impact:

a. **Description:** Consider the environmental impact of materials, including their sustainability, recyclability, and potential hazards.

b. **Factors to Consider:**

I. **Environmental Footprint**: Assess the environmental footprint of materials, including energy consumption, emissions, and waste generation.

II. **Recyclability:** Choose materials that are recyclable or biodegradable to minimize environmental impact and comply with sustainability goals.

Factors Affecting Corrosion Prevention:

1.Chemical Compatibility:

a. **Description**: Corrosion prevention begins with selecting materials that are compatible with the chemicals present in pharmaceutical processes.

b. **Factors to Consider:**

I. **Chemical Resistance**: Choose materials that are resistant to corrosion from acids, alkalis, solvents, and other chemicals used in the process.

II. **Compatibility Testing**: Conduct compatibility testing to ensure the selected materials can withstand exposure to process fluids without undergoing corrosion.

2. Environmental Conditions:

a. **Description:** The operating environment of the pharmaceutical plant, including temperature, humidity, and chemical exposure, can influence corrosion rates.

b. **Factors to Consider:**

I. **Temperature and Humidity**: Consider the effects of temperature variations and humidity levels on corrosion rates and select materials accordingly.

II. **Chemical Exposure**: Assess the concentration and type of chemicals present in the environment to determine the level of corrosion protection required for materials.

3. Surface Preparation:

a. **Description: Proper** surface preparation is essential for enhancing the corrosion resistance of materials and promoting the formation of protective oxide layers.

b. **Factors to Consider:**

   I. **Cleaning**: Ensure surfaces are thoroughly cleaned to remove contaminants and debris that can accelerate corrosion.

   II. **Passivation:** Treat metal surfaces with passivation treatments to remove surface impurities and promote the formation of a protective oxide layer.

4. Material Composition:

a. **Description**: The composition of materials, including alloying elements and impurities, can influence their corrosion resistance.

b. **Factors to Consider:**

   I. **Alloy Selection**: Choose materials with alloy compositions that enhance corrosion resistance, such as stainless steel grades with added chromium, nickel, or molybdenum.

   II. Impurity Control: Minimize the presence of impurities in materials that can compromise their corrosion resistance, such as sulfur or phosphorus in steel.

5. Design Considerations:

a. **Description**: Proper design of equipment and infrastructure can minimize corrosion risk by reducing stagnant areas and promoting fluid drainage.

b. **Factors to Consider**:

   I. **Avoidance of Crevices**: Design equipment with smooth surfaces and avoid crevices or dead spaces where fluids can accumulate and promote corrosion.

   II. **Proper Ventilation**: Ensure adequate ventilation to prevent the buildup of corrosive gases and fumes that can accelerate corrosion.

6. Protective Coatings and Linings:

a. **Description**: Applying protective coatings or linings to metal surfaces can provide an additional barrier against corrosion.

b. **Factors to Consider:**

I. **Coating Selection**: Choose coatings that are compatible with the operating environment and provide effective corrosion protection.

II. **Application Method**: Ensure proper application of coatings to achieve uniform coverage and adhesion to metal surfaces.

7. Maintenance Practices:

a. **Description**: Regular inspection and maintenance of equipment and infrastructure are essential for identifying and addressing corrosion issues before they escalate.

b. **Factors to Consider:**

I. **Inspection Schedule**: Implement regular inspection schedules to detect corrosion early and take corrective actions.

II. **Cleaning and Repairs**: Perform routine cleaning and maintenance to remove corrosion products and repair damaged or corroded surfaces promptly.

8. Regulatory Compliance:

a. **Description:** Compliance with regulatory standards and guidelines is critical for ensuring the safety, quality, and integrity of pharmaceutical products.

b. **Factors to Consider:**

I. **Regulatory Requirements**: Ensure corrosion prevention measures comply with relevant regulatory standards, such as FDA regulations and GMP guidelines.

II. **Documentation**: Maintain documentation of corrosion prevention practices and inspections for regulatory compliance and auditing purposes.

THEORIES OF CORROSION

Understanding the theories of corrosion is essential for effective prevention and mitigation strategies in pharmaceutical plant construction. Here are the key theories of corrosion and their implications for corrosion prevention:

1. Electrochemical Theory:

The electrochemical theory of corrosion provides a fundamental understanding of how corrosion occurs at a molecular level. It describes corrosion as an electrochemical process involving two main reactions: oxidation and reduction. This theory helps in developing effective corrosion prevention strategies and materials selection criteria. Let's delve into the details:

1. Anodic Reaction (Oxidation):

a. **Description**: The anodic reaction involves the dissolution of metal atoms into the electrolyte solution, resulting in the formation of positively charged metal ions.

b. **Equation**: The general equation for the anodic reaction is represented as follows:

c. Metal→Metal ions+Electrons

d. Metal→Metal ions+ElectronsFor example, in the case of iron corrosion (rusting), the anodic reaction can be represented as:

e. $Fe \rightarrow Fe2++2e-$

f. **Process**: At the anode (corroding metal surface), metal atoms lose electrons and enter the electrolyte solution as positively charged ions. This process is facilitated by the presence of corrosive agents such as acids or oxygen.

2. Cathodic Reaction (Reduction):

a. **Description:** The cathodic reaction involves the reduction of species present in the electrolyte, typically oxygen or hydrogen ions, consuming electrons in the process.

b. **Equation:** The general equation for the cathodic reaction is represented as follows:

c. Oxygen/Hydrogen ions+Electrons→Water/Hydrogen gas

d. Oxygen/Hydrogen ions+Electrons→Water/Hydrogen gasFor example, the cathodic reaction involving oxygen reduction can be represented as:

e. $O_2+4H^++4e^-\rightarrow 2H_2O$

f. **Process**: At the cathode (typically a metallic surface or an electrode), oxygen or hydrogen ions present in the electrolyte gain electrons and react to form water or hydrogen gas, respectively.

3. Overall Corrosion Process:

a. **Description:** Corrosion occurs as a result of the simultaneous occurrence of the anodic and cathodic reactions, coupled with the flow of electrons through an external circuit.

b. **Electrochemical Cell**: The corrosion process can be described as an electrochemical cell, with the metal surface acting as the anode and the electrolyte as the cathode. The flow of electrons from the anode to the cathode through the external circuit completes the corrosion cell.

Implications and Prevention:

1. **Cathodic Protection:**
   a. **Description**: Cathodic protection methods involve supplying electrons to the metal surface to counteract the anodic corrosion reaction.
   b. **Methods**: Techniques include sacrificial anode systems (e.g., zinc or magnesium) and impressed current systems.
2. **Corrosion Inhibitors:**
   a. **Description**: Corrosion inhibitors are chemicals added to the electrolyte solution to reduce the rate of corrosion by inhibiting either the anodic or cathodic reactions.
   b. **Types**: Inhibitors can be organic or inorganic compounds that form protective films on metal surfaces or alter the electrochemical properties of the solution.
3. **Material Selection:**

a. **Description**: Understanding the electrochemical behavior of materials is crucial for selecting corrosion-resistant materials for specific applications.
b. **Selection Criteria**: Materials with passive oxide layers (e.g., stainless steel) or inherent corrosion resistance are preferred for environments where corrosion is a concern.

The electrochemical theory of corrosion provides a fundamental understanding of how corrosion occurs at a molecular level. It describes corrosion as an electrochemical process involving two main reactions: oxidation and reduction. This theory helps in developing effective corrosion prevention strategies and materials selection criteria. Let's delve into the details:

2. Pourbaix Diagrams:

a. **Description**: Pourbaix diagrams, also known as potential-pH diagrams, illustrate the thermodynamic stability regions of different chemical species in aqueous solutions as a function of pH and electrode potential.
b. **Purpose:** They provide valuable insights into the corrosion behavior of metals by indicating the conditions under which a metal will corrode, passivate, or remain stable in a given environment.
c. **Components:**
   I. **pH**: Represents the acidity or alkalinity of the solution.
   II. **Electrode Potential (Voltage)**: Indicates the tendency of a metal to undergo oxidation or reduction reactions.
   III. **Species Stability Regions**: Different regions on the diagram represent the stability of various chemical species (e.g., metal ions, oxides, hydroxides) at specific pH and potential values.
d. **Interpretation:**
   I. **Stable Regions**: Materials are thermodynamically stable in regions where their corresponding species are predominant.

II. **Passivation**: Passivation occurs when a protective oxide layer forms on the metal surface, shifting the potential to a more noble (positive) value.

III. **Corrosion**: Corrosion occurs when the metal is in a region where its soluble species (e.g., metal ions) are stable, leading to dissolution.

e. Application:

I. Engineers and materials scientists use Pourbaix diagrams to predict the corrosion behavior of metals in various environments and select appropriate materials for specific applications.

II. They aid in designing corrosion-resistant alloys and protective coatings by understanding the conditions that promote passivation or corrosion.

3. Uniform Corrosion:

a. **Description:** Uniform corrosion is a type of corrosion characterized by the even dissolution of metal over the entire exposed surface, resulting in a uniform loss of material thickness.

b. Mechanism:

I. **Electrochemical Process**: It occurs via electrochemical reactions where metal atoms are oxidized (anodic reaction) and dissolve into the electrolyte, while electrons flow through the metal to a cathodic site where reduction reactions occur.

II. **Uniformity:** Uniform corrosion occurs uniformly across the entire surface exposed to the corrosive environment.

c. Causes:

I. **Homogeneous Environment**: Uniform corrosion typically occurs in environments where the corrosive agents are evenly distributed, leading to uniform attack on the metal surface.

II. **Constant Conditions**: Uniform corrosion may occur under stable conditions where factors such as temperature, humidity, and chemical composition remain relatively constant.

d. **Effects:**

I. **Material Loss**: Uniform corrosion leads to a gradual loss of material thickness, which can compromise the structural integrity of components over time.

II. **Reduced Lifespan: If** left unchecked, uniform corrosion can lead to premature failure of equipment and structures, resulting in safety hazards and costly repairs.

e. **Prevention:**

I. **Material Selection**: Choose corrosion-resistant materials appropriate for the specific environment and application.

II. **Protective Coatings**: Apply coatings or surface treatments to create a barrier between the metal surface and the corrosive environment.

III. **Control Environmental Factors**: Maintain optimal environmental conditions and implement corrosion monitoring programs to detect and address corrosion issues early.

Pourbaix diagrams provide insights into the conditions under which uniform corrosion is likely to occur by indicating the stability of metal species in different environments. Understanding these diagrams helps in selecting materials and implementing corrosion prevention strategies effectively. Additionally, knowledge of uniform corrosion mechanisms aids in designing structures and equipment to mitigate its effects.

4. Localized Corrosion:

a. **Description:** Localized corrosion refers to corrosion that occurs selectively at specific sites on a metal surface, leading to the formation of localized damage such as pitting, crevice corrosion, or stress corrosion cracking.

b. Types:

I. **Pitting Corrosion**: Characterized by the formation of small pits or craters on the metal surface due to localized attack.

II. **Crevice Corrosion**: Occurs in narrow gaps or crevices where stagnant solutions can form, leading to accelerated corrosion.

III. **Stress Corrosion Cracking (SCC)**: Results from the combined action of tensile stress and corrosive environments, leading to crack initiation and propagation.

c. Mechanism:

I. **Initiation**: Localized corrosion often begins at sites where the protective oxide layer on the metal surface is compromised or where the environment promotes localized attack.

II. **Propagation**: Once initiated, corrosion can propagate rapidly within the localized area, leading to deeper penetration and structural damage.

d. Causes:

I. **Microenvironments:** Localized corrosion occurs in regions where there are variations in the chemical composition, pH, or oxygen concentration, creating microenvironments conducive to corrosion.

II. **Shielding Effects**: Certain geometrical features, such as crevices or surface defects, can shield parts of the metal surface from the bulk solution, promoting localized attack.

III. **Mechanical Stress**: Stress corrosion cracking occurs in materials subjected to tensile stress in combination with a corrosive environment, leading to crack initiation and propagation.

e. **Effects:**

   I. **Structural Damage**: Localized corrosion can result in severe damage to metal components, compromising their structural integrity and functionality.

   II. **Failure Risk**: The presence of localized corrosion increases the risk of sudden failure, especially in critical components such as pipelines, tanks, or structural elements.

f. **Prevention:**

   I. **Material Selection**: Choose materials with high resistance to localized corrosion, such as stainless steels with added alloying elements or corrosion-resistant alloys.

   II. **Surface Finish**: Ensure smooth surfaces and minimize surface defects to reduce the likelihood of localized corrosion initiation.

   III. **Environmental Control**: Maintain uniform environmental conditions and avoid stagnant solutions to minimize the risk of localized corrosion.

5. Environmental Effects:

a. **Description**: Environmental factors such as temperature, humidity, chemical composition, and atmospheric pollutants can influence the rate and mechanism of corrosion.

b. **Temperature and Humidity:**

   I. **Effect:** Higher temperatures and humidity levels can accelerate corrosion rates by promoting chemical reactions and increasing the availability of corrosive agents.

   II. **Mitigation:** Implement temperature and humidity control measures to maintain optimal conditions and minimize corrosion rates.

c. **Chemical Composition:**

I. **Effect:** The presence of aggressive chemicals such as acids, alkalis, chlorides, or sulfides can significantly increase corrosion rates and promote localized attack.

II. **Mitigation**: Choose materials resistant to the specific chemicals present in the environment and implement corrosion prevention strategies such as protective coatings or inhibitors.

d. Atmospheric Pollutants:

I. **Effect**: Atmospheric pollutants such as sulfur dioxide, nitrogen oxides, or industrial emissions can react with moisture in the air to form corrosive agents, accelerating metal degradation.

II. **Mitigation:** Implement pollution control measures and protective coatings to minimize the impact of atmospheric pollutants on metal surfaces.

e. Microbial Activity:

I. **Effect**: Microorganisms present in the environment can promote corrosion by producing corrosive by-products or altering the local chemical composition.

II. **Mitigation:** Implement measures to control microbial growth and activity, such as biocides or regular cleaning and sanitation protocols.

Microbial corrosion, also known as microbiologically influenced corrosion (MIC), is a type of corrosion caused or accelerated by the presence and activity of microorganisms. Let's explore microbial corrosion in detail as part of the theories of corrosion:

1. Mechanisms of Microbial Corrosion:

Microbial corrosion involves complex interactions between microorganisms, metals, and the surrounding environment. Several mechanisms contribute to microbial corrosion:

a. **Electrochemical Processes**: Microorganisms can facilitate electrochemical reactions on metal surfaces, accelerating corrosion processes. They can act as catalysts, promoting the transfer of electrons between the metal surface and corrosive agents in the environment.
b. **Biogenic Agents**: Certain microorganisms produce corrosive by-products such as organic acids, hydrogen sulfide (H_2S), ammonia (NH_3), or sulfuric acid (H_2SO_4) through metabolic processes. These by-products can directly attack metal surfaces and promote corrosion.
c. **Biofilm Formation**: Microorganisms often form biofilms on metal surfaces, creating a protective environment that traps corrosive agents and promotes localized corrosion. Biofilms provide a conducive environment for microbial growth and metabolic activities, exacerbating corrosion processes.
d. **Localized Attack**: Microbial corrosion tends to occur in localized areas where microbial activity is concentrated or where biofilms form. This localized attack can lead to pitting, crevice corrosion, or stress corrosion cracking.

2. Factors Influencing Microbial Corrosion:

Several factors influence the occurrence and severity of microbial corrosion:

a. **Microbial Community**: The composition and diversity of microbial communities present in the environment can affect the types and rates of corrosion. Different microorganisms produce varying corrosive by-products and metabolic activities.
b. **Environmental Conditions**: Factors such as temperature, pH, humidity, oxygen concentration, and nutrient availability influence microbial growth and metabolic activity, thereby affecting corrosion rates.
c. **Metal Properties**: The composition, surface characteristics, and corrosion resistance of metals influence their susceptibility to microbial corrosion. Some metals are more resistant to microbial attack than others.

d. **Fluid Dynamics**: Fluid flow patterns and turbulence can influence the distribution of microorganisms and corrosive agents on metal surfaces, affecting the localization and severity of corrosion.
e. **Presence of Nutrients**: Microorganisms require nutrients such as carbon, nitrogen, and phosphorus for growth and metabolism. The availability of nutrients in the environment can impact microbial activity and corrosion rates.

3. Prevention and Control:

Preventing microbial corrosion requires a multi-faceted approach that addresses both the microbial factors and the environmental conditions conducive to corrosion:

a. **Biocide Treatment**: Applying biocides or antimicrobial agents can help control microbial growth and activity in industrial systems, reducing the risk of microbial corrosion.
b. **Materials Selection**: Choosing corrosion-resistant materials and coatings that are less susceptible to microbial attack can mitigate the effects of microbial corrosion.
c. **Environmental Control**: Maintaining optimal environmental conditions, such as pH, temperature, and fluid flow, can help minimize microbial activity and corrosion rates.
d. **Regular Monitoring and Maintenance**: Implementing routine monitoring and maintenance programs can help detect microbial corrosion early and take corrective actions to prevent further damage.
e. **Biofilm Control**: Strategies to prevent or remove biofilms from metal surfaces, such as mechanical cleaning, chemical treatments, or ultrasonic cleaning, can help mitigate microbial corrosion.

CHAPTER – 20

MATERIALS OF PHARMACEUTICAL PLANT CONSTRUCTION, CORROSION AND ITS PREVENT – II

Mr. Sachin Singh

Assistant Professor, Rajiv Gandhi Institute of Pharmacy, Faculty of Pharmaceutical Science & Technology, AKS University Satna, MP-India

ABSTRACT:

Corrosion, a persistent challenge in various industries, manifests in different forms depending on environmental conditions and materials involved. Types of corrosion include:

1. Uniform Corrosion: Occurs uniformly across the surface, leading to gradual material loss. Prevention involves selecting corrosion-resistant materials and applying protective coatings.
2. Galvanic Corrosion: Results from the electrical coupling of dissimilar metals in the presence of an electrolyte, causing accelerated corrosion of the less noble metal. Prevention methods include using compatible metals or insulating them to prevent direct contact.
3. Pitting Corrosion: Creates localized pits or holes on the metal surface, often due to localized chemical attack. Prevention includes maintaining uniform protective coatings and controlling environmental conditions.
4. Crevice Corrosion: Occurs in narrow crevices or gaps where stagnant corrosive agents accumulate, leading to localized corrosion. Prevention involves design modifications to eliminate crevices or using crevice-free materials.
5. Stress Corrosion Cracking (SCC): Results from combined tensile stress and corrosive environments, leading to cracking without significant corrosion visible on the surface. Prevention includes stress relief

treatments, material selection, and controlling environmental factors. Effective prevention of corrosion involves understanding the properties of ferrous (containing iron) and nonferrous metals (lacking significant iron content), selecting appropriate materials based on their resistance to specific corrosive environments, and applying protective measures such as coatings, inhibitors, or cathodic protection. Inorganic nonmetals like ceramics and glasses, and organic nonmetals such as plastics and composites, also play crucial roles in corrosion prevention by offering inert or chemically resistant alternatives to metals in corrosive environments.

Basic material handling systems are essential in industries for safely transporting and processing materials throughout production processes. These systems include conveyors, lifts, bins, and silos designed to handle materials efficiently while minimizing contamination risks and ensuring worker safety. Proper design and material selection in handling systems contribute to operational efficiency and product quality, while also addressing corrosion concerns through appropriate material choices and protective measures.

TYPES OF CORROSION AND THERE PREVENTION

1. Uniform Corrosion:

Description: Uniform corrosion occurs uniformly over the entire exposed surface of a material, resulting in a gradual loss of material thickness.

Prevention:

a. **Material Selection**: Choose materials with high resistance to uniform corrosion, such as stainless steel grades like 316L or 304.
b. **Protective Coatings**: Apply corrosion-resistant coatings such as epoxy or polymer coatings to create a barrier between the metal surface and the corrosive environment.
c. **Maintain Optimal Environmental Conditions**: Control factors like temperature, humidity, and chemical exposure to minimize corrosion rates.

2. Pitting Corrosion:

Description: Pitting corrosion is characterized by localized corrosion attack, resulting in small pits or craters on the metal surface.

Prevention:

a. **Material Selection**: Choose materials with high resistance to pitting corrosion, such as stainless steel grades with added alloying elements like molybdenum (e.g., 316L or 316Ti).

b. **Surface Finish**: Smooth surfaces and avoid imperfections to reduce the likelihood of pitting initiation.

c. **Maintain Proper Passivation**: Passivate stainless steel surfaces to promote the formation of a protective oxide layer that inhibits pitting corrosion.

3. Crevice Corrosion:

Description: Crevice corrosion occurs in narrow gaps or crevices between metal surfaces or between a metal surface and another material, where oxygen and other corrosive agents are restricted.

Prevention:

a. **Proper Design**: Design equipment with minimal crevices and ensure proper sealing to prevent the entrapment of corrosive agents.

b. **Material Selection**: Choose materials with high resistance to crevice corrosion, such as stainless steel grades with low carbon content and molybdenum additions.

c. **Regular Inspection and Maintenance**: Inspect crevices regularly for signs of corrosion and address any issues promptly.

4. Stress Corrosion Cracking (SCC):

Description: Stress corrosion cracking is the formation and propagation of cracks in a material under the combined influence of tensile stress and a corrosive environment.

Prevention:

a. **Material Selection**: Choose materials resistant to stress corrosion cracking, such as duplex stainless steels or nickel-based alloys.
b. **Stress Reduction**: Minimize residual stresses during fabrication and operation to reduce the susceptibility to stress corrosion cracking.
c. **Control Environmental Factors**: Avoid exposure to corrosive environments known to promote stress corrosion cracking, such as chlorides or sulfides.

5. Intergranular Corrosion:

Description: Intergranular corrosion occurs along grain boundaries of a material, often due to sensitization or depletion of alloying elements near the grain boundaries.

Prevention:

a. **Material Selection**: Choose materials with high resistance to intergranular corrosion, such as stabilized stainless steel grades (e.g., 321 or 347) that prevent sensitization.
b. **Heat Treatment**: Perform post-weld heat treatment or solution annealing to restore the corrosion resistance of sensitized materials.
c. **Avoid Contaminants**: Minimize exposure to contaminants that promote intergranular corrosion, such as welding flux residues or chlorides.

6.Microbiologically Influenced Corrosion (MIC):

Description: MIC occurs when microorganisms alter the local environment, accelerating corrosion processes on metal surfaces.

Prevention:

a. **Sanitary Practices**: Implement rigorous cleaning and sanitation protocols to prevent microbial colonization on metal surfaces.
b. **Biocides**: Add biocides to process fluids to inhibit microbial growth and mitigate the risk of MIC.

c. **Material Selection**: Choose materials resistant to MIC, such as stainless steel alloys with high chromium content.

FERROUS AND NONFERROUS METALS

In pharmaceutical plant construction, both ferrous and nonferrous metals are utilized for various applications, each with its own advantages and considerations regarding corrosion prevention. Let's explore ferrous and nonferrous metals in detail, along with their corrosion characteristics and prevention methods:

Ferrous Metals:

1. **Stainless Steel:**
   a. **Description**: Stainless steel is a corrosion-resistant alloy of iron, chromium, and sometimes other elements like nickel or molybdenum. It is widely used in pharmaceutical plant construction due to its excellent corrosion resistance, mechanical strength, and sanitation properties.
   b. **Corrosion Resistance**: Stainless steel exhibits high resistance to corrosion in a wide range of environments, including acidic and chloride-rich environments commonly found in pharmaceutical processes.
   c. **Prevention**: Passivation treatments are often applied to stainless steel surfaces to enhance their corrosion resistance. Regular cleaning and maintenance also help prevent corrosion in stainless steel equipment.
2. **Carbon Steel:**
   a. **Description**: Carbon steel is an alloy of iron and carbon, with small amounts of other elements. It is less corrosion-resistant than stainless steel but is still used in pharmaceutical plants for structural components and non-critical applications.

b. **Corrosion Resistance**: Carbon steel is susceptible to corrosion, especially in acidic or humid environments. Without proper protection, it can undergo uniform corrosion or localized corrosion such as pitting or crevice corrosion.
c. **Prevention:** Protective coatings, such as epoxy or zinc coatings, can be applied to carbon steel surfaces to prevent corrosion. Regular inspection and maintenance are essential to identify and address corrosion issues promptly.

Nonferrous Metals:

1. **Aluminum:**
   a. **Description:** Aluminum is a lightweight, nonferrous metal with good corrosion resistance. It is commonly used in pharmaceutical plant construction for structures, piping, and equipment components.
   b. **Corrosion Resistance**: Aluminum forms a protective oxide layer on its surface, providing corrosion resistance in many environments. However, it can be susceptible to corrosion in acidic or alkaline conditions.
   c. **Prevention:** Anodizing or protective coatings can enhance the corrosion resistance of aluminum surfaces. Avoiding contact with incompatible materials and controlling environmental conditions can also help prevent corrosion.
2. **Copper:**
   a. **Description**: Copper is a ductile and malleable metal with excellent electrical and thermal conductivity. It is used in pharmaceutical plants for piping, heat exchangers, and electrical components.
   b. **Corrosion Resistance**: Copper exhibits good corrosion resistance in most environments, but it can undergo corrosion in acidic or

saline conditions. Corrosion of copper surfaces often results in the formation of greenish copper oxides (patina).

c. **Prevention**: Protective coatings or surface treatments can be applied to copper surfaces to prevent corrosion. Controlling pH levels and avoiding exposure to aggressive chemicals help mitigate corrosion risk.

3. **Titanium:**
   a. **Description**: Titanium is a lightweight, strong, and corrosion-resistant metal. It is used in pharmaceutical plants for equipment and components exposed to highly corrosive environments.
   b. **Corrosion Resistance**: Titanium exhibits exceptional corrosion resistance in a wide range of corrosive environments, including strong acids and chlorides. It forms a stable oxide layer that protects the underlying metal from corrosion.
   c. **Prevention:** Due to its inherent corrosion resistance, titanium typically requires minimal corrosion prevention measures. Proper design and fabrication techniques are essential to maintain its corrosion-resistant properties.

Corrosion Prevention:

1. **Material Selection:** Choose materials with appropriate corrosion resistance for the specific process conditions.
2. **Protective Coatings**: Apply corrosion-resistant coatings or surface treatments to metal surfaces to create a barrier against corrosive agents.
3. **Passivation**: Treat stainless steel surfaces with passivation treatments to enhance their corrosion resistance.
4. **Environmental Control**: Maintain optimal environmental conditions, such as pH, temperature, and humidity, to minimize corrosion rates.

5. **Regular Inspection and Maintenance**: Implement regular inspection and maintenance programs to identify and address corrosion issues promptly.

INORGANIC AND ORGANIC NONMETALS

Inorganic and organic nonmetals play important roles in pharmaceutical plant construction, particularly in sealing, insulation, and chemical resistance applications. Let's explore their use, corrosion characteristics, and prevention methods:

Inorganic Nonmetals:

1. **Glass:**
   a. **Description:** Glass is a versatile inorganic nonmetal with excellent chemical resistance and transparency. It is commonly used in pharmaceutical plants for laboratory equipment, storage vessels, and sight glasses.
   b. **Corrosion Resistance**: Glass is highly resistant to corrosion from most chemicals used in pharmaceutical processes. However, it can be susceptible to attack by strong alkalis or hydrofluoric acid.
   c. **Prevention**: Proper handling and storage of glass equipment can prevent mechanical damage, which may compromise its corrosion resistance. Avoid exposing glass to incompatible chemicals to prevent corrosion.
2. **Ceramics:**
   a. **Description**: Ceramics are inorganic nonmetallic materials composed of metallic and nonmetallic elements bonded together through ionic or covalent bonds. They are used in pharmaceutical plants for lining equipment, insulating components, and manufacturing tools.
   b. **Corrosion Resistance**: Ceramics exhibit high resistance to corrosion from most chemicals, including acids, alkalis, and

organic solvents. They are also resistant to high temperatures and thermal shock.

c. **Prevention:** Proper selection of ceramic materials based on their chemical compatibility with the process environment is crucial to prevent corrosion. Regular inspection and maintenance can identify any damage or wear on ceramic components.

Organic Nonmetals:

1. **Plastics:**
   a. **Description**: Plastics are organic polymers with a wide range of chemical compositions and properties. They are used extensively in pharmaceutical plants for piping, fittings, seals, and lining applications.
   b. **Corrosion Resistance**: The corrosion resistance of plastics varies depending on their chemical composition and structure. Many plastics, such as polyethylene (PE), polypropylene (PP), and polyvinyl chloride (PVC), offer excellent resistance to corrosion from acids, alkalis, and organic solvents.
   c. **Prevention:** Proper selection of plastic materials based on their chemical compatibility with the process fluids is essential to prevent corrosion. Regular inspection and maintenance can identify any degradation or deterioration of plastic components.

Corrosion Prevention:

1. **Material Selection**: Choose materials with high corrosion resistance and chemical compatibility for specific process conditions.
2. **Surface Coatings**: Apply protective coatings or linings to metal surfaces to create a barrier against corrosive agents.
3. **Proper Handling and Maintenance**: Handle and maintain equipment and components properly to prevent mechanical damage, which may compromise their corrosion resistance.

4. **Environmental Control**: Maintain optimal environmental conditions, such as temperature, humidity, and chemical exposure, to minimize corrosion rates.
5. **Regular Inspection and Testing**: Implement regular inspection and testing programs to identify and address corrosion issues promptly.

BASIC OF MATERIAL HANDLING SYSTEMS

Material handling systems are essential components of pharmaceutical plant construction, facilitating the movement, storage, and processing of raw materials, intermediates, and finished products. Let's explore the basics of material handling systems in pharmaceutical plants, along with considerations for corrosion prevention:

Basic Material Handling Systems:

1. **Conveyors:**
   a. **Description**: Conveyors are mechanical systems used to transport materials horizontally, vertically, or at an incline within a facility. They can be belt conveyors, screw conveyors, pneumatic conveyors, or roller conveyors.
   b. **Corrosion Prevention**: Choose corrosion-resistant materials for conveyor components exposed to moisture, chemicals, or harsh environments. Regular cleaning and maintenance can prevent the buildup of corrosive substances on conveyor surfaces.
2. **Storage Systems:**
   a. **Description**: Storage systems, such as bins, silos, and racks, are used to store raw materials, intermediates, and finished products in pharmaceutical plants. These systems may utilize manual, automated, or robotic handling.
   b. **Corrosion Prevention**: Select materials for storage systems that are resistant to corrosion and compatible with the stored materials.

Proper ventilation and humidity control can prevent the accumulation of moisture, reducing the risk of corrosion.

3. **Material Transfer Systems:**
    a. **Description:** Material transfer systems are used to move materials between different processes or equipment within a pharmaceutical plant. Examples include pumps, valves, and piping systems.
    b. **Corrosion Prevention**: Choose materials for transfer systems that are compatible with the chemical properties of the materials being transferred. Use corrosion-resistant coatings or linings for metal components exposed to corrosive fluids.
4. **Packaging Systems:**
    a. **Description**: Packaging systems are used to package pharmaceutical products into containers, such as bottles, vials, or blister packs, for distribution and storage.
    b. **Corrosion Prevention**: Select packaging materials that are corrosion-resistant and suitable for the storage conditions of the pharmaceutical products. Proper sealing and moisture control can prevent corrosion of packaging materials.
5. **Automation and Robotics:**
    a. **Description:** Automation and robotics are increasingly used in pharmaceutical material handling systems to improve efficiency, accuracy, and safety.
    b. **Corrosion Prevention**: Choose materials for automated systems that are resistant to corrosion and wear. Regular maintenance and lubrication of robotic components can prevent corrosion and prolong their lifespan.

Corrosion Prevention in Material Handling Systems:

1. **Material Selection**: Choose materials for handling systems that are resistant to corrosion and compatible with the chemicals and environmental conditions present in the pharmaceutical plant.
2. **Protective Coatings**: Apply corrosion-resistant coatings or linings to metal components exposed to corrosive fluids or environments.
3. **Proper Design**: Design material handling systems with features such as proper drainage, ventilation, and access for cleaning and maintenance to prevent the buildup of corrosive substances.
4. **Regular Inspection and Maintenance**: Implement regular inspection and maintenance programs to identify and address corrosion issues promptly. Replace or repair corroded components as needed to prevent equipment failure.

www.ingramcontent.com/pod-product-compliance
Ingram Content Group UK Ltd.
Pitfield, Milton Keynes, MK11 3LW, UK
UKHW061132310726
14090UKWH00035B/784